Shakespeare
in a
Divided America

James Shapiro

FABER & FABER

First published in 2020
by Faber & Faber Ltd
Bloomsbury House
74–77 Great Russell Street
London WC1B 3DA

Typeset by Faber & Faber Ltd
Printed and bound in the UK by CPI Group (UK) Ltd, Croydon CR0 4YY

A CIP record for this book
is available from the British Library

ISBN 978–0–571–33888–7

10 9 8 7 6 5 4 3 2 1

For my brother Michael

Contents

American soldier in Vietnam, with the Folger Shakespeare
The Taming of the Shrew in his helmet.

Introduction

Read by almost everyone at school, staged in theaters across the land, and long valued by conservatives as highly as by liberals, Shakespeare's plays remain common ground, one of the few places where Americans can meet and air their disparate views. For well over two centuries, Americans of all stripes—presidents and activists, writers and soldiers—have also turned to Shakespeare's works to give voice to what could not readily or otherwise be said.

That engagement dates back to before the Revolutionary War, when Hamlet's famous soliloquy—"To be, or not to be"—was appropriated both by defenders of British rule and by those seeking to overthrow it. Not long after, Shakespeare's contentious histories offered the Founding Fathers, all too aware of the vulnerabilities of the government they had created, a road map for where the young republic might be heading. Those who read these plays "with a view to . . . the treachery, perfidy, treason, murder, cruelty, sedition, and rebellions of rival and unbalanced factions," President John Adams warned, would "find one of the most instructive examples for the perusal of this country." A prescient Adams even reworked a passage from *Henry V* to show how a foreign despot might collude in putting a more pliable leader in the White House.

Yet in those early years of the republic it seemed improbable that Americans would adopt England's national poet as their own. They had fought the British in 1776 and in 1812 would again be at war. Moreover, the strain of puritanism entrenched in the northern colonies was rabidly anti-theatrical. The Quaker William Penn, who founded the Pennsylvania colony, had attacked "the infamous plays" of writers like Shakespeare and helped enact laws suppressing their performance. In 1774 the first Continental Congress was still admonishing colonists to shun theaters. Pennsylvania only ended its ban on playgoing in 1789 and Massachusetts, the last holdout, in 1793.

How Shakespeare won over America in the early nineteenth century is something of a mystery. The absence of rivals had a good deal to do with it. So too did the growing familiarity with his works. Actors from Britain toured the land with a repertory rich in Shakespeare while schoolbooks featured his famous speeches. One of them, McGuffey's *Reader*, first published in 1836, sold more than 120 million copies over the next eighty years. Another, Scott's *Lessons in Elocution*, found its way into the humblest of American homes, including the log cabin in which Abraham Lincoln was raised. Yet there was more to it than the lack of competitors and Shakespeare's widespread availability in schoolbooks and cheap editions. The French author Alexis de Tocqueville, gathering material for his book *Democracy in America*, noted that he first picked up a copy of *Henry V* in a log cabin while touring the United States in 1831, and added that there "is hardly a pioneer's hut that does not contain a few odd volumes of Shakespeare." A half century later, the German writer Karl Knortz said of America that "there is certainly no land on the whole earth in which Shakespeare and the Bible are held in such high esteem."

It helped that in a Bible-obsessed nation, Shakespeare's language sounded so similar to that of the *King James Version* (1611), contributing to the sense that his plays were a kind of secular scripture. Yet it was more than the *thee*s and *thou*s of Elizabethan English that drew Americans to his words. Many of the issues that preoccupied Shakespeare and his contemporaries in the late sixteenth century—the dangers of autocratic rule; the imagined threat posed by those of different races, religions, or nationalities; the slippery boundaries of gender—were still unsettling to nineteenth-century Americans. Shakespeare had usefully framed these as conflicts (resolved through bloodshed in his histories and tragedies, and more peacefully, if provisionally, in his comedies), social and political collisions that could be readily viewed through the prism of America's past and present. Yet much of the mystery of "Why has America embraced Shakespeare?" remains unsolved. All one can safely say is that Shakespeare took root in the United States because he spoke to what Americans cared about. But his plays were not interpreted by everyone in the same ways, especially as divisions deepened between social classes, between the industrial North and slaveholding South, between new waves of immigrants and earlier settlers, as well as between those who believed in America's Manifest Destiny and those wary of such imperial ambitions.

At first glance it seems almost perverse that Americans would choose to make essential to their classrooms and theaters a writer whose works enact some of their darkest nightmares or most lurid fantasies: a black man marrying then killing a white woman; a Jew threatening to cut a pound of a Christian's flesh; the brutal assassination of a ruler deemed tyrannical; the taming of a wife who defies male authority. *Hamlet* alone touches on incest, suicide, drunkenness, adultery, and fratricide. As I write these words in November 2018, a news report describes how parents of students at Mitchell High School in Bakersville, North Carolina, were shocked to discover that a performance of the satirical 1987 adaptation *The Complete Works of William Shakespeare (Abridged)* at the school included "suicide, alcohol consumption, and 'bad language.'" What they seem to have found even more objectionable was a same-sex kiss. The troubled parents later gathered in a prayer circle before circulating a petition calling for the local school board to "ban any group from performing in the District if they promote 'Homosexuality, Incest, Suicide, or any other [*sic*] that would be contrary to life.'" It's hard to invent a

3

better example of how Shakespeare speaks to the fears that divide us as a nation. Yet calls for censorship will not make those divisions (and what some may find disturbing) disappear. His writing continues to function as a canary in a coal mine, alerting us to, among other things, the toxic prejudices poisoning our cultural climate. At some deep level Americans intuit that our collective nightmares are connected to the sins of our national past, papered over or repressed in the making of America and its greatness; on occasion, Shakespeare's plays allow us to recognize if not acknowledge this.

It turns out that who gets to perform in Shakespeare's plays is a fairly accurate index of who is considered fully American. As far back as the 1820s, when Ira Aldridge had to move from New York to London in order to play Othello, Shylock, and other roles denied to African Americans in the United States, those who aren't accepted as truly American—because they don't look or sound the part—have been rejected when it comes to being cast as one of Shakespeare's heroes or heroines. Their experience is epitomized in a short story, "The School Boy Hamlet," published in 1946 by the Japanese American writer Toshio Mori in the *Pacific Citizen*, a San Francisco-based newspaper that during the war moved to Utah's Topaz War Relocation Center, a euphemism for what was more or less a concentration camp, where Mori and other Japanese Americans—most, like himself, American born—were incarcerated after the attack on Pearl Harbor. "The School Boy Hamlet" is about a young Japanese American living in San Francisco before the war who has an overwhelming desire to play Hamlet on Broadway. It's a compulsion that takes over his life, which he spends rehearsing speeches from the plays. His family and even his only friend eventually abandon him because he cannot understand what everybody else sees but will never tell him directly: there's no way that someone of his ethnicity will be cast as Hamlet. Mori's story crystallizes the prejudices and unspoken assumptions that everybody in America in the 1940s understood—except, sadly, for the protagonist of the story, Tom Fukunaga, who doesn't fit contemporary notions of what a hero like Hamlet should look like. Community in Shakespeare's plays is often built on (and quietly critiqued for) its principle of exclusion—we need only think of the puritanical Malvolio in *Twelfth Night* or Shylock the Jew in *The Merchant of Venice*, who are both left out of the charmed circle of inclusion at play's end. American identity has been formed on analogous lines: we define ourselves against those whom we reject, keep out, or lock up.

To write a comprehensive history of Shakespeare in America that would take us from East Coast to West Coast and from Revolutionary times until our own is an impossible task. There is simply too much territory and too long a time span to cover, and individual and regional responses to his work are too varied to reduce to generalizations. As much as many want to believe in the universality of his plays, it is more accurate to say that while they may be read by almost everyone, we often disagree about what they mean and how they ought to be staged. The experience of seeing *Othello* performed in the antebellum South (where it was quite popular, though the title role was only played by white actors who darkened their skin color) could not have been more different than watching Paul Robeson play Othello in 1943 on Broadway (the first time an African American would do so). The pressure of the times matters. The "G.I. *Hamlet*" performed by and for infantrymen fighting in the Pacific in 1944 was a far cry from a production Abraham Lincoln saw during the Civil War in Washington. And Lincoln's understanding of *Macbeth* was radically different from that of the actor and white supremacist, John Wilkes Booth, who assassinated him.

Instead of attempting a rushed survey, I have chosen to drill down more deeply into eight defining moments in America's history, hoping that a sustained analysis of core samples from those years might reveal features of our past that are otherwise less visible to us. In the course of a career spent researching and writing about Shakespeare, I gravitated early on toward studying particular years in depth, devoting nearly a quarter century to learning all that I could about two consequential years in his life. I came to know more about the preoccupations of Londoners in 1599 and 1606 than I did about political concerns in my own nation's past. But this focus shifted as my forays into advising local productions of the plays kindled an interest in Shakespeare in the United States. This led in turn to my assembling an anthology for the Library of America on what Americans had written about Shakespeare. While undertaking research for that volume I stumbled upon material I had never heard of or only knew about in a cursory way. It was a revelation. Reading the reformer Jane Addams's 1895 essay "A Modern Lear" (on the recent Pullman workers' strike) uncovered more about the bloody conflict between labor and management in Gilded Age America than anything I had ever been taught in school. Mary McCarthy's skewering essay "General Macbeth" in 1962 exposed the hollowness of our military-industrial complex during the Cold War as powerfully as her friend Hannah Arendt would expose the banality of evil in her book *Eichmann in Jerusalem* the following year.

This new direction in my work brought me into the orbit of Americans in positions of authority for whom Shakespeare clearly mattered. President Bill Clinton provided a foreword to my anthology in which he recalled his early engagement with the plays in Hot Springs, Arkansas, where memorizing lines from *Macbeth* in high school taught him about "the perils of blind ambition, and the emptiness of power disconnected from higher purpose." I entered into an extended exchange over the politics of who wrote Shakespeare with retired Supreme Court Justice John Paul Stevens, who had written to me about it. I was invited to speak at Bohemian Grove, a secretive retreat north of San Francisco, where, it was my impression, mostly mainstream and wealthy Republicans (all men, as women were excluded), many of whom knew Shakespeare's works well, gathered every July. And I was asked to participate in a mock appeal of Shakespeare's Shylock, presided over by Supreme Court Justice Ruth Bader Ginsburg, in Venice. My limited role there was to engage in conversation with fellow Shakespearean Stephen Greenblatt; we essentially stalled for time while Ginsburg and her fellow judges reached their verdict. But the event gave me an opportunity to observe the exacting and brilliant Justice Ginsburg closely, and it was hard to ignore the messages of gender equality and religious tolerance implicit in her rulings: she declared that Portia should go to law school, and Shylock was to have his loan returned to him and his coerced conversion to Christianity nullified. Supreme Court Justices weren't supposed to go around promoting their ideological views; I saw how Shakespeare proved an effective way of doing so indirectly.

At the same time, I was learning more about how Americans with considerably less power or status responded to Shakespeare. Since 2012, in addition to my work as an English professor at Columbia University, I've served as the Shakespeare Scholar in Residence at the Public Theater in New York, assisting ninety-minute Mobile Unit performances of Shakespeare that tour local prisons and community centers. Shakespeare's plays are rich in the extremes of experiences—injustice, separation, violence, revenge—and it was soon obvious that while I might have been more familiar with Shakespeare's language, these playgoers grasped far better than I what was at stake in the plays. Some of those imprisoned, such as the women in the Bedford Hills Correctional Facility—as engaged and responsive an audience as I have ever witnessed—had seen a half dozen or more of the plays. Watching their reactions to professional productions of *Macbeth* and *Romeo and Juliet* was both humbling and illuminating.

While all this deepened my interest in how Shakespeare mattered to Americans, it was the election of Donald Trump in 2016 that convinced me to write about Shakespeare in a divided America. After the election, I headed to some of the red states in the South—lecturing and talking with audiences about America's Shakespeare in Alabama, Kentucky, Texas, and Tennessee—to grapple with what, from inside my blue state bubble, I had failed to understand about where the country was heading. I wasn't the only one turning to Shakespeare to make sense of the moment. On the eve of the election, Stephen Greenblatt published a powerful op-ed in the *New York Times* likening Trump to a Shakespearean tyrant. And a month after Trump was elected, Oskar Eustis, the artistic director of the Public Theater, decided to respond to this seismic event by directing a production of *Julius Caesar* the following summer at the Delacorte Theater. The open-air Delacorte is located in Central Park, and since Joe Papp built it in 1962, spectators—by now, more than 5 million—have flocked to see Free Shakespeare in the Park. Fifty thousand more would see this timely *Julius Caesar*. Because that production, and reactions to it, powerfully shaped my understanding of much of what follows in these pages, it will help if I describe it here at some length.

Julius Caesar hadn't been staged at the Delacorte in many years, and Shakespeare's account of the end of the Roman republic and the rise of autocratic rule (marking the end of democracy in the West for nearly two thousand years) spoke directly to the political vertigo many Americans were experiencing. As Eustis told *New York Magazine*, "The election of Trump really reveals to us that what we thought of as norms were really historically limited and may change completely." He hoped that staging *Julius Caesar* could "provide a cathartic experience for those of us who are losing our minds. What I could feel in myself and in the audience is that we were playing out this violent fantasy and, by playing it out, puncturing its power."

This was the fourth time since the 1980s that Eustis would direct *Julius Caesar,* and his understanding of the play had evolved over the years. "When I first did this," he said, "my stance was that Cassius was right, Brutus was wrong, and that the only thing they did wrong was that they didn't go far enough." He likened his earliest take on it to Bertolt Brecht's late play *The Days of the Commune,* which argued "that the Paris Commune failed because they didn't go far enough. They didn't actually decide to hang on to power. They just tried to stay pure." Thirty years later Eustis had come to a different understanding: "It's not that I think Brutus is right. It's not that I think Julius Caesar is right. What I'm watching is a group of people struggling with how" to "take political power," and how then, "does that political power reflect their values?" For Eustis, Antony is "somebody who can take power, but has no idea how to make that reflect" his values. With "Brutus and Cassius, you have the case of people who don't know how to take power." And with Caesar and Octavius, "you have people who are able to take power and who are able to use that to reflect their values, which is to have power. Power becomes an end in itself. And that of course is the destruction of democracy."

My work at the Public Theater has also involved helping out with the pair of large-scale Delacorte Shakespeare productions every summer. This has typically meant joining the company for the first week or two of rehearsals when the text is unpacked and analyzed, and before that helping directors prepare a working script. Eustis knew the play's opening moves, its gambits, traps, and endgame. He also knew, as anyone who has tackled the play soon learns, that *Julius Caesar* is broken backed, the second half—mostly involving a quarrel between Brutus and Cassius, followed by a blur of confusing battle scenes culminating in their self-inflicted deaths and the triumph of Antony and Octavius—invariably a letdown, never quite matching the drama of the buildup to Caesar's assassination.

9

I didn't direct, couldn't act, and wasn't a dramaturge, but I was invited into the rehearsal room because I could explain what Shakespeare's words meant and speak about the play's Elizabethan contexts. Eustis recognized the power and precision of Shakespeare's words and his cast understood that a deeper knowledge of that language offered vital clues to their characters' actions and motivations. My small role meant that I could watch what turned out to be a remarkable production take shape, then see it performed at the Delacorte as many times as I liked.

One reason why *Julius Caesar* is rarely staged nowadays is that its large cast (so many of whom deliver major speeches) demands so many talented actors. In this respect it differs from *Hamlet, Macbeth, Othello, Romeo and Juliet,* and *Richard III*—Shakespeare plays that have long dominated the American theater—which could be staged with just a star or two. Eustis was charismatic and the Public Theater a showcase for top actors. He quickly assembled a strong cast, their faces familiar from television, film, and Broadway shows, including Corey Stoll as Brutus, John Douglas Thompson as Cassius, Nikki M. James as Portia, and Teagle Bougere as Casca. Eustis had initially toyed with the idea of having a woman play both Calpurnia and Octavius. In the end, he decided against that and cast Tina Benko as Calpurnia and Robert Gilbert as Octavius. In what turned out to be an inspired decision, he cast Elizabeth Marvel (who had just played the president of the United States on *Homeland*) as Antony.

It would be a modern-dress rather than a "toga" production, set in contemporary America, with giant banners depicting George Washington and Abraham Lincoln framing the stage. A tall, blond Caesar, dressed in a business suit and wearing overlong blue or red ties, resembled Donald Trump, and an elegant and Slavic-accented Calpurnia his wife Melania. When Eustis told me early on about what he was envisioning, I asked whether he would reach out to

Alec Baldwin, who had a long history at the Public Theater and whose wicked impersonation of Donald Trump on *Saturday Night Live* had infuriated Trump and captivated viewers—and he shook his head. I had misunderstood: this was not going to be satiric. He cast Gregg Henry as Caesar; familiar to moviegoers from his many roles as a tough guy, Henry was slimmer and younger than Trump, but his gait, intonation, and swagger perfectly captured those of the new president.

Eustis drew on his own previous experience as well as decades of seeing versions of the play directed by others, though the longest shadow over his production was cast by one directed by Orson Welles in 1937 at Broadway's Mercury Theatre. This landmark show had been America's first major modern-dress Shakespeare. And, whether directors were aware of it or not, it would profoundly influence all subsequent American productions of the play. Arguably, no other interpretation of *any* Shakespeare play in America would exercise so powerful a gravitational pull on its successors.

The 22-year-old Welles, fresh from his success with an innovative "Voodoo" *Macbeth* in Harlem the previous year, again broke sharply with tradition. His production cut two ways. It was, as Welles later said, "overtly anti-fascist." The pro-Caesar camp dressed in military garb and gave fascist salutes, and Joseph Holland's Caesar, with his jutting chin, even bore a passing resemblance to Mussolini. The subtitle that Welles added—*The Death of a Dictator*—made his political slant unambiguous. Yet Welles refused to celebrate the conspiracy or depict Brutus (whose role he kept for himself) as noble. Quite the contrary. He saw Brutus as an "impotent, ineffectual, fumbling liberal; the reformer who wants to do something about things but doesn't know how and gets it in the neck in the end. He's dead right all the time, and dead at the final curtain," a "bourgeois intellectual, who, under a modern dictatorship, would be the first to be put up against a wall and shot." Reviewers at the time struggled, without much success, to reconcile the production's warnings about the dangers of fascism with its equal insistence on the limits and cluelessness of liberalism. Welles, who saw both sides, was drawn to the play precisely "because Shakespeare has feelings for and against everyone in it."

Welles's production was also notable for its insights into emerging media and their capacity to manipulate the masses and undermine democracy. Newsreels at the time showed how carefully choreographed large-scale rallies in Germany and Italy were stirring up bigotry and nationalism. His production cost roughly $6,000, a pittance for a Broadway show—but Welles insisted on using the latest in playhouse technology, installing thirteen 500-watt "uplights" to create the so-called Nuremberg effect, reproducing for Broadway audiences some of the frightening impact of a Nazi rally.

For two centuries, directors had cut a scene that comes shortly after Caesar's murder which threatened to undermine the nobility of the conspirators; including it might suggest that they too had acted like a bloodthirsty mob. Welles restored this scene, and for many playgoers and reviewers it was the most searing one in his production. In it, a poet named Cinna wanders out in the evening and is accosted by fellow citizens who, stirred up by Antony, are angrily seeking out supporters of the conspiracy. He protests that he is Cinna the *poet* and not Cinna the conspirator, and tries to escape, but they surround then brutally murder him—their anti-elitism signaled in their desire to "Tear him for his bad verses" (3.3.31).

While most of the mob in Welles's version was dressed like working-class Americans, a few wore paramilitary garb, and the scene suggested that mob violence and fascistic tendencies were domestic issues, not merely foreign ones. As Welles told the *New York Times*, "It's the same mob . . . that hangs and burns negroes in the South, the same mob that maltreats the Jews in Germany." For Welles, the heart of the play was the assassination scene, the funeral orations, and the death of Cinna. He ruthlessly cut what followed, eliminating the proscription scene (in which an ascendant Antony and Octavius callously horse-trade over which of their political enemies in Rome they will kill off), and radically reduced Acts four and five to fewer than three hundred lines.

Welles was focused on fascist Europe, Eustis on Trump's America. Eustis too retained the scene in which Cinna is assaulted. The part of the doomed poet was movingly played by Yusef Bulos, a Jerusalem-born actor well into his seventies. In an encounter that evoked recent acts of police brutality across America, he is subjected to a "stop and frisk" and harshly beaten. Eustis also included the proscription scene; in his staging of it, Cinna the poet, assaulted and arrested earlier, is summarily executed along with Trebonius and others either implicated in the assassination of Caesar or unluckily swept up in the crackdown that followed. The final two Acts of the play, while shortened, still ran to roughly nine hundred lines, and the fast-paced production, which ran without an intermission, lasted two hours.

The show, which began as the sun was setting in Central Park, opened with a brief prelude, a "day-after-the-Hillary-defeat" moment, during which playgoers were invited to walk about the flower-strewn stage and were given markers to share their thoughts on long paper scrolls taped to walls. This somber interlude was interrupted by the arrival onstage of a group of white men wearing red "MAKE ROME GREAT AGAIN" baseball caps, who proceeded to poster over the handwritten reflections. Someone was shoved and a body went flying (it was as yet impossible to know who was an actor and who a surprised member of the audience). Confused spectators who had wandered onstage were hurriedly ushered off as Flavius, speaking for those on the losing side of the now divided nation, rebuked the celebratory mood of the aggressive newcomers; the opening lines of the play now had a timely edge: "Hence!

Home, you idle creatures, get you home! Is this a holiday?" (1.1.1–2).

Though the play bears his name, Caesar appears in only three scenes (not counting his brief return as a ghost). Eustis made the most of them. Gregg Henry's Caesar first appears onstage in the play's second scene, in full campaign mode, waving and smiling, gestures that always drew responsive cheers from the mostly liberal spectators, who were happy to play along (Trump had won less than a fifth of the vote in New York City). Other, nonverbal details further linked Trump and Caesar, and these too were mostly received with smiles or the shock of recognition. In Shakespeare's text, Caesar asks Antony to touch Calpurnia before he runs in a footrace on the Feast of the Lupercal, to ensure her fertility; Gregg Henry's Caesar, in demonstrating to Antony what he means, engages in what Trump had referred to as grabbing women "by the pussy." It was one thing to hear Trump brag about doing it in the notorious *Access Hollywood* tape; it was another to see a man resembling the president casually grab a woman's crotch. And it helped motivate a subsequent moment when a Trump-like Caesar reaches back to grab his wife's hand, only to have it brushed away—Calpurnia's gesture recalling Melania's on a tarmac when she was accompanying her husband on a state visit but clearly wanted no part of him at that moment.

Eustis didn't have to work very hard to identify Trump with Caesar. Like Caesar, Trump was easily flattered and scornful of political adversaries. Trump's obsession with his rivals' appearance gave new weight to Caesar's remarks about Cassius—"Yond Cassius has a lean and hungry look. He thinks too much. Such men are dangerous. . . . Would he were fatter" (1.2.194–98). When John Douglas Thompson's Cassius subsequently ran onstage waving a "RESIST" banner and wearing one of the pink "pussyhats" worn by thousands of postelection protesters, you could look around the Delacorte and see smiles and nods, as many in the audience made a very personal connection to the action. More than anything else, Caesar's arrogance uncannily anticipated Trump's. When he is asked to explain why he refuses to go to the Senate and says "The cause is in my will: I will not come. / That is enough to satisfy the Senate" (2.2.71–72) his petulance almost always provoked laughter. Like Trump, Caesar seemed easily persuaded by the last person who speaks to him. Calpurnia, who partly disrobes and joins a naked and cigar-smoking Caesar in a Trumpian gold-plated bath-tub, is relieved after persuading him not to go to the Senate— then looks on helplessly as Decius enters and, with a few flattering words, gets him to change his mind.

Eustis, who had remained faithful to Shakespeare's words throughout, decided to add three of his own—or rather Trump's own. After Casca recounts how Antony thrice offered Caesar a crown, and Caesar refused it, sensitive to how this might appear to the disapproving people, and then swooned, Brutus asks him what happened next. In Shakespeare's original, Casca recounts how Caesar won over the crowd by saying, "if he had done or said any-thing amiss, he desired Their Worships to think it was his infirmity" (1.2.269–71). Casca then witheringly adds: "Three or four wenches where I stood cried 'Alas, good soul!' and forgave him with all their hearts. . . . if Caesar had stabbed their mothers they would have done no less" (1.2.271–75). Eustis, recalling Trump's boast during his campaign that he "could stand in the middle of Fifth Avenue and shoot somebody and I wouldn't lose any voters," amended Casca's words, so that he now said: "If Caesar had stabbed their mothers *on Fifth Avenue*, they would have done no less." As Teagle Boug-ere spoke this line he gestured behind him toward Fifth Avenue, a block or so to the east, collapsing for a moment ancient Rome, Elizabethan London, and the site of the production.

Until this moment the not-so-subtle hints of a Trump-like Cae-sar were of a piece: they were played for laughs and highlighted

Trump's bluster. But they had steered clear of Trump's darker, bullying side that for many Americans rendered him unfit for the office of the presidency. That would change when Caesar, expecting to be crowned, enters the Senate. The audience was primed. Even those who hadn't recently read or seen the play half-remembered from tenth-grade English classes that his assassination was imminent. Gregg Henry stood at a podium as he recited Caesar's lines, drifting into self-praise and insisting on his superiority to all those gathered there. When he asks, "What is now amiss / That Caesar and *his* Senate must redress?" (3.1.32–33), that *his* recalled Trump's habit of speaking in proprietary ways ("*my* generals"). At that point, an Iranian-born woman, Marjan Neshat—the kind of person Trump could never quite treat respectfully—stepped forward and addressed Caesar flatteringly: "Most high, most mighty, and most puissant Caesar, / Metellus Cimber throws before thy seat / An humble heart——" (3.1.34–36).

But before she can finish, Caesar brusquely cuts her off: "I could be well moved, if I were as you" (3.1.59). And working himself up into a tirade, he mocks her "Low-crookèd curtsies, and base spaniel fawning" (3.1.44) accompanying these words with an ugly gesture which he clearly thinks is funny—jerkily flailing his arms and hands—that recalled what for many was the low point of Trump's presidential campaign, when he mocked the disability of Serge Kovaleski, a *New York Times* reporter who suffered from a medical condition that impeded the movement of his right arm and hand. For those at the Delacorte who hated Trump, that cruel gesture was a reminder of how sinister a leader he was, the kind on whom you wished the worst. A few moments later, that wish came true. First Casca, then Cassius, Metellus Cimber and the rest of the conspirators stabbed the Trump-like Caesar as they dragged him down from the podium. As he fought for his life they knifed him repeatedly before Brutus delivered the fatal blow. As Caesar bled out, Brutus sprawled backwards, in shock at what he and the others had just done.

After seeing this riveting scene staged a few times, I turned my attention to how those seated around me were reacting to it. Many were slack-jawed; others covered their faces. Night after night a deathly silence descended on the house. On two occasions that silence was punctuated by the sound of a lone playgoer applauding, in each instance clapping just once or twice, as the pleasure of seeing a fantasy fulfilled was overtaken by embarrassment or shame. I would not have been surprised if on any given night this first sound of clapping might have triggered a groundswell of involuntary applause, much as it does at the end of every theatrical performance. But that never happened. There was just a long and uncomfortable silence.

That silence was only broken when Cinna at last cried out, "Liberty! Freedom! Tyranny is dead!" (3.1.79). As the conspirators regained their footing, stooping and washing their hands and daggers in Caesar's blood and holding them aloft, something quite unnerving happened, night after night. In ones and twos, outraged playgoers, most of them on the young side, began to stand up and angrily shout about what they were witnessing. Within a short time nearly fifty of them, scattered through the house, were on their feet, waving their fists, shouting recriminations, and expressing outrage. Brutus struggled to be heard above the din. I watched this outburst, as well as the anxiety of some of those seated near the protesters, with interest. Unlike those caught off guard by their outrage, I knew that they were additional cast members that Oskar Eustis had planted throughout the Delacorte. Until now four dozen of them had been sitting quietly, indistinguishable from other actors or from spectators in this modern-dress production. Eustis was not the first director of this play to employ supernumeraries, but he was the first to use them in such a way.

Eustis had set a trap. He was offering a counterpoint, a rival perspective. It was as if he had slammed on the brakes and 1,800 playgoers were experiencing whiplash. What had we been wishing for? By giving voice to the opposition, he was forcing on playgoers a set of moral questions not unlike those Brutus was struggling with: Do the ends justify the means? How do we reconcile our values with our desires? As Eustis put it in a radio interview during previews: "Brutus is hoping that this assassination will be seen as a liberation. But the moment the knives come out it is a horror show. It is nothing but a horrible tragic event that leads to terrible results. So I don't have a moment of thinking, 'I am promoting assassination as a technique or making light of the murder of the leader of the country,' not at all."

That last sentence points to what Eustis understood were the risks of his approach: the resistance, in an increasingly polarized America, to hearing more than one side of a story. In insisting on allowing opposing voices to question the motives of the conspirators, Eustis was staying true to something essential to the play's handling of Caesar's assassination, which Shakespeare had set on a razor's edge. *Julius Caesar* offers as many arguments justifying the assassination as it does condemning it. Every speech can be read two ways. It boiled down to whom you believed and trusted. As good an argument can be made that Caesar was wrongfully slaughtered as one in support of Brutus' conclusion that it was better to kill a potential tyrant than allow him to amass power and destroy the republic.

Shakespeare's habit of presenting both sides of an argument is especially characteristic of his Roman tragedies: Does Lucius mount a coup at the end of *Titus Andronicus*, backed by foreign soldiers, or is this simply a restoration of order? Are Antony and Cleopatra tragic figures or rather "a strumpet's fool" and a "Triple-turned whore"? (1.1.13; 4.12.13). Does *Coriolanus* celebrate the defeat of authoritarianism or lament its loss? In so habitually offering competing perspectives, and in assuming that his audiences were capable of appreciating this, Shakespeare was very much of his age, a product of an Elizabethan educational system that trained young minds to argue *in utramque partem*, on both sides of the question. Eustis, in urging us to confront the moral quandaries of *Julius Caesar* and in injecting oppositional voices that challenged the violent action of the conspirators, assumed that contemporary audiences were no less up to the task. In an age in which so many were quick to dismiss the views of the other side that was a risky assumption.

Watching the production's tipping point, when first Brutus and then Antony speaks directly to the crowd, I often thought of this. One was trying to justify the conspirators' violent actions, the other turn an increasingly frenzied onstage crowd against them. It felt like changing the channel from MSNBC to Fox News. Elizabeth Marvel's Antony at first fails miserably when addressing her "Friends, Romans, countrymen" (3.2.75); she seemed stiff, almost robotic, in her delivery. The supernumeraries, initially swayed by Brutus, now shout her down. Marvel could barely be heard as she slumped to the ground, utterly defeated. But she then suddenly shifted tactics and slowly won the crowd to her side.

It was a bravura performance, one of the highlights of the production. Marvel's Antony briefly mentioned Caesar's will but only returned to it when the crowd around her was fully primed. The last time I had seen a group of people so itching with expectation—"read us the will! Caesar's will!" (3.2.150)—was when Oprah Winfrey told her television show's live audience that small gift boxes would be passed to everyone, one of which would contain a key to a new car. When she gave them permission to open the boxes, everyone screamed for joy—for each box contained one of those car keys. It was much the same with the dozens onstage gathered around Antony when Marvel read from the will and described what Caesar had left them. The emotional appeal of a savvy political leader and that of a television personality became indistinguishable:

> Moreover, he hath left you all his walks,
> His private arbors, and new-planted orchards,
> On this side Tiber; he hath left them you,
> And to your heirs forever—common pleasures,
> To walk abroad and recreate yourselves.
> Here was a Caesar! When comes such another?
>
> 3.3.248–53

In rehearsals, Marvel started pronouncing the verb *recreate* (in the sense of "walking abroad and *enjoying* yourselves") in the next-to-last line as *re-create*. Her choice was inspired, and tapped into that American conviction that we can easily re-create ourselves—personally, religiously, politically. The moment in which the dozens of supernumeraries, drunk with the excitement of it all, raced off wielding makeshift weapons to do Antony's bidding—driving Brutus and Cassius from Rome—marked a political re-creation and the end of the republic.

On opening night, Oskar Eustis took to the stage before the performance began, and had this to say about how both theater and democracy depend upon competing points of view:

> This play . . . warns about what happens when you try to preserve democracy by nondemocratic means. And . . . (spoiler alert) . . . it doesn't end up too good. But at the same time, one of the dangers that is unleashed by that is the danger of a large crowd of people, manipulated by their emotions, taken over by leaders who urge them to do things that not only are against their interests, but destroy their very institutions that are there to serve and protect them. This warning is a warn-

ing that's in this show, and we are really happy to be playing that story tonight. . . . I am proud to say . . . that we are here to uphold the Public's mission. And the Public's mission is to say that the culture belongs to everybody, needs to belong to everybody, to say that art has something to say about the great civic issues of our time, and to say, that like drama, democracy depends on the conflict of different points of view. Nobody owns the truth. We all own the culture.

His insistence that democracy depends on the expression of competing viewpoints echoed the language of one of the principles guiding public discourse since the end of World War II. The war and its immediate aftermath had taught Americans about the threat to democracy in countries where the people were fed only a single version of what passed for truth. In 1946 the Federal Communications Commission, which controlled licenses to America's media frequencies, issued an extraordinary ruling, which came to be called the "Fairness Doctrine":

> If, as we believe to be the case, the public interest is best served in a democracy through the ability of the people to hear expositions of the various positions taken by responsible groups and individuals on particular topics and to choose between them, it is evident that broadcast licensees have an affirmative duty generally to encourage and implement the broadcast of all sides of controversial public issues over their facilities.

Radio and television stations were now required to present a diverse set of viewpoints as a way of best serving the American people and preserving democracy from demagoguery. Though challenged from time to time, the Fairness Doctrine would remain in force until the 1980s, when it came under assault under Ronald Reagan's push to deregulate. It was further undermined in 1986 by a 2–1 ruling by the DC Circuit of the US Court of Appeals; the two judges in the majority, Robert Bork and Antonin Scalia, declared that the doctrine was only a doctrine, not a law. Enforcement soon stopped and it was repealed a year later.

It doesn't take much imagination to predict what followed: the rapid rise of partisan programming and the emergence of echo chambers, as Americans retreated to their respective camps, some turning to right-wing media, others to liberal commentators and websites. Talk during the Obama years of restoring the Fairness Doctrine was met by stiff resistance from the Right; nothing came of it, as Sean Hannity characterized the effort as "an assault on the First Amendment" and Newt Gingrich dismissed the Fairness Doctrine as "Affirmative Action for liberals." By the time that Eustis urged that "democracy depends on the conflict of different points of view" on opening night, it was too late. Those on the political Right could only see one side of the story being enacted onstage: the brutal assassination of President Donald Trump. And they were bent on stopping it. I'll return to that—and its implications for the future of Shakespeare in America—in the final chapter.

WE MAY EXPERIENCE Shakespeare's plays communally in classrooms and theaters, but we react to them in highly personal ways, and in the chapters that follow I have tried to be especially attentive to that. Each of these chapters delves deeply into how (in most cases) a pair of individuals have experienced Shakespeare. The focus of each chapter is limited to a play or two, and each revolves around a significant social or political conflict in the nation's history. My choices also reflect a desire to capture the extraordinary range of ways in which Americans have experienced Shakespeare, through solitary reading, amateur and professional performances, and adaptations of the plays in musicals, movies, and large-scale civic spectacles. My hope is that, taken together, these stories offer a fresh perspective on the history of the United States over the past two centuries, one that may shed light on how we have arrived at our present moment, and how, in turn, we may better address that which divides and impedes us as a nation.

"The Fruits of Amalgamation," E. W. Clay.

CHAPTER 1

1833: Miscegenation

On New Year's Eve of 1835, former president John Quincy Adams wrote a long letter to a friend about *Othello*. Three months later most of that letter appeared in *American Monthly Magazine* as an essay on "The Character of Desdemona." In it, Adams vilifies Desdemona for desiring and then marrying a black man:

> My objections to the character of Desdemona arise not from what Iago, or Roderigo, or Brabantio, or Othello says of her; but from what she herself does. She absconds from her father's house, in the dead of night, to marry a blackamoor. She breaks a father's heart, and covers his noble house with shame, to gratify—what? Pure love, like that of Juliet or Miranda? No! Unnatural passion; it cannot be named with delicacy. Her admirers now say this is criticism of 1835; that the color of Othello has nothing to do with the passion of Desdemona. No? Why, if Othello had been white, what need would there have been for her running away with him?

Adams has little patience for critics who accuse him of misreading the play in light of the increasingly fraught racial politics of America in 1835, and even less for those who in recent years had begun to claim that Desdemona's "love for Othello is not unnatural, because he is not a Congo negro but only a sooty Moor." Othello himself says that he is black (and had been "sold to slavery" (1.3.140) earlier in his adventurous life). For Adams, there can be only one conclusion: "the passion of Desdemona for Othello is unnatural, solely and exclusively because of his color," and because of this "her elopement to him, and secret marriage with him, indicate a personal character not only very deficient in delicacy, but totally regardless of filial duty, of female modesty, and of ingenuous shame."

Contemporaries may well have been surprised to see these words appear under the former president's familiar initials—"J. Q. A."—and not simply because of the harsh views expressed here. Adams, a tireless writer, whose correspondence and daily journal entries totaled many thousands of pages, was widely admired as one of the most literate individuals of his day. But he was also a cautious politician, extremely reticent about expressing his opinions in print, especially controversial ones, so published surprisingly little in his long career, and absolutely nothing on interracial marriage.

Stranger still, he was doubling down on a companion piece he had just published (that had prompted the attack on the "criticism of 1835"). This too was on Shakespeare—"Misconceptions of Shakspeare Upon the Stage"—and had appeared earlier that month in the *New England Magazine*. While this first essay dealt with his views on King Lear and Juliet, it included a few choice words for Desdemona's interracial marriage that anticipated his subsequent and longer diatribe. As this earlier essay unfolds, it becomes increasingly clear that it is Desdemona's physical intimacy with Othello that so discomforts Adams: "her fondling with Othello is disgusting." That essay similarly concludes that "the great moral lesson of the tragedy of *Othello* is, that black and white blood cannot be intermingled in marriage without a gross outrage upon the law of Nature; and that, in such violations, Nature will vindicate her laws." Insistent on being understood, Adams puts this even more bluntly. Any pity we might feel as we watch Othello kill Desdemona must give way to the grim satisfaction that she got what was coming: "when Othello smothers her in bed, the terror and the pity subside immediately into the sentiment that she has her deserts."

Why had a former president and now member of Congress felt it necessary to weigh in publicly not once, but twice, and so unflinchingly, on Desdemona's interracial marriage? It's the sort of claim that we might expect from a Southern slaveholder. But John Quincy Adams was from Massachusetts, which as far back as 1783 had renounced slavery. More puzzling still, Adams was widely recognized as one of the leading abolitionists in the land. He had spearheaded the opposition to the Gag Rule (intended to prevent petitions against slavery from being acknowledged by Congress), would fight against the annexation of Texas and thereby the creation of additional slave states, and would soon successfully argue the *Amistad* case (in which he defended captured African slaves) before the Supreme Court. Adams's advocacy led to a spate of death threats. His congressional opponent (and later Confederate general) Henry Wise called him "the acutest, the astutest, the archest enemy of southern slavery that ever existed"—and Wise didn't mean this as a compliment.

Disturbing prints by the Philadelphia artist E. W. Clay that circulated in 1839 tried to stir up racial antagonism through depictions of interracial mingling, called at the time amalgamation (the term "miscegenation" was not invented until 1864). In one of those prints, "Practical Amalgamation," a black man and woman are seated on a couch, each with a white lover. Behind them, in framed portraits, three men look down approvingly on the scene: Arthur Tappan (a fierce abolitionist about whom it was reported, falsely, that he was married to a black woman); Daniel O'Connell (who was the Irish leader of the Catholic Emancipation movement and another strong abolitionist); and, on the right, J. Q. Adams. How could a man seen by opponents of interracial union as one of their greatest foes publish a pair of essays condemning Desdemona for marrying a black man and claiming that in her murder at his hands she got what she deserved?

A partial answer, at least to what precipitated Adams's surprising decision to publish his views on Desdemona, can be traced

27

"Practical Amalgamation," E. W. Clay.

back to a disastrous encounter at a dinner party a few years earlier. The occasion was the arrival in the United States of one of the most celebrated Shakespeare actors of the day, Fanny Kemble. The Kembles were British theatrical royalty. Fanny Kemble's uncle and aunt, John Philip Kemble and Sarah Siddons, had been the greatest Shakespeare actors of their time, and Fanny's father, Charles Kemble, who had performed alongside his famous siblings in minor roles, was a notable actor in his own right, and joint owner of the Covent Garden Theatre. Her mother acted as well. When threatened with bankruptcy in 1829, her parents persuaded the nineteen-year-old Fanny Kemble to enter the family business. She studied the role of Juliet for three weeks, then made a triumphant debut at Covent Garden in October 1829. She was an immediate success, and the family's financial ruin was averted. Fanny Kemble was quick at learning parts (a new one every month, including those of Portia and Beatrice) and was enormously popular, both onstage and in London's social scene, where as a well-informed and engaging conversationalist she more than held her own. With the retirement, decline, and deaths of John Philip Kemble, Sarah Siddons, and the no less celebrated Edmund Kean, Fanny Kemble stood at or very near the pinnacle of the London theater world.

By 1832 she was not only acting in plays but also writing them. By then, however, insolvency again threatened. Charles Kemble persuaded his reluctant daughter to accompany him on what turned out to be a lucrative two-year tour of the United States. Fanny Kemble was at the peak of her career when she arrived in the States, a celebrity as much as a star performer. Her warm reception in prominent circles in Britain had ensured that even in American states known for their suspicion of actors she would be a much sought-after guest.

The Kembles set sail in August 1832 and the following month began performing in New York. Audiences (as well as suitors) flocked to see Fanny Kemble. The praise in the *New York Evening Post* was typical: Fanny Kemble conveyed "an intensity and truth never exhibited by an actress in America." A young Walt Whitman, only thirteen or so at the time, secured a seat and later recalled, "Fanny Kemble! . . . Nothing finer did ever stage exhibit." At subsequent stops in Philadelphia and Washington, DC, she met with prominent writers and politicians, including President Andrew Jackson (and let slide his complaints about "scribbling ladies" who fomented political controversy).

Her arrival in Boston in April 1833 was keenly awaited. Securing the Kembles as dinner guests during their brief stay could not have been easy, but George Parkman, a wealthy physician, managed to do so. Because it was true, or because he knew that he had to flatter the former president to get him to travel the nine miles from Quincy for the dinner, Parkman told him that Fanny Kemble had requested his presence. Either way, it worked. Adams wrote in his journal that "the young lady was desirous of being introduced to me. And I could but say that it would be very pleasing to me. . . .

As a sort of personage myself, of the last century, I was flattered by the wish of this blossom of the next age, to bestow some of her fresh fragrance upon the antiquities of the past." While acknowledging here the great gap in their ages—he was now 66, she 23—Adams doesn't admit to other gulfs separating them. Kemble represented a British perspective on the morality and politics of the plays, he an American one. She embodied Shakespeare onstage; the only Shakespeare he cared about was on the page. She mingled with leading writers and politicians on both sides of the Atlantic and confidently expressed her views; he remained convinced of women's "imperfections" and "the frailties incidental to their physical and intellectual nature." Adams seems to have decided before they met that Kemble was overrated, her handsome looks and fine mind over-praised; he noted snidely in his journal a few days before the dinner that "Fanny Kemble [passes here] for a great beauty, and a great genius, both of which with the aid of fashion and fancy, she is."

Parkman invited only a dozen or so guests to the dinner party. Some of the men were accompanied by their wives—but not Adams, though his British-born wife, Louisa, who had a strong interest in Shakespeare, had just joined him in Quincy, arriving from Washington the day before. She may not have been invited along because she was exhausted from the long trip; or it may be that this was one more instance of Adams's conviction that women should not be involved in political or literary life (as Louisa Adams herself put it, her husband "had always accustomed me to believe, that women had nothing to do with politics; and as he was the glass from which my opinions were reflected, I was convinced of its truth"). In any case, he came alone and was seated next to Fanny Kemble. Adams was underwhelmed. He made an early night of it, arriving back home before eleven. The following morning he dutifully recorded in his journal that he had "had much conversation with Miss Kemble, chiefly upon dramatic literature; but it differed not from what it might have been with any well educated and intelligent young woman of her age." It's hard to tell whether his dismissiveness was due to overly high expectations or, as seems more likely, a failure to take a young woman seriously.

Kemble also recorded her impressions. She was shocked by what Adams had to say about Shakespeare's plays, including *Othello*, so taken aback that she gulped down her water (and almost her glass too) and thought it best not to respond:

> Last Saturday I dined at————'s, where, for my greater happi-
> ness, I sat between————and————. . . . Presently Mr.————
> began a sentence by assuring me that he was a worshipper
> of Shakespeare, and ended it by saying that *Othello* was dis-
> gusting, *King Lear* ludicrous, and *Romeo and Juliet* childish
> nonsense; whereat I swallowed half a pint of water, and nearly
> my tumbler too, and remained silent,—for what could I say?

Kemble doesn't elaborate on what disgusted Adams about *Othello* or what in particular had reduced her to silence. There the matter might have rested, destined to be forgotten, like countless uncomfortable exchanges between ill-matched dinner guests. Except that two years later—in part because of longstanding commitments, in part because she saw herself as a writer—Fanny Kemble decided to publish a two-volume journal of her American tour, including her recollections of that evening. Its publication led to a storm of protest and excellent sales.

By then Fanny Kemble had married an American, Pierce Butler, who had likely insisted on her inserting dashes in place of real names, to spare those exposed or embarrassed by what she had written. But we know that it was Adams whom she speaks of here, because years later, at the request of a close friend, she filled in those blanks herself in a copy of the printed edition now in Columbia

University's rare book collection. And those dashes didn't stop those who bought her book from filling in the blanks; even before it was published, as copies of her manuscript circulated, that guessing game was being played up and down the East Coast. If anything, the omissions generated even more gossip and finger-pointing. And everyone seemed to know that she was speaking of John Quincy Adams.

When in the autumn of 1835 word reached Adams of the publication of their exchange, he was mortified. Seeking either to help or to fan the flames, George Parkman invited Adams to write an extended response on blank pages of Parkman's recently purchased copy of Fanny Kemble's book. In his long entry, Adams blames "Miss Kemble, [who] appears to have misapprehended the purport of my remarks upon the plays of Shakespeare." If she disagreed with him, she should have said so: "I hoped to elicit from her, either her assent to them, or some observations which might have served me to rectify my opinions." Parkman, with Adams's permission, took Adams's essay to the publisher of the *New England Magazine*, where it was immediately printed, stripped of its opening and closing remarks about Fanny Kemble.

Though the essay was only signed "A," it was clear to many that its author was the former president, and his views were harshly condemned in the press. Adams was stung. What had begun as "a merely casual and very desultory conversation with Miss Fanny Kemble" had now gone national. The critic for the Philadelphia *National Gazette* refused to accept his claim that Othello was black, arguing that Adams had racialized the play in a way that Shakespeare hadn't intended: "Othello should not be so conceived, either as a Negro or Ethiop, but as Shakespeare took him from the Spanish poetry of the day, . . . a Moorish Chieftain." And while warmly agreeing with Adams that "it would seem, then, that Shakespeare was, even in his day, a firm Anti-Amalgamationist," the chivalric

Virginian reviewer for the *Alexandria Gazette* felt that Adams had nonetheless unfairly defamed "one of the best and purest of Shakespeare's female characters." Adams now felt attacked from both sides, a not unfamiliar position for the cautious former president. He was sufficiently self-aware to know that his subsequent long essay on Desdemona and her love for Othello was a tedious and "self-defensive dissertation," but he couldn't hold back, and agreed to have it published under his initials.

While his attack was directed against amalgamation, it focused less on Othello than on the headstrong white woman who desires him. Adams parts company with those who saw the greater threat of interracial mingling stemming from the fantasy of hypersexualized black men, from whom white daughters had to be protected. In this respect, the essay does double duty for Adams: Shakespeare's play confirmed both his deep anxiety about the dangers of mixing the races as well as the threat posed by disobedient women. His own long marriage to a wife who had proved indispensable to his political success had done little to soften Adams's views. Ironically, and almost surely unknown to him at the time, the very month that Adams would write on *Othello*, his wife Louisa would comment on the play herself in her own private diary, reflecting on "the petty spite" and "degrading littleness" of "political life" that produces "the Iago-like attack of smooth'd faced hypocrites" who "wear the mask of friendship, to stab more securely the victims whom they assail." We don't know enough about what was by all accounts a strained relationship to speculate about how his essay on Desdemona's character indirectly touches upon Adams's own marriage.

IT TURNS OUT that John Quincy Adams had brooded about *Othello*, race, and Desdemona's unnatural desires back in his undergraduate days at Harvard—which may explain why he so

33

strenuously rejected the charge that what he thought about Desdemona's marriage was "criticism of 1835." In 1786 Massachusetts reenacted its law against racial intermarriage (which dated to 1705) while eliminating prohibitions against interracial fornication (to protect white men who had sex with black women outside the bounds of wedlock). That same year a nineteen-year-old John Quincy Adams chose to speak about *Othello* to fellow members of his Harvard club. In that address he tried out some of the arguments to which he would later return. Even as an undergraduate he refused to accept the popular view that *Othello* was "the most perfect of all" of Shakespeare's plays; it couldn't be, because the "very foundation upon which the whole fabric is erected appears injudicious, disgusting, and contrary to all probability." He doesn't elaborate on what he means by "disgusting," though it's not hard to guess. The young Adams also found it unbelievable that the senators of Venice would trust the state in the hands of Othello and didn't think it "natural that a young lady so virtuous and chaste as Desdemona is represented would, as Brabantio expresses it, 'Run from her guardage to the sooty bosom of such a thing as him, to fear, not to delight.'" Even then, the greater share of blame is shouldered by Desdemona.

In September 1785, the year before young Adams delivered this speech, his parents, Abigail and John Adams, saw Sarah Siddons and John Philip Kemble, Fanny Kemble's aunt and uncle, star as Desdemona and Othello on the London stage. A letter that Abigail Adams wrote to her son about it gives some sense of how thrilling she found the production: "I did not go into fits, nor swoon, but I never was so much pleased with any person I ever saw upon any theatre." Other than saying that she would have preferred seeing Siddons play a role other than Desdemona, Abigail Adams never mentions race in her letter and there's no record of any other conversation between mother and son about *Othello*.

Yet when Abigail Adams wrote to everyone else about this performance of *Othello*, her letters were all about her deep discomfort with watching a black man fondling a white woman (even though she knew that it was a white actor playing Othello in blackface). She wrote to her sister Elizabeth Smith Shaw that "I lost much of the pleasure of the play, from the sooty appearance of the Moor. Perhaps it may be early prejudice; but I could not separate the African color from the man, nor prevent that disgust and horror which filled my mind every time I saw him touch the gentle Desdemona." She was even more explicit about her ambivalence when she wrote to her son-in-law, William Stephens Smith. I've included in this original-spelling transcription the cross-outs and second thoughts that convey her agitation:

I was last Evening however at Drury Lane and Saw for the first time Mrs. Siddons. Grace was in all her steps heaven in her Eye And every Gesture dignity and Love. She appeard in the tradegy of Othello, and acted the part of Desdemona. Othello was represented blacker than any affrican. Whether it arises from the prejudices of Education or from a real natural antipathy I cannot determine, but my whole soul shuderd when ever I saw the sooty <~heretik?~> More touch the fair Desdemona. I wonder not that Brabantio thought Othello must have used Spells and magick to have won her affections. <~The Character of Othello~> Through the whole play <~is that of a Noble Generous open Manly~> the Character of Othello is Manly open generous and noble, betrayed by a most artfull villan and a combination of circumstances into an action that his Soul abhored. <~but I So powerfull was prejudice that I could not seperate the coulour from the Man and by which means~> That most incomparable Speach of Othellos lost half its force and Beauty, because I could not Seperate the coulour from the Man.

Abigail Adams here gets at the heart of the problem: was her unease in watching a black man "touch the fair Desdemona" a "natural antipathy" or something learned or taught, "the prejudices of Education"? Though she doesn't answer that question, it's an extraordinarily honest response; as someone who strenuously opposed slavery, Abigail Adams's revulsion, whatever its source, clearly made her feel uncomfortable. Her self-doubt stands in sharp contrast with the reaction to the play of her eldest son, who never questioned his own disgust at reading about or watching an interracial couple touching each other: he *knew* it was a violation of natural law.

WHEN IN 1834 Fanny Kemble left the stage and married Pierce Butler (who had pursued her during her American tour), she had not understood that much of the Butler family fortune derived from a slave plantation in Georgia, the second largest in the state, which her husband inherited two years after their wedding. Fanny Kemble was now mistress to more than six hundred slaves. At the end of December 1838, she traveled with her husband and their two young daughters from their home in Philadelphia to the plantation on Butler Island, Georgia, where they resided until May. What she saw there of slavery and the sexual exploitation of black women she found horrific, and it would help destroy an already crumbling marriage.

Kemble kept a journal on this trip too, in the form of long letters to a friend in Massachusetts, Elizabeth Dwight Sedgwick. In the entry for January 1839 she describes the visit of a slave named Morris, who wished to be baptized. Her account turned from his features to generalizations about "a certain African tribe from which the West Indian slave market is chiefly recruited, who have these same characteristic features . . . They are a tall, powerful people, with remarkably fine figures, regular features, and a singularly warlike and fierce disposition." It was a description that led her in turn to the imagined racial characteristics of Shakespeare's tragic hero: "I do not think Morris, however, could have belonged to this tribe, though perhaps Othello did, which would at once settle the difficulties of those commentators who, abiding by Iago's very disagreeable suggestions as to his purely African appearance, are painfully compelled to forego the mitigation of supposing him a Moor and not a negro."

Her reflections on Othello as a black man (rather than a lighter-skinned Moor) led her back to her conversation on that topic with John Quincy Adams. "Did I ever tell you of my dining in Boston . . . and sitting by Mr. John Quincy Adams, who, talking to me about Desdemona, assured me, with a most serious expression of sincere disgust, that he considered all her misfortunes as a very just judgment upon her for having married a 'nigger?'" That last word, which she indicates is quoted verbatim, comes as a shock. It may well explain why a stunned Fanny Kemble kept gulping her water and was reduced to silence. Still, it's hard to believe that a leading abolitionist and one of the best educated men of his day really spoke of Othello in this way. Did people in Boston at the time even use that word? Apparently, they did. To cite but a pair of examples: a British author, William Faux, visiting Boston in February 1819, writes that the "contempt of poor blacks, or niggers, as they are called, seems the national sin of America," and in the early 1830s the Massachusetts abolitionist Lydia Maria Child described how "the very boys of this republic would dog [the] footsteps" even of "a colored man with the dress and deportment of a gentleman" with "the vulgar outcry of 'Nigger! Nigger!'"

Kemble's recollection of Adams's remarks led to additional and sardonic thoughts about the play and slave culture in America. Why don't American productions just come out and, with a slight edit, say what their audiences privately think about Othello? In proposing this, she shows an actor's ear for the sneering ways in which the word was uttered in the slaveholding South:

I think, if some ingenious American actor of the present day, bent upon realizing Shakespeare's finest conceptions, with all the advantages of modern enlightenment, could contrive to slip in that opprobrious title, with a true South Carolinian anti-abolitionist expression, it might really be made quite a point for Iago, as, for instance, in his first soliloquy—"I hate the nigger," given in proper Charleston or Savannah fashion, I am sure would tell far better than "I hate the Moor."

For Adams, marriage between blacks and whites was largely theoretical; he may never have met an interracial couple, or if he did, never acknowledged it. But for Kemble, the fruits of amalgamation were visible everywhere she turned in Georgia.

Kemble wryly notes that while her husband railed against sexual relations between whites and blacks, anyone could see that masters and overseers engaged in sex with enslaved women: "I cannot help being astonished at the furious and ungoverned execration which all reference to the possibility of a fusion of the races draws down upon those who suggest it; because nobody pretends to deny that, throughout the South, a large proportion of the population is the offspring of white men and coloured women." She then demolishes the claim men like her husband and Adams made that amalgamation was against natural law. If it were truly unnatural, why are laws needed to prohibit it? If so monstrous, why are all these white men busily impregnating black women?

After her four-month stay in Georgia, Fanny Kemble never returned to the plantation. She separated from her husband, finally divorced him in 1849, and returned to the London stage (where, for the first time, she played Desdemona, and deliberately broke from tradition, resolving, as she put it, to make "a desperate fight of it" in the "smothering scene" rather than "acquiesce with wonderful equanimity," as her predecessors in the role had done). Butler retained custody of their daughters and used that leverage to delay the publication of her journal about life on the plantation.

LONG BEFORE MOST AMERICANS, Adams had a keen sense of where slavery, tolerated and indeed practiced by many of the nation's founders, would inexorably lead. Because of this, *Othello* meant something quite different for him than it had for his father, John Adams, America's second president, who though not a slave owner himself, and against slavery on principle, tolerated it, as others did, because it was politically expedient to do so. Back in the 1760s, a 33-year-old John Adams, still making his way in the world, could even liken his own unsettled life to Othello's—"a life of *here and everywhere*, to use the expression, that is applied to Othello, by Desdemona's father. Here and there and everywhere, a rambling, roving, vagrant, vagabond life." For John Adams, in these pre-Revolutionary War days, Othello's blackness doesn't even register; for his son, whose generation inherited the problem of slavery, it was all that mattered.

In 1820 John Quincy Adams reconstructed in his journal a cordial conversation he had had with John C. Calhoun, secretary of war and a staunch defender of slavery, over what emancipation would mean for America. The two played out the moves. Abolish slavery, Calhoun said, and the South would immediately break with the North and ally itself with Great Britain. When Adams pointed out that this meant "returning to the colonial state," to his surprise Calhoun agreed, saying that this departure would have been forced on the South. A naval blockade of the North would follow, then undoubtedly an invasion of the South and a bloody civil war. Neither man could see further than that—though both recognized that the abolition of slavery would mean the end of the compromise that had resulted in the United States of America. While he "pressed the conversation no further," Adams reflected in his journal what might

39

follow a "universal emancipation of the slaves": "the extirpation of the African race on this continent, by the gradually bleaching process of intermixture, where the white portion is already so predominant." How Adams felt about the possibility of this "bleaching" and a fully interracial nation is not recorded, but the context suggests that it was undesirable. It would be the only time in his voluminous journal entries that he broached the issue of amalgamation.

If in 1820 emancipation still seemed distant (and few in the country at that time shared his prescience), a decade later, civil strife over the issue of slavery seemed far more likely. Nat Turner's short-lived and bloody slave rebellion (and the ensuing and frenzied retaliation) took place in August 1831 and slavery laws in the South quickly became more restrictive. In the North, the number of antislavery societies ballooned from 1832, when the first was founded, to 1836, when the number reached 350. In December 1831 Adams inaugurated his congressional career by introducing abolitionist petitions, but did so with the caveat that he did not "countenance and support" those calling for the abolition of slavery; he was simply defending the constitutional right to petition. When challenged by a zealous abolitionist to explain this seeming contradiction, Adams explained that pressing further "would lead to ill-will, to heart-burnings, to mutual hatred, where the first of wants was harmony; and without accomplishing anything else." Adams was still a reluctant abolitionist, struggling to find middle ground, hoping to preserve the union of North and South while insisting on the principle that slavery violated a higher natural law. As a recent biographer puts it, "Adams remained something of a sleeping giant between this brief foray [of 1833] and his awakening to his antislavery role in January 1836." Adams's resolve strengthened considerably in 1836, which was also the year that his essay on "The Character of Desdemona" was published. That year he ingeniously opened up a new front on the war on slavery, invoking a "war powers" argument and threatening martial law.

Shortly after, Adams finally admitted to himself in a journal entry that opposing slavery "is a cause upon which I am entering at the last stage of life, and with the certainty that I cannot advance it far; my career must close, leaving the cause at the threshold. To open the way for others is all I can do. The cause is good and great."

IF WE RELY on his daily journal entries and his vast correspondence as evidence, Adams had not given much thought to Desdemona's "unnatural" union with Othello for nearly a half century after his undergraduate speech on the subject, a period in which he went on to serve as a diplomat, ambassador, secretary of state, senator, and then president of the United States. It was only after leaving the White House in 1829, when he began to wrestle with how committed he intended to be to the abolitionist cause, that their interracial marriage once again began to preoccupy him. The first inkling of this occurs in May 1830, in a letter he wrote to his son Charles. He had been reading the fragments of Cicero's oration on "Roscius the Comedian," he explained, which addressed a property issue concerning a slave—trained as an actor by Roscius but owned by another Roman—who is killed. Who ought to collect damages, his owner or the man who taught him his craft?

Adams, trained as a lawyer, considered this question's potential contemporary application, for such a property dispute might well arise in the American South between a slave owner and a tradesman who had taught a slave his craft. The case prompted another thought. While slaves may not be taught to read in America, they might profitably be taught to act in leading black roles: "The managers of our theatres might take the hint; and except where it is felony to teach them to read, might teach many a slave to make excellent Othellos, Zangas, and Jubas—In my exposition of Othello's character he ought to have no other representative." Adams wrote with the assurance that his son knew who Zanga, the avenging black hero of Edward Young's *The Revenge* (1721), was, as well as Juba, the Numidian prince of Joseph Addison's *Cato* (1712). His antislavery polemic touching on the failure to educate slaves might have ended there, but Adams could not stop himself, and added: "As the people of Maryland and Virginia breed slaves for exportation to the cotton and sugar plantations, why should they not breed them for stage players and husbands to Desdemonas?" Adams couldn't seem to invoke Othello without his thoughts drifting to that "unnatural" scene in which a trained black actor would marry a white Desdemona.

He was not alone in fantasizing luridly about Othello and Desdemona. E. W. Clay invited viewers to do the same in another of his racist prints from the late 1830s, called "The Fruits of Amalgamation." Hanging on the wall above the interracial couple and their children is a portrait of "Desdemona and Othello." It may look like a quiet domestic scene, but the threat of the violence that a black man may inflict upon his white wife—imagined to be the inevitable fruits of such a union—is foreshadowed in the scene from Shakespeare's play, and even subliminally figured in the angle of the black husband's arm (the same as Othello's, who is about to smother Desdemona).

Adams and Clay weren't the only ones invoking Othello during these heady times. Adams's fierce opponent in the House, James Henry Hammond, of South Carolina, who believed that slavery was "the greatest of all the great blessings which Providence has bestowed upon our glorious region," invited his fellow congressmen to imagine a nightmarish future in which an Othello would be seated alongside them. The real threat for Hammond was political, not sexual: a talented and ambitious black man cut in Othello's mold dominating whites politically, even one day serving as president of the United States. Like Adams, Hammond found it easier to speak of Shakespeare's fictional character than to name an actual, threatening African American person:

Are we prepared to see them mingling in our legislation? Is any portion of this country prepared to see them enter these halls and take their seats by our sides, in perfect equality with the white representatives of an Anglo-Saxon race—to see them fill that chair—to see them placed at the heads of your Departments; or to see perhaps some Othello . . . gifted with genius and inspired by ambition, grasp the Presidential wreath and wield the destinies of this great Republic? From such a picture I turn with irrepressible disgust.

The 1830s proved a difficult time for those, like Adams, trying to stake out an increasingly untenable position of favoring abolition while opposing amalgamation. The incoherence of this position was mirrored in legislative battles: while in 1836 Massachusetts legislators revised state law to include "explicit instructions that the biracial offspring of interracial couples were deemed illegitimate," they reversed themselves seven years later, voting to repeal the ban on marriage between whites and "Negroes, Indians, or Mulattos." There could be no middle ground. It was either unnatural and illegal or natural and permissible. Those like Adams trying to split the difference were left arguing that people were free—but that freedom did not extend to the right to marry someone of a different race.

Adams couldn't stop obsessing now about Othello and Desdemona, and began rehearsing to those in his circle, in letters as well as in conversation, his riff about the play's interracial problem. So, in September 1829, when dining with his son Charles, Adams "disclosed his singular views" of Othello and Macbeth, which, Charles recorded, "rather amuse than convince me." And in February 1831, he wrote to Pennsylvania author and politician Charles Jared Ingersoll about Desdemona as a "wanton trollop" who received her just punishment for "falling in love with a blackamoor." Later that year, while dining in New York City with the legal scholar James Kent,

Adams tried out his theory once again: "I said I took little interest in the character of Desdemona, whose sensual passions I thought over-ardent, so as to reconcile her to a passion for a black man." Kent chose not to let the argument pass unchallenged, for Adams admits in his journal that Kent "did not entirely agree with him in this estimate of Desdemona; his son still less." Adams may have been rigid but he was not stupid—and if his congressional record is any indication, he knew the difference between a winning and a losing argument. He must have recognized that he wasn't gaining any converts to his views on Desdemona's lust for Othello, yet he persisted, and by the time that he encountered Fanny Kemble eighteen months later, he was pressing this argument more aggressively than ever.

What he told her, and then so uncharacteristically elaborated on in print, seems to have allowed Adams to cling to a position short of genuine freedom and equality for former slaves. His tentative steps toward becoming a committed abolitionist seem to have required a counterweight, and he found it in this repudiation of amalgamation. Shakespeare gave him much to work with. By directing his hostility at Desdemona rather than Othello, he was able to sidestep criticizing black men. And it proved more convenient to attack a headstrong young fictional woman than a living one, though it's clear he could be hostile to both. It is not a great leap to consider his essay on "The Character of Desdemona" as a rebuke of Fanny Kemble, who had publicly embarrassed him. While her name was excised before Adams's response was published, she haunts it. As with race, so with gender: Shakespeare licensed Adams to say what he otherwise was too inhibited or careful to say—or say so honestly. For a very intelligent man, he seems to have been extraordinarily clueless about how he sounded—or about how much he was revealing about his most deeply held convictions. He never admitted to or wrestled with in the privacy of his journals how disgusting he found interracial marriage or how at odds this disgust was with his abolitionist convictions; yet he felt free to share these feelings with friends, with Fanny Kemble, and eventually with the world, but only through his reflections on Shakespeare.

Adams remained proud of what he had written about Desdemona's character, so much so that when in 1839 a leading American actor, James Hackett, who was assembling a collection on Shakespeare, asked if he could republish the pair of essays, Adams agreed, and recorded that this "extension of my fame is more tickling to my vanity than it was to be elected President of the United States. I pray God to forgive me for it, and to preserve me from falling in my last days into the dotage of self-adulation." Hackett included both essays in his *Notes, Criticisms, and Correspondence upon Shakespeare's Plays and Actors*, published in 1863, a copy of which he sent to President Abraham Lincoln. What Lincoln thought of his predecessor's essays is lost to us.

Adams died in 1848, so didn't live to see this belated publication, nor another that also came out in 1863: Fanny Kemble's *Journal of a Residence on a Georgian Plantation in 1838–1839*. Had he seen her book he might have been infuriated by what she now revealed of their conversation, yet perhaps mollified by a letter appended to the end of the book, written by Kemble in late 1862 in response to being asked whether she considered herself an abolitionist. From what she had seen, Kemble wrote, hypocritical and self-interested Northerners, "with the exception of an inconsiderable minority of its inhabitants," have "never been at all desirous of the emancipation of the slaves." Their position on abolition only changed with "the gradual encroachment of the Southern politicians upon the liberties of the North," which provoked "resistance on the part of Northern statesmen." In the same volume in which she had earlier castigated Adams for having called Othello a "nigger," she singled out for special praise the efforts of one of those progressive Northerners: "the life-long opposition to Southern pretensions by John Quincy Adams."

45

Ulysses S. Grant (*left*) and Alexander Hays,
at Camp Salubrity, Louisiana, 1845

CHAPTER 2

1845: Manifest Destiny

In the summer of 1845 more than half of the US Army was ordered to head to the Mexican border. The soldiers set up camp on disputed territory south of the Nueces River, in Corpus Christi. Four thousand strong, it was the largest deployment of American troops since the War of 1812. Yet the objectives of their mission remained unclear, even to its commanders. Had this "Army of Occupation" been dispatched to the border as a threat, to nudge Mexico into surrendering its claims to Texas—formally annexed by the United States the previous March—in exchange for a substantial cash payment? Or had President James K. Polk sent them there to provoke Mexican troops and trigger a war of conquest that could lead to a land grab of more than a million square miles and extend the reach of slavery?

Weeks then months dragged by as the troops, encamped in neat rows along the shoreline, drilled and awaited orders. Before they landed, only a few dozen people lived in the small coastal trading post; but the arrival of thousands of soldiers in Corpus Christi quickly drew a parallel army of camp followers—a "vast horde of liquor-selling harpies." The outcome was predictable. One of the officers described Corpus Christi at the time as "the most murderous, thieving, gambling, cut-throat, God forsaken hole in Texas." Soldiers combated boredom, dysentery, rattlesnakes, and torrential downpours with gambling and brawling, and patronized the saloons and brothels that had sprung up near their encampment.

In early November, hoping to curb the fistfights and dissipation, Captain John B. Magruder oversaw the building of an "Army Theater" within the encampment, large enough to hold eight hundred spectators. He and other young officers, many of whom had been classmates at the US Military Academy at West Point, fell to work, painting scenery and rehearsing plays that they themselves would perform. The theater took two months to build. It opened on January 8, 1846, and played to packed houses, though admission was not cheap: a box seat cost a dollar and a place in the pit half that (at a time when soldiers were paid seven dollars a month). The opening production was James Sheridan Knowles's *The Wife*, a decade-old play about a wife's suspected infidelity that owes much to *Othello*. For soldiers anxious about wives and sweethearts left behind, a plot that in the end celebrated a devoted wife's fidelity was a smart choice. But an alternative and brutal outcome, in which male anxieties find an outlet in violence, is never far from thought. The play's epilogue, spoken by its heroine, Mariana (the "wife" of the title), makes this, and its relationship to Shakespeare's grim model, explicit; in it, Mariana recounts how she had "dreamed each night, I should be Desdemona'd," though luckily she avoids the fate of Shakespeare's heroine, since, as she puts it, "my Othello, to his vows more zealous— / Twenty Iagos could not make him jealous!"

The officers also decided to stage *Othello*—and most likely began rehearsing it in November. One might think that a play about a black man eloping with a white woman would have been objectionable or taboo in the South, but the opposite is true: in the quarter century before the Civil War, *Othello* was regularly staged in slave states (with bronzed-up white Othellos); twenty times, for example, in Memphis, Tennessee, and twice that many times in Mobile, Alabama. The issues of race and amalgamation had a particular resonance for those gathered in Corpus Christi, because victory in a war with Mexico meant introducing slavery into territory where it was now illegal and raising the prospect of the large-scale intermingling of white Anglo-Saxon blood with what was called the Mexican "race."

Far more than most playgoers, they would have recognized that *Othello* was also about the frustrations of military life, in which soldiers seek relief in drinking, fighting, and the embrace of camp followers. Iago's grievances at the outset of the play would also have sounded familiar, given the often-bitter conflicts among the officers gathered in Corpus Christi over who had precedence: those with brevets (temporary promotions based on merit) or those who held seniority in rank the old-fashioned way (as Iago puts it "where each second / Stood heir to the first"). And, of course, it was a play about manliness and the fear of cuckoldry.

A popular lieutenant, Theodoric Porter, was chosen to play Othello. But finding the right officer to play Desdemona proved a tougher challenge. Lieutenant James Longstreet—one of many at Corpus Christi who would later play a leading role in the Civil War—was first asked to play her, but he stood six feet tall and was unusually athletic, a football player, and was deemed physically wrong for the part. The company then settled on a West Point classmate and friend of both Porter's and Longstreet's who was 5 feet, 7 inches tall and a slight 135 pounds. His name was Ulysses S. Grant. We don't know whether Grant had much interest in or exposure to Shakespeare, but at this point in his life he seems to have had a strong intellectual bent: he was a skilled painter and an avid reader of contemporary fiction, and we know that on his way to West Point from his home in rural Ohio he had taken advantage of going to the theater while passing through Philadelphia.

It's hard to shake the familiar grizzled image of Grant, whose steely visage stares back from the front of fifty-dollar bills. But that image dates from decades later in his life, after he served as commander of the Union army that defeated the Confederacy, and then as eighteenth president of the United States. Grant was chosen to play Desdemona because of his looks and perhaps his voice too (J. D. Elderkin, who served with him in this campaign and admired Grant, recalled that "he was always a very mild-spoken man, he spoke like a lady almost"). Occasionally, biographers draw attention to what was considered his "girlish" features as a young man, none more so than W. E. Woodward, whose popular *Meet General Grant* (1928) pressed this point hard: "Young Grant had a girl's primness of manner and modesty of conduct. There was a broad streak of the feminine in his personality. He was almost half-woman, but the strand was buried in the depths of his soul." Woodward offers no source for his claim, repeated by others, that in "the army before the Mexican War he was called the 'Little Beauty' by the officers of his regiment."

All this would seem exaggerated were it not supported by what Longstreet recalled of their days at the Academy when interviewed by the *New York Times* at the time of Grant's death in 1885: "As I was of large and robust physique I was at the head of most larks and games. But in these young Grant never joined because of his delicate frame." Longstreet also recalled Grant's "fragile form" and how his "distinguishing trait as a cadet was a girlish modesty." A rare photograph of a youthful and beardless Grant survives from the year before he shipped off to Corpus Christi. Age 22 or so, Grant is on the left, alongside his racing horse, Dandy, and might easily pass for one of Shakespeare's cross-dressed heroines. When she first set eyes on him at this time, Emma Dent, his future sister-in-law, thought Grant looked "as pretty as a doll." It's not that surprising, then, to learn that Longstreet, in an unpublished interview he gave around 1890, remembered how "Grant took part in the theatricals which we had at Corpus Christi and used to do the girl's parts. He looked very like a girl dressed up."

THERE ARE MOMENTS when nations change course. Americans often assign names to these turning points: "the Boston Tea Party," "Pearl Harbor," "9/11." The year 1845 was one of these pivotal moments. Grant himself later acknowledged the epochal and costly nature of the decision the nation faced that year. The way he saw it, what started in Corpus Christi would, after horrendous loss of life in the Civil War, end at Appomattox, with the defeat of the South. Mexico, he wrote, was "of incalculable value; but it might have been obtained by other means. The Southern rebellion was largely the outgrowth of the Mexican war. Nations, like individuals, are punished for their transgressions. We got our punishment in the most sanguinary and expensive war of modern times." The Mexican–American War redefined the physical boundaries no less than the moral ones of a republic-turned-empire, for it would serve as a proving ground for aggressive and militant territorial expansion, grounded in a fervent conviction that it was America's God-given right to claim (and if need be, seize) all lands from East to West Coast. The inspired name for this conviction, introduced into the national vocabulary in the summer of 1845, was "Manifest Destiny."

For John L. O'Sullivan, the journalist who coined this term, annexing Texas was a catalyst for this new sense of national purpose: "It is now time for the opposition to the annexation of Texas to cease . . . It is time for the common duty of patriotism to the country to succeed—or if this claim will not be recognized, it is at least time for common sense to acquiesce with decent grace in the inevitable and the irrevocable." A cheerleader for American exceptionalism, O'Sullivan mocked those bent on "thwarting our policy and hampering our power, limiting our greatness and checking the fulfillment of our manifest destiny to overspread the continent allotted by Providence for the free development of our yearly multiplying millions." O'Sullivan's appeal to God and country and his assurance that "the boundless future will be the era of American greatness" were a winning combination.

Many abolitionists recognized the dangers of expansionism and tried to derail it. But they came across as weak and elitist. It wasn't easy challenging the swagger of those who thought defeating both the Mexican and British military and extending American dominion to the Pacific would be accomplished with little cost or sacrifice. O'Sullivan had argued that it was pointless to look to the past: "We have no interest in the scenes of antiquity, only as lessons of avoidance of nearly all their examples." In response, but to no avail, Shakespeare's authority was mustered by Robert Charles Winthrop, a member of the House from Massachusetts and one of those who opposed the annexation of Texas "now and always." He addressed his fellow congressmen in early 1845, deriding naïve warmongers who urged their fellow Americans to "muster our fleets in the Pacific, and march our armies over the Rocky Mountains, and whip Great Britain into a willingness to abandon her pretensions" to the Pacific Northwest. "I have wishes that some Philip Faulconbridge were here to reply," he argued, "as he does in Shakespeare's *King John*, to some swaggering citizen of Angiers:

> ——Here's a large mouth, indeed,
> That spits forth Death and mountains, rocks and seas
> Talks as familiarly of roaring lions
> As maids of thirteen do of puppy dogs.
> What cannoneer begot this lusty blood?
> He speaks plain cannon fire, and smoke and bounce.
>
> (2.1.458–63)

Winthrop knew his Shakespeare, and trenchantly paraphrases the rest of the speech: "And against whom are all these gasconading bravadoes indulged? What nation has been thus bethumpt and bastinadoed with brave words?" Yet his efforts to shame politicians (whose manhood was all talk and who let others do the fighting for them) in the end proved fruitless.

The confluence of technological and demographic changes that marked this effort to make America great in the 1840s now seem painfully familiar. The rise of the telegraph, coupled with the widespread introduction of steam engines on waterways and rails, accelerating the movement of goods and people, revolutionized traditional notions of time and space. Old and familiar ways were further upended by a changing labor landscape, marked by increasing industrialization, the loss of jobs to women (who could be paid less), and a rise in immigrant labor, as the influx of foreigners in the 1840s nearly tripled, with more than 1,700,000 new arrivals, mostly Irish and German, competing for jobs and housing.

Inherent in Manifest Destiny was a belief in manly superiority. Like a headstrong wife, Mexico had to be taught a lesson, roughed up a bit. President Polk's negotiator in Mexico, John Slidell, wrote to the secretary of state in March 1846 that "We shall never be able to treat with her . . . until she has been taught to respect us." A poem—"They Wait for Us"—published in the propagandistic *National Songs, Ballads, and Other Patriotic Poetry Chiefly Relating to the War of 1846*, offers a more personal version of such thinking, imagining a young Mexican wife longingly awaiting the arrival of the Yankee invaders, "Whose purer blood and valiant arms, / Are fit to clasp her budding charms." The poem goes on to justify her act of cuckoldry; she needs a real man, for her Mexican husband's once "manly mind," long "vanquished by the subtile clime," is now "sunk in sloth."

In her book *Manifest Destiny and the Antebellum American Empire*, Amy S. Greenberg has illuminated how competing versions of manliness collided at this time in America. A restrained masculinity that embraced moderation, virtue, domesticity, and sobriety—a "manhood derived from being morally upright, reliable, and brave"—was being elbowed out by a more martial manhood, one characterized by a greater tolerance for excess, alcohol, physicality, and domination. This model had a special appeal for workingmen who felt left behind in an age of rapid economic transformation—changes that little benefited them—and so turned, in hope and frustration, to America's frontier.

The military encampment in Corpus Christi in the autumn of 1845 offered about as extreme and concentrated a version of martial manliness as might be found anywhere. And the building of the Army Theater (and soon, a second and commercial Union Theater, in which professional actors performed) can be seen as an attempt to temper this dangerously aggressive world with a more restrained model. But what those well-meaning officers hadn't realized was that their theatrical efforts would force them to confront the discomfort they themselves felt about manliness. It explains why, in the end, though he rehearsed the part of Desdemona, Grant was not allowed to perform it. Longstreet recalled in his unpublished interview that "Lieutenant Porter who was to play the part of Othello objected. . . . Porter said it was bad enough to play the part with a woman in the cast, and he could not pump up any sentiment with Grant dressed up as Desdemona."

It's unclear whether Porter's reported use of the word "sentiment" carries a hint of the residual dictionary sense of "amatory feeling or inclination." If we take him at his word, it sounds like Porter, something of a method actor, couldn't muster the physical desire for Grant demanded by the role (not least of all, one imagines, in the scene in which Othello arrives in Cyprus and lovingly kisses Desdemona). But that explanation feels unsatisfying, a placeholder for something that neither Porter nor Longstreet could quite admit to.

Five years after his unpublished interview Longstreet finished his memoir, *From Manassas to Appomattox* (1895). He had been at the center of many of the bloodiest and most consequential battles in his nation's history, in both the Mexican–American and Civil Wars. That he devotes attention to this anecdote about amateur theatrics a half century after these rehearsals of *Othello* took place, and even remembered the conversations the young officers had, suggests that what happened, though seemingly trivial, had made an indelible impression. In this memoir, Longstreet returns to the issue of "sentiment," though this time Grant's rather than Porter's. And he adds a clarifying detail; in this version, he edits out how good Grant looked in a dress, and has Porter shift the blame onto men playing women's parts: "after rehearsal Porter protested that male heroines could not support the character nor give sentiment to the hero."

The episode offers the rarest of glimpses into anxieties about what it meant to be a white man at this unsettled time in American history, when, as the historian Harry Watson memorably put it, "all white men would be equal, at least in theory, but no one else would be the equal of a white man." Shakespeare helps clarify what was happening at this moment in America, for the performance of his plays forced to the surface the cultural tensions and shifts that otherwise prove so difficult to identify and might otherwise have remained submerged. In the end, Longstreet writes, a professional actress was brought in to replace Grant: "we sent over to New Orleans and secured Mrs. Hart, who was popular with the garrisons in Florida." Gertrude Hart arrived in time to rehearse and perform the lead on opening night of *The Wife*. In December, Grant went on a monthlong expedition that took him to San Antonio and Austin, and it is unlikely that he would have rehearsed the part of Desdemona after Hart's arrival.

Grant never wrote about his experiences performing at the Army Theater. Still, a future general and president saw the world, for a brief moment, through the eyes of a white woman in love with a black man. Curiously, it was around this time that the clean-shaven Grant decided at long last to grow a beard. Perhaps, on the eve of his first military campaign, his reputation for girlish looks was not something he wanted to cultivate. He wrote to his fiancée three months later, on February 7, 1846, "Julia if you could see me now you would not know me, I have allowed my beard to grow two or three inches long." But, Longstreet recalled, Grant didn't give over playing "the girl's parts" in other plays; Grant would have done so as a bearded lady rather than as one easily mistaken by his fellow soldiers for a desirable woman. In early March, the Army Theater was torn down and the army broke camp and marched south to the Rio Grande. The time for theatrics was over.

ON DECEMBER 29, 1845, as the young officers in Corpus Christi were preparing to open their Army Theater, playgoers were gathering five thousand miles away at London's Haymarket Theatre to see a much-anticipated production of *Romeo and Juliet*, starring a pair of American siblings in the title roles. *Romeo and Juliet* had been one of the most popular of Shakespeare's plays in the late eighteenth century, staged in London roughly five hundred times from 1750 to 1800. But by 1820 the number of productions had fallen off, on both sides of the Atlantic. In New York City, for example, there are records of fifteen productions between 1754 and 1806, but only four over the next twenty years. When it was performed in the early nineteenth century, critics and playgoers were invariably disappointed. Part of the problem was Romeo's character, which required an actor dashing enough to carry off a romantic first kiss at the Capulets' party and engage in furious swordfights in which he kills Tybalt and then Paris. Yet the same actor had to be convincingly unmanly when he declares, "O sweet Juliet, / Thy beauty hath made me effeminate." And he needed to be even more wrought in the scene in the friar's cell, where he falls on the floor, weepy and self-pitying, as Friar Lawrence chastises him: "Art thou a man? Thy form cries out thou art; / Thy tears are womanish . . . Unseemly woman in a seeming man" (3.1.12–13; 3.3.110–13). Nineteenth-century British critics, desperate to protect Shakespeare's hero from charges of effeminacy, resorted to hairsplitting: "Of all the male persons of the drama that we can think of, Romeo, without being in the least effeminate (we hope our readers will find the distinction intelligible) is the most feminine."

From the time that Richard Burbage, the star tragedian of Shakespeare's playing company, first thrilled Elizabethan play-goers in the role, and from the Restoration up through the late eighteenth century, one leading man after another succeeded in making the role his own. The play ought to have been a hit during the Romantic era. But as norms of manhood began to change, mir-roring the split between martial manliness and effeminacy within Romeo himself, male actors found the role increasingly unplayable. The leading English tragedians of the early nineteenth century—John Philip Kemble, Samuel Phelps, Charles Kean, and William Macready—all stumbled, some badly, in the role, or only excelled in parts of it. The polite, courtly (and often aging) Romeos that reigned on both sides of the Atlantic were duds.

The performance at the Haymarket Theatre in December 1845 offered an alternative, for the part of Romeo was to be performed by a woman, Charlotte Cushman, and that of Juliet by her younger sister, Susan. And the Cushman sisters (nicknamed the "American Indians" by the British actors who filled out the cast) promised to restore much of what had long been cut. Cushman's Romeo was an immediate sensation. The enthusiastic review in the London *Times* was representative:

> It is enough to say that the Romeo of Miss Cushman is far superior to any Romeo that has been seen for years. The dis-tinction is not one of degree, it is one of kind. For a long time Romeo has been a convention. Miss Cushman's Romeo

is a creative, a living, breathing, animated, ardent, human being. The memory of playgoers will call up Romeo as a collection of speeches delivered with more or less eloquence, not as an individual. Miss Cushman has given the vivifying spark, whereby the fragments are knit together. . . . To drop to more material considerations, Miss Cushman looks Romeo exceedingly well.

Cushman was not the first woman to play Romeo. Ellen Tree had done so in London in 1832, with Fanny Kemble as her Juliet. Others in England soon followed—including Caroline Rankley, Felicita Vestvali, Fanny Vining, Margaret Leighton, and Esmé Beringer. But even before Tree, American women had begun playing the part; in New York City alone Mrs. Barry played Romeo in 1827, followed by Lydia Kelly in 1829, Mrs. Hamblin in 1832, Mrs. Barnes in 1833, and Mrs. Lewis in 1836. Records of nineteenth-century performances are spotty at best—and even fewer cast lists survive—but George C. D. Odell, who combed through archives and assembled this evidence in his fifteen-volume *Annals of the New York Stage*, identified fourteen other women who took to the stage as Romeo after Cushman's London debut—and that was in New York City alone, at a time when Shakespeare was performed in many towns and cities across America. In an ugly aside, Odell places the blame for what he thought was a terrible idea on Cushman herself, rather than to something larger percolating in the culture: "Miss Cushman's homely features and lack of feminine charm drove her to masculine characters; her success in them helped to perpetuate throughout the best years of the century the very bad custom of female Romeos, Hamlets, etc." While there were still men who played Romeo at the time, for a brief and crucial period in the mid-nineteenth century, Romeo had become a woman's part. And no woman was as celebrated in the role as Charlotte Cushman—almost forgotten today, but in her own day a superstar, the greatest American actress of the nineteenth century.

Cushman's early aspirations as a singer—she was reportedly a fine contralto—had foundered when, forced into soprano parts, she injured her voice. She changed careers in her late teens and her potential as an actor was recognized early on, following her debut as a strong-willed Lady Macbeth at the age of 19, in 1836. But Cushman soon saw that if she didn't want to be a bit player—and at the outset of her career she was performing upwards of forty different minor roles a year—she would have to carve out a distinctive theatrical identity. Given the parts in the repertory available to women, that would not be easy.

Even when enjoying success as Lady Macbeth, Cushman knew that she would always be subordinate to her male leads; she wasn't particularly happy with them nor they with her, especially as her reputation grew. A fellow actor, George Vandenhoff, wrote of her assertive Lady Macbeth that "one feels that if other arguments fail with her husband, she will have recourse to blows." Edwin Booth, no less intimidated, confessed that when playing Macbeth alongside her, he felt like crying out, "Why don't you kill him? You are a great deal bigger than I am." For her part, as she later told the critic William Winter, she resented playing against "such little men." She stood only five feet six inches, so this had less to do with height than with stage presence. Winter, an admirer, saw this as central to her appeal: "You might resent her dominance, and shrink from it, calling it 'masculine'; you could not doubt her massive reality nor escape the spell of her imperial power."

Cushman gravitated to so-called breeches parts, including Rosalind in *As You Like It* and Viola in *Twelfth Night*, comedies in which the heroines disguise themselves in men's attire, and was soon recognized as "undoubtedly the best breeches figure in America." Critics were struck by how completely she transformed herself into a man: she looks, one wrote, "in every inch a man; and a man she is in voice and manner also, and gesture . . . Her mind became masculine as well as her outward semblance; and on the assumption of her manly garb she would seem to have doffed all the constraint of her sex." But this sort of flirtation with cross-dressing was a far cry from passing as a man (and not simply playing a woman briefly disguised as one). Cushman decided to take the next step and play male leads. In the course of her long and distinguished career she would go on to play more than forty such roles, though no part she played would have the cultural impact of her Romeo.

She prepared for her London debut as Romeo with extraordinary care. She had quietly assayed the part early in her career, the first time in April 1837 while still a stock player in Manhattan (a reviewer for the *New York Courier* noted that "her love scenes with Juliet were beautifully rendered," and if she "would give to the impassioned scenes more fire, and to her grief more emphasis, her Romeo would be indeed a faultless performance"). Though records of this are scarce too, it appears that this year she also performed the role in Albany as well as in New Orleans, then took another turn at it in Philadelphia in 1843. These early and brief forays made clear to her the particular hurdles she faced in playing Romeo, both professional and personal.

While reviewers would praise her naturalism as Romeo—"there is no trick in Miss Cushman's performance"—that effect can also be seen as an accumulation of techniques she had honed over time. She had a particular genius for signaling or disguising the conventional habits of one gender or the other. Experienced actors of the day such as John Coleman marveled at this talent. "As a rule," Coleman writes, actresses who cross-dressed "betray their female origin by quaint little movements, their lower limbs are apt to cling helplessly together, the knees instinctively bowed inward." Not Cushman. She didn't try to disguise her "ample and majestic bust," he concludes, a bit bizarrely, yet her figure "might have been that of a robust man." Cushman also understood how critical it was to capture Romeo's turmoil in the balcony scene as well as in the friar's cell, so put special effort into them; audiences were thrilled by her "agonized, distracted look" in the latter, "the frantic expression of the face, the deadly determination." Vandenhoff, who played Mercutio in her Philadelphia performance, lent her his sword, hat, and cloak, taught her some fencing moves, and later took credit for the "masculine and effective style" in which she killed Tybalt and Paris. Yet he never mustered the courage to tell Cushman to her face what he later committed to paper: "Romeo requires a *man*, to feel his passion, and to express his despair. A woman, in attempting it, 'unsexes' herself to no purpose"; there "should be a law against such perversions."

Cushman borrowed freely from the technique of two stars she had acted alongside, Edwin Forrest and William Macready. Both men were talented and egotistical—but there their resemblance ended. Forrest was America's first great native-born actor. Barrel-chested and muscular, he cultivated the persona of the brash, hypermasculine American male. Even the *New York Times* gushed about this, arguing that he was the embodiment of the new type of man the country now needed: "Standing before them in his colossal strength of form, his chiseled and massive features the indices of an iron will, he seems the type of the American man before whose indomitable energy the wilderness of the New World has receded." Forrest was wildly popular with young, white, working-class men. And he was deeply uncomfortable with strong women (including his English wife, whose divorce settlement he unsuccessfully contested for eighteen years). Forrest had publicly caned a man who criticized him in the newspapers, paid a ridiculous amount for a statue of himself as Coriolanus, and was both a friend and a supporter of President Andrew Jackson, who embodied his sort of masculinity in the political sphere. Forrest's career was carried along by the swift currents of "Jacksonian democracy"—that catch-phrase (and oxymoron) for the political realignments in the 1830s and 1840s that came to be identified with the nation's seventh president: anti-elitist, racist, manly, expansionist, nationalist, in favor of limited regulation and a more powerful presidency, and mostly good for white men.

Macready was everything Forrest was not. Though no less self-centered (he was the kind of actor who trimmed the lines of others in the cast and demanded that others retreat to the rear of the stage while he hogged the footlights), Macready was also admired by the cultural elites, whose friendship he cultivated. His restrained acting style, which tended to the naturalistic and psychological, capitalized on his expressive features and strong voice. Macready had strongly supported Cushman at the outset of her career, encouraging her to make her fortune in London. While Cushman was likened to Forrest as a brash American, she bore a closer physical resemblance to Macready. The English humorist Gilbert Abbott à Beckett in London made much of this likeness: "What figure is that which appears on the scene? / 'Tis Madame Macready—Miss Cushman, I mean. . . . In the chin, in the voice, 'tis the same to a tittle. / Miss Cushman is Mister Macready in little." His poem also reveals how much Cushman lifted from Macready, including many of his trademark gestures, the "walk on the toes," the "bend of the knee, the slight sneer of the lip, / The frown on the forehead, the hand on the hip." A keen observer of his rivals, Forrest saw the resemblance too, and privately mocked Cushman as "a Macready in petticoats."

Charlotte Cushman's decision to make her London debut as Romeo in late 1845 was badly timed: Anglo-American relations had recently begun to fray over rights to the Pacific Northwest, a territorial dispute that since the War of 1812 had remained unresolved; it was agreed that both Americans and British subjects could dwell and trade in the large swath of Oregon Territory that covered present-day Idaho, Oregon, Washington, Wyoming, and Montana as well as parts of British Columbia. The situation had been heading toward a quietly negotiated diplomatic resolution until James Polk inflamed matters during his presidential run by linking American territorial ambitions in Mexico with those in the Pacific Northwest. He did so to win voting blocks in a hotly contested election: the Oregon Territory—presumably without slaves—would balance out the acquisition of slave states in land carved out from Mexico.

By the time that Polk gave his inaugural address in March 1845, this campaign promise was now policy, as Polk made clear that America's claim to Oregon was both "clear and unquestionable." British warships anchored off the coast of the Pacific Northwest, as Polk asked Congress on December 2, 1845, to give the British notice that America was terminating its agreement to jointly occupy this territory, while in the Senate there were calls for war with Britain. It's unlikely that Polk wanted to embroil the US military on two fronts; but he gambled that war in the Pacific Northwest was the last thing the British needed at this moment. Though powerful, the British Empire had its hands full dealing with armed conflicts with the Maori in newly colonized New Zealand, even as they were embroiled in the First Afghan War, and, closer to home, dealing with famine in Ireland. But whether all this posturing in Washington was a bluff remained unknown in December 1845.

Two weeks before Cushman's London debut as Romeo, a long editorial ran in the *London Times* that made clear the British saw (and were not pleased by) what was taking place in the United States: "If then we seek for some more considerable cause of the agitation now raging in the Union, on the subject of Oregon, it may without much difficulty be identified with the popular passion which so recently gratified itself by the annexation of Texas, and which must now be regarded as the predominating principle

63

of the foreign policy of the United States." The editorial then took a sharper tone, making clear that this change in foreign policy to what we now call "America First" threatened to turn the young republic into an absolutist regime:

> By annexing Texas and by laying claim to exclusive sovereignty in Oregon, without submitting to arbitration or compromise, the United States have already done what no state in Europe—no, not the strongest and most unscrupulous of them all, would have dared to attempt, or could have perpetuated with impunity. Such acts belong to a more barbaric time, and they have usually been prompted by the lawless passions of absolute princes.

The problem, then, was a product of both the "popular passion" of the American people and the "lawless passions" of their leaders. The immediate political context in which Cushman took the stage was not conducive to a warm welcome; for any American with a passionate acting style, or playing a passionate role, the dangers of guilt by association were inescapable.

London audiences that had previously applauded Edwin Forrest now turned against him. And reviewers found it convenient to use Cushman as a stick to beat her fellow countryman. The same critic who eviscerated Forrest for his Othello also said that it was "impossible to speak too highly" of Cushman's Emilia in the same production (she was also praised for her "boldness," pronounced the "American Siddons," and deemed undervalued "on the other side of the Atlantic"). It maddened Forrest that Cushman's acting style depended on much the same brash American style as his own, yet only she was praised for it. He sniped that Cushman "is not a woman, let alone being womanly." It would be the last time the two would work together. But it was a great stroke of luck for Cushman that Forrest served as a lightning rod for anti-American sentiment. The appeal of a passionate and distinctively American acting style had not diminished; but it was now only acceptable in a woman, especially when playing a man.

Like every other actress of the day, Cushman knew that the personal lives of women who performed publicly were closely scrutinized, and one who dared embrace another woman onstage even more so. Cushman made sure that she was known as a regular churchgoer and as an unmarried woman secured the reputation as one who was not seen consorting with men. Some must have seen past this, including the female admirer in London who told another after watching Cushman play Romeo—after a pause and with a "light laugh"—that "Miss Cushman is a very dangerous young man." But had most London playgoers known (and not just subliminally grasped) that she was a woman who loved other women—the term "lesbian" did not even enter the vocabulary until 1890—they may well have repudiated her, so one more thing that Cushman had to do in preparing for her high-risk London debut was restrict familiarity with her sexual orientation to her loyal circle of women friends. When she sailed from America she had to leave behind her lover, Rosalie Sully, with whom she had exchanged vows, and until her stardom was assured, and even thereafter, she was assiduous about managing her public persona.

Knowing how realistically she planned to perform the play's most erotic scenes, she also chose her Juliet carefully, scraping together enough money to bring her sister to England, hoping that critics would have less to complain about if two sisters shared the stage (though Susan's domestic situation—her husband having abandoned her and their young child—had not gone down well in Edinburgh, where the sisters had performed together in advance of the London opening). Cushman was no doubt relieved to read in the *Morning Advertiser* after opening night that her sister's appearance as Juliet "diminished, in a great degree, any unpleasant feeling that might otherwise have been entertained." It was only after her success was assured that she turned to other, and younger, Juliets.

Once her fame was secure, Cushman felt freer to dress as she liked, appearing in public in "a man's hat and coat, a man's collar and cravat, [and] wellington boots, which, so far from attempting to conceal, she displayed without reticence or restraint," and "led to speculations which it would be indecorous to repeat." Back in America, she "astonished" locals (as the *Cleveland Plain Dealer* reported in 1851) by her "fine appearance" at her hotel dressed from head to toe "in masculine attire—hat, coat, unmentionables and all." Cushman had a number of long-term lovers, including the English actor Matilda Hays and the American sculptor Emma Stebbins. She called Stebbins "Her Juliet," and Mary Devlin signed her letters to Cushman as "Your Juliet," confirming how fully identified Cushman was with this role—one that she preferred above all others.

She retained her manly demeanor even when heckled. There's a wonderful anecdote of her playing Romeo at the National Theatre in Boston during the 1851–52 season, with Sarah Anderton as her Juliet, when "in the midst of one of the most romantic passages between the lovers, some person in the house sneezed in such a manner as to attract the attention of the whole audience, and everyone knew that the sneeze was artificial and derisive." Hearing that man snort, "Cushman instantly stopped the dialogue, and led Miss Anderton off the stage, as a cavalier might lead a lady from the place where an insult had been offered her." Whether she was still in character or simply being herself at that moment—and it's probably impossible to draw a sharp distinction—she "then returned to the footlights and said in a clear, firm voice, 'Some man must put that person out, or I shall be obliged to do it myself.'" The crowd loved it, and as the "fellow was taken away; the audience rose *en masse* and gave three cheers for Miss Cushman, who recalled her companion and proceeded with the play as if nothing had happened." Years later Cushman recalled that she "got more cheers for that irregular interpolation than for any of the scenes written for the original Romeo." It's not surprising, for in that moment she threaded the needle perfectly, acting gallantly without overstepping the mark, willing to take matters into her own hands if necessary, but positioning the lout who intentionally sneezed as the aggressor whose behavior needed to be publicly and collectively repudiated.

Cushman's London debut produced an unprecedented outpouring of criticism on both sides of the Atlantic. Most of the reviews were raves; a few were patronizing. All of them returned, obsessively, to what happens to masculinity when a woman can so convincingly play a man. The *Athenaeum*, while conceding that this was "one of the most extraordinary pieces of acting, perhaps, ever exhibited by a woman," made clear that this achievement was decidedly not a good thing: "The instances . . . are rare in which the heroes of tragedy have been personated by other than men: but such mistakes have occurred, and will occur again. The interests of Art, however, require that certain limits should be set to this license, which, as we are informed, has already been carried to excess in America." Others, like the critic for the *Morning Chronicle*, while acknowledging that what everyone was witnessing was a "delicate, perhaps a dangerous, experiment," couldn't quite deal with the fact that he forgot that this Romeo was a woman: "Perhaps the most extraordinary feature of Miss Cushman's performance was, that the idea that we were looking at a woman never once crossed us. We hardly know whether, in writing this, we are penning down a compliment or not." No less an authority than Queen Victoria, who went to see Cushman's Romeo, weighed in: "No one would ever have imagined that she was a woman, her figure and her voice being so masculine."

As is so often the case in the theater, there was a gap between what people saw and what they projected upon the performers or simply imagined seeing. A video clip of Cushman's performance would no doubt disappoint, failing to capture its allure. The sole surviving photograph, a publicity shot of Cushman dressed as Romeo, taken four or five years after her London debut when she was playing the part in America and wearing the same costume, conveys little of what made her performance so thrilling. And yet, as late as 1858 (at age 42) she was still being hailed by American reviewers as "in face, form, and general make-up, a most perfect specimen of the impetuous and yet loving Romeo":

Charlotte Cushman as Romeo, c. 1854.

Compare this with the illustration of her performance that ran in the *Illustrated London News* a few days after she first appeared as Romeo on the London stage. This broad-shouldered, smoldering lover whose face Juliet caresses is likely closer to what playgoers imagined that they saw:

Charlotte Cushman as Romeo and Susan Cushman as Juliet at the Haymarket Theatre, January 1846.

For some, Cushman's performance threatened longstanding notions of propriety. The critic for the *Spirit of the Times* was not alone in worrying about the effects on Cushman of performing masculinity, the kind of damage that Lady Macbeth had brought on herself: "She is a woman and we cannot but be shocked at the unsexing of the mind and heart which she must undergo at assuming such a character as Romeo." Even as the planned eight-night run extended to eighty, and toured elsewhere in Britain, and soon, in a triumphant return home, in America's major cities, a backlash kicked in. The writer most threatened by Cushman's performance was an Englishman, George Fletcher, who hated the idea of that hybrid, a "she-Romeo," and wrote at length about "the disgustingly monstrous grossness of such a perversion." It is the erasure of difference in Cushman's performance, so praised by others, that unnerves Fletcher:

> It is idle to talk (as we find certain critics doing at the time) as if there was nothing in the performance itself to remind one's very physical apprehensions that the *soi-disant* impassioned hero was a woman. That any male auditors could think so, would surely prove that we live in a time when there are men with so little manhood as to have almost lost all sense of the essentially different manner in which this passion, especially, manifests itself in the two sexes respectively.

Fletcher simply cannot accept that others can forget that Cushman is a woman; for him it must remain an impossibility, or rather something best banished from consciousness. He's left to argue that Cushman misrepresents Shakespeare's hero by hypersexualizing Romeo through "the most vulgarly selfish and headlong will and appetite," a distortion made worse by "the nasal utterance and awkward vowel pronunciation of her country." The only way to wash away the stain of her "unnatural personation" is for a manly and patriotic Englishman to take up the challenge and expel "the intensely gross misconception of it lately impressed on the minds of so large a portion of the London public."

Cushman succeeded not only, as her various admirers have argued, because she was a superb actor who captured both Romeo's tough and feminine sides, but also because she understood her cultural moment and its confused craving for and repudiation of a manly manhood. Upon returning in 1850 to America, where she played Romeo at the Astor Place Opera House, her performance had to be halted in the middle of the second Act because the sustained applause went on for so long. The *New York Evening Post* noted that "she drew together as large an audience as we have seen at any time in that building," adding, in way of explanation, that the "part of Romeo is remarkably well adapted to the little more than feminine and little less than masculine qualities of Miss Cushman." Six months on, newspapers were still reporting that the crowds that came to see her were unprecedented: "We have never before seen such a large assemblage within the walls of the Broadway Theatre."

By this time the Mexican–American War was over. The troops that marched south from Corpus Christi in March 1846 soon engaged Mexican forces, and Congress declared war on Mexico on May 13. By then, Theodoric Porter, who had so recently played Othello, was dead, killed in a skirmish, his body never recovered. By war's end in 1848, roughly a sixth of the more than 100,000 American soldiers who fought in the victorious campaign were dead, the highest rate of fatalities of any American war. Now that America had won, the state of Texas got a lot larger, and parts or all of Nevada, Utah, California, Arizona, Colorado, New Mexico, and Wyoming would soon be ceded by Mexico to the United States. The military campaign was so successful that some wanted to push on further south into Central America—but the thought of even larger-scale amalgamation checked that impulse. In the Northwest, despite nationalist cries of "Fifty-Four Forty or Fight!"—alluding to the northern boundary of Oregon, with its latitude line of 54 degrees, 40 minutes, and so a catchphrase for the effort to extend the border as far as Alaska—the Senate approved in June 1846 the Oregon Treaty with Great Britain. The British gave America most of what it demanded, setting the border at the forty-ninth parallel (ceding what is now Oregon, Washington, Idaho, and parts of Montana and Wyoming). But the huge territorial expansion came at a terrible price. As Ulysses S. Grant foresaw, the "wicked war" that began in Texas led inexorably to the Civil War killing fields of Antietam, Gettysburg, Bull Run, and the Wilderness. By 1865, the fires that fueled Manifest Destiny were extinguished, along with the lives of more than 700,000 Confederate and Union soldiers. Martial manliness was, many now saw, a hollow and dangerous thing.

This also marked the end of the age of female Romeos. After the war, a couple of women gave readings from the part, but only one is recorded as having acted it on the New York stage—Miss Marriot, in 1868. Before the war, the *New York Times* could declare that "there is in the delicacy of Romeo's character something that requires a woman to represent it," and the character's "luscious language . . . seems strange on the lips of a man." After the war, such sentiments disappeared from print. A less manly acting style—exemplified by the "poetic" Hamlet of Edwin Booth, "his heart too tender, and his will too weak for the circumstances of human life" (as his admirer William Winter put it) was now in vogue. Once men could comfortably play a Romeo who could at times appear effeminate, they reclaimed the role.

In 1874, New Yorkers lined Fifth Avenue to honor Charlotte Cushman's retirement from the stage, and she was similarly celebrated across the land. A contemporary, writing after Cushman's death in 1876, recounts that her loss "was regarded in America almost as a national catastrophe." Cushman is now all but forgotten; the story Americans like to tell of their past cannot easily accommodate her. Near the end of her acting career, on March 1, 1873, Cushman performed in Washington, DC. President Ulysses S. Grant, three days before his second inauguration, came to see her perform, and wanted to meet her afterward. But Cushman didn't care to talk to him, explaining why in a letter to a friend a few days later: President Grant was "at the theater on Friday. I did not see him—for I had no curiosity." Had she known that a cross-dressed Grant had once rehearsed the part of Desdemona she might have been more curious.

*Great Riot at the Astor Place Opera House, New York,
on Thursday evening, May 10, 1849.*

CHAPTER 3

1849: Class Warfare

A fatal shot tore through the neck of Asa Collins, a 45-year-old real estate agent, as he stepped off a Harlem Railroad car in lower Manhattan. A few blocks away, Bridget Fagan, a 30-year-old housekeeper out shopping, was felled by a shot that struck her below the right knee; amputation failed to save her life. George W. Gedney, a 34-year-old Wall Street broker, caught a shot that shattered his skull. An African American woman, whose name nobody thought to record, was shot and badly wounded at the corner of Lafayette Place. They were all innocent bystanders. Most of those who died on the evening of May 10, 1849, were shot deliberately while taking part in a violent riot outside the Astor Place Opera House. More than a score were killed and a hundred or so wounded. Newspapers reported that the bloodshed was unprecedented: the "massacre on Thursday night in front of the Opera House was, in the number and character of its victims, the most sanguinary and cruel that has ever occurred in this country," a "wholesale slaughter."

The New York State militia had been mustered to suppress the riot at Astor Place, where a huge crowd, estimated at somewhere between 10,000 and 24,000, gathered to protest a performance of *Macbeth* by the British actor William Macready. The more hot-headed among the crowd, unable to force their way into the theater, attacked the majestic building itself. The militia's presence did little to deter them, nor did a warning volley fired over their heads. As the increasingly emboldened rioters hemmed in the police and militia, pelting them with cobblestones, the order was given to fire directly at the crowd. Successive volleys rang out until the rioters, realizing at last that the soldiers weren't firing blanks, retreated. Some, calling for revenge, promised to return in force the following day.

The story went national, the *New Orleans Daily Crescent* reporting that what "began in madness ended in blood." That "madness" was so widely known that it didn't need to be repeated: a feud between Shakespeare actors. As one local paper put it: "Our city has been intensely agitated, a riot of a most outrageous and disgraceful character has taken place, the military has been called out, property destroyed, blood shed, and, for the last thirty-six hours, New York has worn the aspect of a civil war, all because two actors had quarreled." It would be more accurate to say that while the Astor Place riots had their origins in a theatrical controversy, this proved to be less a cause than a complex means of channeling long-simmering anger over a host of divisive social issues, many of them amplified by their Shakespeare connection.

Press accounts traced the source of the violence to an earlier Shakespeare performance. William Macready was touring Scotland in March 1846, and opened his engagement at the Edinburgh Theatre with *Hamlet*. He played to a full house, though, as the hypersensitive star complained in his diary, they "gave less applause to the first soliloquy than I am in the habit of receiving." That the audience was initially cool may in part be explained by the 53-year-old Macready's odd appearance: he wore a sort of dress whose waist reached to his armpits, oversize gloves, and a satin undershirt that looked dirty. A fellow actor described the effect as "positively grotesque." Yet all went well enough until the moment in Act 3 when Hamlet tells Horatio, "I must be idle" (3.2.89), just before *The Mousetrap* is staged.

Scholars, then as now, are divided over what Hamlet means by this. For some, it's an indication that he must appear indifferent. That's what the actor James Hackett thought at the time: Hamlet must appear "listless and unoccupied, in order that his guilty uncle, the king, might disregard his presence." Not everyone agreed, including nineteenth-century editors convinced that because Hamlet intends to feign madness, acting idly here "signifies the aimless going hither and thither which marks an idiot." Macready preferred this interpretation, and while he didn't exactly move "hither and thither" aimlessly as the Danish court is seated, he came pretty close (and, as it happens, his movement recalls Anthony Scoloker's description in 1604 of how the first actor to play Hamlet, Richard Burbage, would "run mad"). Hackett, who had seen him play Hamlet, describes how Macready "assumed the manner of a silly youth, tossed his head right and left, and skipped back and forth across the stage five or six times before the footlights, at the same time switching his handkerchief, held by a corner, over his right and left shoulder alternately."

At just this moment in Macready's Edinburgh performance, he was loudly hissed. A young John Coleman, from his vantage point onstage as Horatio, remembered it vividly years later as "a hiss like that of a steam engine." Macready, upon hearing it, was stopped in his tracks and "became livid and absolutely hysterical with rage." Badly derailed, Macready sat down onstage and struggled to collect himself. Coleman looked up into the box seats and spotted the perpetrator, the American actor Edwin Forrest: "I can see him now. The square brow, the majestic head, the dark eyes flashing forth defiance." The house went quiet and the other actors stood around waiting. The audience too was silent, until a voice rang out from the gallery: "Throw him out." Forrest rose and slipped out of the playhouse, while Macready, Coleman writes, "like a man possessed, leaped into the breach, apparently inspired by the ordeal through which he had passed."

It's not obvious what drove Forrest to hiss so vehemently and why in turn it so upset Macready. This sort of theatrical disruption was pretty minor by contemporary standards, and the practice of hissing goes back at least as far as Elizabethan days (Shakespeare even jokes about it, having Puck in the epilogue to *A Midsummer Night's Dream* speak of how he and his fellow actors hope to escape the hissing sound of "the serpent's tongue"). Forrest too was on tour in Scotland, playing in Aberdeen, and had detoured 180 miles out of his way to see Macready perform. He had recently been stung by the mockery of London's critics, some of them friends of Macready, in this, his second extended tour of Britain. He was quicker to blame his rival for working against him behind the scenes than to admit that the English had grown weary of his blustering style. But it's hard not to conclude that watching Macready prance back and forth across the stage, waving his handkerchief daintily in the air, the obsessively masculine Forrest couldn't resist hissing in disapproval of what struck him as his rival's effeminate manner.

Macready's reaction in the days that followed, as the encounter was written up in national newspapers, underscores how wounded he felt and how reflexively he saw the growing quarrel as rooted less in personal animosity (since before this the two actors had gotten along well enough) than in national character: "No Englishman would have done a thing so base . . . I do not think that such an action has its parallel in all theatrical history! The low-minded ruffian!" Forrest remained defiant. He fiercely defended his right to hiss and explained what had provoked his response: "Mr. Macready thought fit to introduce a fancy dance into his performance of *Hamlet*, which I thought, and still think, a desecration of that scene." Forrest returned to the United States and ramped up his own nationalist rhetoric, telling a crowd in Kentucky of his commitment "to bring the American stage within the influence of a progressive movement—[cheers]—to call forth and encourage American dramatic letters—[applause]—and last, not least, to advance to just claims of our own meritorious and deserving actors [applause]." Critics and audiences on both sides of the Atlantic took sides, and the controversy remained a sore point between two of the most famous entertainers of the day.

A couple of years later, in the autumn of 1848, it was Macready's turn to perform on his rival's turf. He had decided to sail to America for a farewell tour. When Forrest learned that Macready would appear at the Arch Street Theatre in Philadelphia for eleven performances, he signed on for a parallel run at the Walnut Street Theatre, a short stroll away. He would go head-to-head with the Englishman. If Macready opened with *Macbeth* on October 19, so would he. And the same held true for *Othello* on October 22, *Lear* on October 27, and *Hamlet* on closing night. And on those nights of the run when Macready was performing non-Shakespearean roles, Forrest responded with a pair of nationalist melodramas he had commissioned in a contest to promote American dramatists, playing to his strengths and to his Jacksonian principles. So on November 21 and 28, when Macready staged an adaptation of a German play, *The Stranger*, Forrest appeared in *Metamora*, in which he played a noble Native American driven to violence (who dies cursing the English), and then in *The Gladiator* as Spartacus, who heroically leads the fight against oppressive Roman masters. And if the political counterpoint was not obvious enough, when Macready took the stage as King Henry VIII on November 30, Forrest played the brash hero in *Jack Cade*, a commissioned American play about the doomed leader of a popular uprising made famous by Shakespeare in *Henry VI, Part 2*. It didn't much matter that both actors were by now quite wealthy (earning as much as fifty dollars or more for every performance) or that Macready chafed against the British class system and was considering settling in America; Macready was now positioned, by Forrest and his vocal American supporters (and by his own words), as the embodiment of British elitism.

Their feud might have simply exhausted itself at the box office, with the actor who drew the larger crowds declared the victor. The two men crossed paths on the street in Philadelphia and had a chance to clear the air, but neither said a word to the other. While Forrest seethed, Macready was increasingly unnerved by the threat of having his performances disrupted. Before opening night, he was told to expect protesters. Only a few showed up. A penny was thrown at him, then a rotten egg; both missed. The dispute could have ended there, but Macready seized upon a curtain call, rare in those days, to deliver a speech in which he admonished that un-named "American actor" who had so rudely hissed in Edinburgh. It was a costly decision. That was sufficient provocation for Forrest, who retaliated by publishing a letter in the *Public Ledger* mocking Macready for not having the courage to name him, and dismissed his rival as a "superannuated driveller."

Macready changed his mind about settling in the United States ("Let me once get from this country and give me a dungeon or a hovel in any other"). He published a letter of his own threatening legal action and overreacted in advance of his performance of *Othello*, asking for "at least ten police behind the scenes" at the theater. His fears for his safety were unfounded, and that performance, along the rest of the run, passed without further escalation. But if Macready thought that he had put the controversy behind him as he continued his American tour, which would culminate in New York City, he was wrong. In Cincinnati, a playgoer tossed half a sheep's carcass onstage during his "fancy dance" in *Hamlet*—a gesture, Macready thought, of "malevolent barbarism." The quarrel would soon escalate.

MACREADY HAD FIRST TOURED America in 1826 when he was in his mid-thirties, already an established star. He made his New York debut at the Park Theatre, near City Hall, which had opened

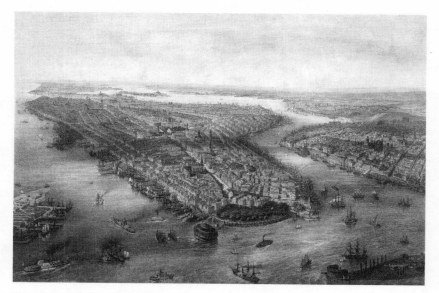

Theodore Muller, *New York and Brooklyn*, c. 1849.

in 1798 and had stood for more than a quarter-century as the metropolis's premier theater. Over time it began to face competition. In 1823 the Chatham Garden Theatre was built, followed two years later by the conversion of the Lafayette Circus into a playhouse. Macready's tour coincided with the opening of what was soon the Park's main competitor, the Bowery Theatre, which could seat 3,500 playgoers.

The growth of New York City between Macready's first visit to New York and his return in 1848 was extraordinary. In 1820 New York was a relatively small, homogenous city: its population was 123,000, only 5,000 of whom were immigrants. By 1850 the population had quadrupled to more than a half million, nearly half—235,000—now foreign-born, mostly from Germany and Ireland. The city had become overwhelmingly white; the 1845 census noted that 12,000 or so—3 percent of the city's population—were "colored"; a century earlier, when slavery was still practiced there, a fifth of the city had been African American. The city had extended as far north as Greenwich Village in the 1820s, and by the year of the Astor Place riots would encompass all of lower Manhattan up to Twenty-Sixth Street. The remaining grid of Manhattan, plotted in 1811, was rapidly filling in.

By 1849 there were many more theaters, and they were playing an increasingly visible role in the city's cultural life. While the Park had burned down, the Bowery was thriving, as were the Broadway, Burton's, the Olympic, Christie's Minstrels, and Chanfrau's, as well as the recently built Astor Place Opera House (which, despite its name, staged plays too in order to turn a profit, just as other theaters put on operas). A move toward branding—with each theater catering to a specific clientele, offering alternative kinds of entertainment—was beginning, but only just beginning. Playgoers could still find a range of offerings, including Shakespeare, staged at almost every venue, and an avid playgoer might go to the Bowery one night and the Park the next.

Some theaters provided access to the pit through a side entrance, others through the main one. Some had slightly higher entry fees than others. But all of New York's theaters—at least until the Astor Place Opera House was built—admitted anyone who could pay for a ticket. A cheap seat cost as little as a quarter (or even half that), which meant that almost everyone, at a time when a day laborer earned roughly a dollar a day and a skilled worker twice that, could afford to see a play. There were no dress codes. No seat (except for boxes) could be reserved in advance. The theater was one of the few places in town where classes and races and sexes, if they did not exactly mingle, at least shared a common space. This meant, in practice, that the inexpensive benches in the pit were filled mostly by the working class, the pricier boxes and galleries were occupied by wealthier patrons, and in the tiers above, space was reserved for African Americans and prostitutes. All knew their place, or were taught to. Macready recalled what happened at the Park Theatre when a "black woman . . . by some mistake had got into the pit," where she was "roughly" handled "amidst shouts of laughter from the white spectators."

In the late 1840s it was comforting to think of the rapidly changing city as it had been, not as it was fast becoming. In a lithograph by Theodore Muller from 1849, Manhattan looks remarkably peaceful. The image also shows that while extending northward, the city was not yet—except for church spires—soaring upward. There weren't many green spaces for relief from those crowded streets: that large patch of green in the middle of the lithograph is the area around City Hall, what we now think of as downtown. Central Park did not yet exist and the densely inhabited part of the city tapers off north of Fourteenth Street, where the two great thoroughfares, Bowery and Broadway, intersect (now Union Square, so named because when the grid was laid out that was where they met). You could say that in the 1840s and 1850s those two streets, one grounded in the notorious Five Points, the other in the financial district—embodying the different classes and aspirations of the city—had been on a collision course, as the metropolis, and its theaters, extended northward along these arteries. They would soon collide, explosively, at Astor Place.

Income inequality had also increased dramatically. Nowadays, we speak of the "One Percent" who command more than their fair share of the nation's wealth; in 1849, their equivalent was called the "Upper Ten Thousand" or the "codfish aristocracy" (so named for the vast sums made in the fishing industry). In 1842, the *Sun* began publishing alphabetical lists of New Yorkers with a net worth greater than $100,000—including more than a dozen millionaires. Even as the rich were getting richer, the poor, especially the just off the boat, were truly impoverished. Street gangs of working-class immigrants were on the rise, their muscle exploited by unscrupulous politicians. The city was deeply divided over abolition. Nativism, in reaction to the unending stream of immigrants, was on the rise. Class divisions had grown sharper too, with unionization and better labor conditions (like a ten-hour workday) as yet a dream. The city's police department was too small and poorly organized to deal with a crisis, and firefighters were still volunteers. The strains went largely unacknowledged.

They only became obvious when rioting broke out. The history of New York City in the eighteenth and nineteenth centuries was punctuated by violent riots, among these the Negro Riots of 1712 and 1741, the Stamp Act Riot of 1765, the Doctors' Riot of 1788, the African Grove Riot of 1823 (in which a black theater was destroyed by a white mob), the Spring Election Riot of 1834, the Abolition Riots of 1834–1835, and the Flour Riots of 1837. More often than not, the rioting originated at a theater: between 1816 and 1834 alone there were twenty-nine theater-related riots in New York City. The last of these was the Farren Riot at the Bowery Theatre, a dress rehearsal for what would happen fifteen years later at Astor Place. In early December 1833, Forrest was to star again in *Metamora*. The other actors had to learn their parts quickly, and the stage manager, George Farren, backed up by a fellow Englishman, Thomas Hamblin, who ran the theater, posted a notice warning that any actor who wasn't off book by the final rehearsal would be fined a night's wages. A popular American actor, D. D. McKinney, was unprepared and read from his script. When he was docked a symbolic dollar (he was earning $15 a week), he angrily refused to accept his wages, declaring that "he cared not for the laws of the theatre." Hamblin fired him. McKinney went to the press and accused Hamblin of acting in a way that was "tyrannical and arbitrary in the extreme, and not to be tolerated by an American public." Hamblin refused to back down. The stakes were further raised when a local butcher accused Farren of having "cursed the Yankees" and "called them jackasses."

The slow-lit fuse ignited rioting seven months later, on July 9, when Farren was to profit from a benefit performance. That same night, a crowd gathered at the Chatham Street Chapel to disrupt an American Anti-Slavery Society meeting. Disappointed to find no abolitionists there, the crowd, swollen to four thousand or so, and stirred up by handbills recounting Farren's insulting words about Americans, decided to head instead to the nearby Bowery Theatre, where they "took possession of every part of the house, committed every species of outrage," and attacked Hamblin, who tried to protect himself from assault by waving an American flag. The angry crowd wasn't easily assuaged, even after they were assured that Farren would be fired. Their hero, Edwin Forrest, who was playing the lead that evening, spoke to them, and the blackface performer George Washington Dixon tried pacifying them by singing the patriotic "Yankee Doodle Dandy" as well as the racist "Zip Coon." They didn't disperse, however, until a large contingent of watchmen arrived, whereupon they turned their rage once again against the abolitionists, charging down to Rose Street, where they trashed the home of a leading abolitionist, Lewis Tappan, and for the next week ran amok against other antislavery campaigners and attacked African American homes and churches. The theater, not for the last time, found itself at the center of a riot, one fueled by a heady mixture of racism, nationalism (spurred by anti-British sentiment), hostility toward abolition, and economic anxiety.

As the story of the Farren Riot suggests, there were many reasons why theaters in antebellum New York figured so centrally in fomenting civil disobedience. Riots require crowds, and theaters, located in densely populated parts of town, could hold thousands of spectators. And because there were many British actors working in New York's theaters, they were a convenient place to stir up nationalist sentiment. But a more significant reason was that theaters were

85

imagined to be worlds unto themselves and therefore less subject to outside authority. It was a view reiterated in 1849 by an anonymous commentator: "The public and magistrates have been accustomed to look upon theatrical disturbances, rows, and riots, as different in their character from all others . . . and magistrates, looking upon it as a matter between the actors and the audience, have generally refused to interfere, unless there was a prospect of a violent breach of the peace." Theaters were imagined as more contentious versions of town hall meetings, democratic spaces where all could speak their minds; to challenge these unspoken rules was un-American and a provocation.

One of those who recognized the extent to which America's theaters exposed rifts between social classes was a foreigner, Alexis de Tocqueville. In his *Democracy in America* (1835) he notes that the American theater is one of the few places where rich and poor meet, and "there alone do the former consent to listen to the opinion of the latter, or at least to allow them to give an opinion at all." Tocqueville saw that this commingling inevitably favored the disenfranchised: "The pit has frequently made laws for the boxes." The American stage, then, was a potential threat to a nation's financial and cultural elite: "If it be difficult for an aristocracy to prevent the people from getting the upper hand in the theater, it will readily be understood that the people will be supreme there when democratic principles have crept into the laws and manners—when ranks are intermixed—when minds, as well as fortunes, are brought more nearly together."

New York's upper crust responded to such threats by building a new theater in which it could retain its authority. The Astor Place Opera House, built in 1847, financed by the subscriptions of 150 wealthy citizens, deliberately broke with longstanding traditions. The site had been chosen with care, just north of the nine sumptuous townhouses of Colonnade Row, an enclave occupied by some of the city's wealthiest citizens (including, before his death, the fabulously rich John Jacob Astor, after whom the new building was named). The *Spirit of the Times* captures with unintended irony the aspirations of the new theater: "There is a feeling of repose, of security from rude and impertinent interruption, a languor of voluptuous enjoyment." A popular minstrel song mockingly offers much the same sentiment, but does so from the perspective of the excluded, and in a markedly different dialect:

> De Astor Opera is anoder nice place;
> If *you* go thar, jest wash your face!
> Put on your 'kids,' and fix up neat,
> For dis am de spot of de *eliteet!*

New York's *Home Journal* described the new building in luscious detail, from the exterior—"the dark chocolate-colored stone that soon imparts an air of age to edifices constructed of it"—to its lavish interior, where the "facades of the three tiers within" are "all aglitter with gold and silver gildings," a "glorious chandelier . . . hangs from the center of the ceiling," and underfoot, "thick-pictured carpets line the floors with a layer of absorbing silence." It was "the kind of house Titania would have ordered for Bottom to see a play in"—though designed to keep out rude mechanicals like him.

The Opera House could hold 1,800 spectators, half the capacity of competitors. It introduced fixed and numbered seats in the pit (renamed the parquette, what we now call the stalls or orchestra seats), which were covered in red damask; the benches that filled the pit in other theaters were now relocated to a small "cockloft" with an obstructed view, accessible only through a narrow stairway, segregating these spectators from the wealthier subscribers below. And there would be no space set aside for prostitutes; unaccompanied women were not welcome. The message was clear. As the *New York Herald* put it, this was to be "the first authentic organization of the upper classes, congregated under a splendid dome in a respectable quarter of the city." On top of all this, a dress code was instituted—including white or "kid" gloves for men—intended to keep out working-class riffraff.

That dress code rankled. A pseudonymous "American Citizen" complained that "to say to the laboring man you must appear in the Opera House in a black dress coat, white vest, white cravat, and white kid, would be equivalent to telling him he should not enter it at all." The new rules were seen as fundamentally undemocratic: "The Opera House in this city was intended for the exclusive use of those only who could afford to pay high prices for admission, and dress in a peculiar style. But it will be asked: have not people a perfect right to establish a theatre and fix such a rate of prices as they see fit, and require persons to dress in a certain fashion? We answer emphatically, *no*. In this country to do so would be an outrage on the feelings and rights of a vast majority of the people." Others also saw that the changes instituted at the new playhouse crossed a threshold and threatened "the spontaneous cohesion of interest and sympathy which alone binds a republic."

THE FAREWELL PERFORMANCES at the exclusive Opera House by an actor viewed by many as a stand-in for British elitism could not have been worse timed. In addition to ongoing Anglo-American tensions, exacerbated by Britain's callous response to the Irish Famine (which had produced an exodus to America), reports of revolutionary violence that had been sweeping European capitals since February 1848 (including the use of military force to suppress civilian protesters) were discomforting to some and emboldening to others.

In local politics, the Whigs—the party of the rule of law, bank-rolled by the same clientele that frequented the Opera House—had recently defeated the splintered Democrats in New York's mayoral election. In response, antebellum Democrats were doubling down in their populist base, blending "lower-class racism and anti-abolitionism, class and ethnic resentments, and nationalist jingo," as the historian Sean Wilentz puts it, to build an "anti-nativist, red-blooded party of the patriotic workingmen, the eternal foe of the aristocratic, Tory, 'Federal Whig Coon Party.'" That meant relying heavily on the strong-arm tactics of Tammany Hall go-betweens like Isaiah Rynders, who would be a ringleader in the ensuing rioting.

Rynders was a thug and a nativist with a violent past. He thought that mob violence was justified if it reflected the will of the people, and believed "that freedom of speech was a privilege, not a right, especially if such speech insulted Americans or threatened their values or prerogative." Shakespeare was as much a part of his life as fisticuffs. As a young dockhand, Rynders had purchased a copy of the plays and he trained himself to "recite entire scenes from memory." Shakespeare also came in handy when stirring up a crowd; a "singular feature" of Rynders's "campaign addresses when he entered the political fray" was "a mixture of terrible profanity with liberal quotations from the Scriptures and Shakespeare."

In anticipation of Macready's opening night, unusual coalitions were forming. On one side, bankers and leading cultural figures found common ground in championing the British Shakespearean. On the other, nativists opposing the foreigner Macready joined forces with their sometime foes, the immigrant Irish Catholics. Their mutual hatred of the British overrode their differences, and their shared racist views cemented their union. Macready's appearance at Astor Place offered a perfect occasion for a showdown; both sides were confident they would prevail in any confrontation.

Rynders's lieutenant, Ned Buntline, wrote in his newsletter, *Ned Buntline's Own*, "If they mean to have a war, let it begin here!"

Forrest, who was playing to packed houses at the Broadway Theatre, decided to shadow Macready once again, and declared that he too would play Macbeth that evening. Thomas Hamblin at the Bowery did the same, hoping to cash in on the controversy. All three actors played to full and appreciative houses that evening, and Forrest got a huge cheer when he recited Macbeth's timely words, "what purgative drug / Would scour these English hence?" (5.3.57–58). Nearly 10,000 New Yorkers would see one of these three productions of *Macbeth* that night. To put that in perspective, in the past thirty years there have only been three productions of *Macbeth* in all on Broadway. In mid-nineteenth century America, Shakespeare's appeal remained near universal, his works embraced as avidly by the Bowery crowd as they were at Astor Place—if anything, more so. Since the previous May, playgoers at the Bowery could have seen *Macbeth*, *Coriolanus*, *Hamlet*, *Othello*, *Richard III*, *Romeo and Juliet*, *King John*, and *Henry VIII*, while the Broadway offered *Romeo and Juliet*, *Hamlet*, *Othello*, *Macbeth*, *King Lear*, *The Merchant of Venice*, *The Comedy of Errors*, and *Henry IV, Part 1*. Before Macready's scheduled one-month run, the only Shakespeare in the past year at Astor Place had been a benefit starring Edwin Forrest as Macbeth; his supporters didn't hold that against him. Elsewhere, Chanfrau's was offering *Richard III* as well as *Othello* in a double bill with the blackface parody *Otello*. There had even been a pair of burlesque skits greeting Macready on his arrival in America: *Mr. Macgreedy, or A Star at the Opera House* at Chanfrau's and *Who's Got Macready, or A Race to Boston* at the Olympic.

At stake were competing notions of what sort of behavior was acceptable in a theater, as well as diverging American and British approaches to Shakespeare. *Macbeth* that May 7 highlighted these differences. It's a mistake to think of Macready's and Forrest's performances as a showdown between highbrow purist and lowbrow crowd-pleaser: both performers today would seem wildly over-the-top. Shakespeare's Macbeth is bold yet contemplative, committed to a brutal path to power yet tortured by the consequences of that choice, leaving actors considerable leeway in how to approach the role. Yet the play didn't offer an opportunity—as say, *Julius Caesar* or *Coriolanus* did—to explore competing political views; the differences between British and American styles would turn on issues of character. Forrest, in keeping with how he approached most roles, emphasized Macbeth's boldness and played him as "the ferocious chief of a barbarous tribe," a warrior who furiously hurls a goblet over the head of Banquo's ghost and nearly strangles a messenger who brings bad tidings. Forrest showed little interest in exploring Macbeth's reflective side or his guilty conscience. To that end, for example, he altered the punctuation of the soliloquy in Act 1 that begins "If it were done when 'tis done, then 'twere well / It were done quickly" (1.7.1–2), turning self-doubt into confident assertion: "If it were done, when 'tis done, then *'twere well.*" He had an intuitive grasp of what values his fellow countrymen identified with, and gave them a Macbeth, as one admirer put it, who was "a man there to do his three hours' work; brawlingly it may be, sturdily, and with great outlay of muscular power, but there's a big heart thrown in."

Macbeth was Macready's favorite role. He offered playgoers a more thoughtful and tormented hero. Central to his interpretation was how much Macbeth's character is altered after killing Duncan. His "crouching form and stealthy, felon-like step of the self-abased murderer" in this scene was, for many, unforgettable. So too was "the terrible agony of his cry—'Wake Duncan with thy knocking! I would thou couldst!'" (2.2.78) as he averted his face and stretched out his arms "as it were, to the irrecoverable past." And when confronted by Banquo's ghost, Macready "brought out the gnawing of

conscience and the insecurity of ill-gotten power," his haggard features and restless movements making it seem "as if the curse 'Macbeth shall sleep no more' had taken visible effect." Some found in
this approach too much intellect and too little heart. Others were
annoyed by his interminable pauses, through which he conveyed to
the audience a character steeped in thought (a prompter in Bristol
nearly drove Macready mad by feeding him the next line at every
long pause, assuming that he was having trouble remembering the
part). Macready, anticipating method acting by many decades, was
probably the first to have said that "I cannot act Macbeth without
being Macbeth."

Shakespeare leaves unclear whether, at play's end, when Macbeth tells Macduff "I will not fight with thee" (5.8.22), he utters
those words either cravenly or scornfully. Macready spoke them
fearfully, and dies falling upon Macduff's sword, "in yielding
weakness." In contrast, Forrest's manly Macbeth fights to his last
breath. Even after Macduff disarms him and delivers a fatal blow,
he manages to draw a dagger, and, dying, "drives its point into
the stage, where it remains, quivering, by his side, as the curtain
falls"—and the remainder of the play is cut. In this, perhaps more
than in any other Shakespearean role, each man was understood as
cultivating, and ultimately defining, his national character: Forrest
the brash American, Macready the sensitive Englishman.

Another tension was in play, between the homegrown future
and the British-inflected past of Shakespeare in America, and by
extension, where the nation had come from and was headed. Two
days before Macready took to the stage, the *Albion* urged its readers
not to miss him, for the British star was the "last surviving link of
that galaxy of the highest order of histrionic talent that succeeded
Garrick, and which numbered in its ranks the Kembles, the Siddons, O'Neill, Young, and Kean, with all of whom Mr. Macready
was a contemporary." Like many farewell tours, Macready's was

haunted by nostalgia for a reassuring past. You might not be able to put these complicated feelings into words, but seeing Macready perform captured them perfectly. More was at stake, then, than watching an aging star for the last time. Macready's accent, gentle manliness, and propriety represented a world that was being overtaken by everything that Forrest, guiding spirit of the new and for many coarser age of Manifest Destiny, represented. From the box seats, it must have looked like a ruthless Macbeth was killing off the gracious Duncan. But viewed from the pit, the refusal to concede that the old ways—embodied in Macready—had always favored the elite must have been infuriating.

The immediate goal of those opposing Macready was simple: drive him from the stage. But this would not be easy at the Opera House, which was difficult to infiltrate. The solution for Forrest's supporters was to go around to various hotels, buying fifty tickets here, thirty there, and then quietly distribute these to young toughs who understood what was required. Rynders bought some, as did others. We don't know who bankrolled their efforts or whether Forrest knew of these plans, but in the end, roughly five hundred tickets to Macready's *Macbeth* were distributed in this way. While they weren't anticipating any significant disruption, the managers of the Opera House were reassured when New York City's chief of police, George Matsell, accompanied by a few of his men, agreed to be there.

A playgoer who was there that evening recalled how those sitting in "the boxes began to feel anxious" when a "hard-looking crowd" of working-class men, some "in their shirt-sleeves, others . . . ragged and dirty," entered the theater shortly after 7 p.m. A new sound was heard in the Opera House, the "stage reveille" familiar to playgoers at the Chatham or Bowery theaters: a rhythmic rapping and stomping—"Tap! Rap-rap-tap—Tap! Tap! Rap-rap-tap!"—from first-time visitors impatient for the play to begin. Macready mistook what he thought was "the greatest applause, as it seemed, from the whole house." He bowed repeatedly, and, as the noise failed to diminish, began to think, "This is becoming too much." It slowly dawned on him that in addition to cheering and handkerchief-waving supporters, "there was opposition, and that the prolongation of the applause was the struggle against it." He tried waiting it out, to no avail. He even tried addressing the audience, but the protesters would not allow him to be heard. A banner was unfurled, reading *"No apologies—it is too late!"* on one side, and on the other, *"You have ever proved yourself a liar!"* When it became clear that the clamor was not going to subside, Macready told his fellow actors that they would present the play wordlessly—and so they did.

This enraged those keen on disrupting the performance. They hurled eggs and pennies. Potatoes followed, along with lemons, apples, an old shoe, and a bottle of asafetida, a foul-smelling spice, that splashed Macready's costume. It took courage to withstand the onslaught, but Macready and the rest of the cast persisted, through the first Act, then the second. The uproar never ceased. Those trying to disrupt the performance loudly chanted snatches of the witches' choruses. Cries rang out hinting at the larger sources of conflict: "Three groans for the codfish aristocracy!" "Down with the English hog!" and then, mockingly, "Three cheers for Macready, Nigger Douglass, and Pete Williams!" (Frederick Douglass had arrived in New York to speak at the American Anti-Slavery Society Convention, and had been seen walking downtown in the company of two white women; Williams was an African American who owned a saloon in Five Points where whites and blacks danced together). Amalgamation, abolition, and a performance of *Macbeth* by a British actor were all part of the same elitist worldview that had to be forcefully rejected.

The fury of the protesters intensified at the sight of Macready entering in Act 3 wearing a crown. First one chair, then another, then two more came flying onstage from the second tier of seats. The police chose not to intervene and made no arrests. Despite the apparent danger, a reporter for the *New York Herald* seated close to the stage reported that none of what was thrown "appeared to be aimed directly at the person of Mr. Macready." Macready didn't have the luxury of knowing that the chairs crashing onstage a few feet from where he stood weren't meant to hit him. Before things got further out of hand, he bowed to the audience, told a fellow actor that he had fulfilled his obligations, and walked off. The curtain dropped. Undaunted by the experience, and escorted from the theater by friends, Macready left Astor Place, he recorded, "in the best spirits." The victorious protesters spilled out of the theater. Rather than heading home or to nearby saloons for a celebratory round or two, they moved on to the Broadway Tabernacle, intent on breaking up a meeting of the American Anti-Slavery Society.

The following morning Macready decided he had had enough and booked passage home to England. But Macready's supporters saw how much was at risk if thuggish protesters could establish a precedent in this violent way. They had to act quickly. In a remarkably short time, a group of forty-eight leading financial and cultural leaders signed and published a letter urging Macready to continue performing at Astor Place. With this action they assumed center stage; the anonymous author of *Account of the Terrific and Fatal Riot at the New-York Astor Place Opera House* writes that Macready "was to be put down less on his own account, than to spite his aristocratic supporters. The question became not only a national, but a social one. It was the rich against the poor."

Their letter ran in local papers, along with Macready's response. He agreed to perform on Thursday, May 10, and finish what he had started: he would play Macbeth again. Most of those who had signed the letter were politically engaged men of means—real estate developers, bankers, lawyers, editors, and judges—known for their support of the arts. They were joined by some high-profile men of letters, including Washington Irving, Evert Duyckinck, and Herman Melville. Melville's name may have struck some as a surprise, since unlike almost all the other signers, he wasn't a Whig, but rather a Young America Democrat, and committed to establishing a national drama. The controversy was forcing him and many other New Yorkers to take sides, which meant weighing in the balance competing loyalties and interests—financial, personal, aesthetic, political, and ideological—and betraying some of them. It also meant deciding whether, as a writer, you saw yourself, and your work, as highbrow or popular. It could not have been an easy decision for the 30-year-old novelist.

What seems to have tipped the balance for Melville was his changing view of Shakespeare, whose work would so profoundly influence his next novel, *Moby-Dick*. He had only recently started reading the plays closely, having bought his first set of Shakespeare's works a little more than a year earlier, and since then had fallen hard for his works, especially the tragedies. Melville had gone to hear Fanny Kemble read from *Macbeth* and *Othello* and had recently written to his friend (and fellow signer) Evert Duyckinck that "I would to God Shakespeare had lived later, and promenaded on Broadway." An American Shakespeare was clearly needed, though one on the page, not the stage, if Forrest's bluster was the best the theater could offer. When within a year Melville would write "that men not very much inferior to Shakespeare are this day being born on the banks of the Ohio," he might have been pointing at himself.

Much of the evidence about what happened behind the scenes over the next three days is lost or suppressed. We know that this time Macready's followers tried to pack the house. On the other side, Rynders came up with a new strategy. Working out of the Empire

Club, where his Native American Party headquarters were located, he had hundreds of posters printed, then displayed throughout the town, that read:

WORKING MEN,

SHALL

AMERICANS

OR

ENGLISH RULE

IN THIS CITY

The crew of the British steamer have

Threatened all Americans who shall dare to express their

Opinions on this night, at the

ENGLISH ARISTOCRATIC OPERA HOUSE!

We advocate no violence, but a free expression of opinion

To all public men.

WORKINGMEN! FREEMEN!

STAND BY YOUR

LAWFUL RIGHTS!

American Committee.

Having pushed all the right patriotic, nativist, and anti-elitist buttons (without even naming Macready), and invented that bit of fake news about the crew of that British steamer, Rynders then went one step further, posting alongside these inflammatory posters others calling on all Englishmen to come out in force to "sustain your countrymen." With any luck there would be brawling in the streets.

Mayor Caleb Smith Woodhull, sworn in earlier that week, anticipated trouble and arranged for a meeting at City Hall with the theater managers and leading members of his administration. He wanted to call off the performance, but by then it was too late.

Everyone in the room felt the political pressure of the signatories. Woodhull was told by his chief of police that he lacked the manpower to control the crowd if things really got out of hand, so it was decided to call up the militia. No warning was made, however, urging New Yorkers to stay off the street. Meanwhile, workmen boarded up the lower windows of the theater. Late that afternoon, 200 policemen took positions inside the theater and another 125 around it. Farther downtown, two hundred infantrymen of the Seventh Regiment collected ammunition and were joined by two companies of hussars, two troops of horse and one of light artillery.

When the doors to the Opera House opened, employees screened out undesirables whose tickets lacked a special mark on the back. This time around the protesters—fewer than a hundred managed to get in—were badly outnumbered. When a deafening mix of cheers and hissing greeted the British star's first appearance onstage, and agitators cried "Out with him" and shook their fists "in savage fury," Macready laughed at them and used Macbeth's truncheon to point out offenders to the police, who initially refused to intervene, respecting the time-honored right of playgoers to make their feelings known. The management then brought out a sign that read: "The friends of order will remain quiet." It was a neat trick, as only Macready's supporters fell silent. The police at last dragged out some of the most disruptive protesters; the hope was that making an example of a few young men would calm the rest. It worked. The show went on, even though by now it was clear that protesters who couldn't enter were attacking the building. The actors onstage had to compete with the noise and distraction of the tumult, as cobblestones smashed the theater's unprotected upper windows and one hurled through an opening struck and damaged the magnificent chandelier. Word spread that the mob intended to torch the theater.

When his fellow actors implored Macready to shorten the performance, he refused, determined to show a steely resolve, later recalling how he threw himself into the part "whilst those dreadful deeds of real crime and outrage were roaring . . . all around us." He spoke the words "I will not be afraid of death and bane / 'Til Birnam *Forest* come to Dunsinane" (5.3.61–62) so defiantly that Forrest's supporters made a final attempt "to get up a tumult . . . but failed." And when Macready came to the line "Our castle's strength / Will laugh a siege to scorn" (5.5.2–3), his supporters in the audience—in the midst of a furious siege themselves—loudly applauded. *Macbeth* was acted until the final curtain, at which point the remaining playgoers exited through a path protected by soldiers with fixed bayonets.

Outside there was chaos—and had been for the better part of two hours. While Rynders, hoping to keep a low profile, had stayed away from Astor Place that evening, his ally Ned Buntline mobilized supporters in the surrounding streets. When a large pile of cobblestones from a construction site nearby was spotted, Buntline urged his followers to hurl them, in volleys, at the Opera House. The police, badly outnumbered, and having only nightsticks for protection, were also showered with volleys of stones, and those who were injured retreated into the playhouse. Others waded into the crowd and arrested stone throwers and ringleaders, including Buntline himself. There were cries of "Burn the damned den of the aristocracy" and "America rules England tonight, by Jesus." Smaller groups of rioters tried to break down the theater doors. A little before 9 p.m. word was sent downtown: bring up the militia.

The cavalry arrived first but was quickly overwhelmed. Some of the riders were pulled off their mounts, the rest, bloodied, were driven off, but the infantry managed to force their way through the furious crowd. The new mayor, who was on the scene, consulted with his security forces and was told that he needed to give the order to fire; the troops would otherwise be overwhelmed. The mayor equivocated, then slipped away to a nearby hotel, leaving others to give that controversial command. With the situation becoming desperate, the soldiers, dozens of them now bloodied, were ordered to "charge bayonets." But the rioters were by now so close that they yanked muskets out of soldiers' hands. The order was at last given to the troops to fire—though only as a warning shot, over the heads of the rioters. A cry was heard, "They have only blank cartridges, give it to them again," and the protesters resumed the attack, one of them daring the soldiers to fire in earnest: "Take the life out of a free-born American for a bloody English actor?" Another command to fire was given, this time aiming low. The rioters initially retreated toward Lafayette Place before surging forward again. One last time the militia was ordered to fire, this time directly at the mob, which gave way. By now more than twenty people were dead and, on both sides, dozens wounded.

At half past eleven the light artillery arrived on the scene and set up two cannons, one facing Broadway, the other, the Bowery. They had arrived just in time, for it was rumored that "the crowd intended to arm and renew the attack." By one in the morning the remaining protesters had finally dispersed. Astor Place looked like a war zone. Nearby houses were spattered with bullet holes. Littered on the ground were sections of heavy iron railings that had been torn from fastenings and used by the rioters against the military. The Opera House windows were shattered and two of its doors smashed. The surrounding area was strewn with bricks and cobblestones, and there were pools of blood on the sidewalks.

The following morning, newspapers reported that "the excitement today is intense, and fearfully increasing. Nothing else but the *Tragedy of Macbeth* is talked of, or thought of. Knots of men, on every corner, are discussing the affair and we find the liveliest apprehensions are entertained that the terrible scenes of last night will be attempted to be renewed, this evening at night fall." Rumors were rampant. According to one, "firearms had been purchased and obtained in large quantities by persons riotously disposed." Another warned "that there is to be an attack on the Arsenal and an armed demonstration at sundown." There was also talk of making "a sudden rush upon the soldiers about midnight, and to disarm them." The *Telegraph* reported threats that "the Mayor's house . . . will be sacked tonight, also, that the Opera House will be blown up!" Some of the wealthy thought it a good time to leave town. Others hired private security, packed up valuables, and cleaned their pistols. "The town was in a fearful condition," the actor Lester Wallack recalled, "and for several days after was like a city in a state of siege. Some were saying that it was a rascally thing that the people should be shot down and murdered in the streets, and others were arguing that the military had only done their duty." New Yorkers "from the nursery to the work shop, and from the parlor to the counting room" debated who was in the right.

The authorities, fearing more violence, acted aggressively. Dozens were arrested. It was agreed that the damaged Opera House would be closed. The mayor issued a proclamation "deploring the loss of life, urging all citizens to stay home and avoid assembling in public," and warned that rioters did not have a monopoly on violence. Gun shops were searched and their weapons secured at the Arsenal after the mayor's office learned of efforts to rent two thousand muskets. A thousand special deputies, two thousand infantry, as well as a squadron of cavalry and four troops of horse artillery were marshaled.

The opposition plotted their next moves as well. They lacked the firepower of the authorities and were aware that despite the anger at the mayor and the military, talk in the street had begun to turn against them, or at least against violent protest. As the *Morning Express* put it, the "sight of blood had restored peace, and re-enthroned reflection." If they had any hopes of shifting public opinion and of securing the crucial support of the middle class, they would have to rely on oratory. To that end, placards were posted throughout the city, attracting crowds, declaring that "the great Crisis has come": "Will English aristocrats and foreigners be allowed to triumph?" And will citizens "allow themselves to be deprived of the liberty of opinion—so dear to every true American heart?" A second round of posters was plastered around the town, this time urging citizens to join a large rally, followed by a protest march back to Astor Place that evening.

The size of the crowd that gathered downtown on May 11 was estimated at 25,000 or more. Newspapers reported that the opposition had succeeded in attracting "an immense number of citizens of the greatest respectability in demeanor, deportment and appearance"—the crucial middle class they needed on their side. The rally was like a modern-day version of the funeral oration scene in *Julius Caesar*, where the citizens gather after blood has been shed to hear and act on the exhortations of powerful speakers. A series of resolutions were proposed at the outset of the rally calling for the censure and indictment of the authorities and condemning the murder of innocent protesters. *Measure for Measure*, a play that turns on the abuse of civic authority, was quoted (2.2.123) in deriding "the pride, tyranny and inhumanity of those who, '*dressed in a little brief authority*,' have shown a higher regard for the applause of those who courted a fatal issue than for the lives of their fellow citizens." It was also resolved that the time-honored rights of playgoers would not easily be surrendered: while "opposed to all violence, in theatres, or elsewhere, we still insist that citizens have a perfect and indisputable right to express their approbation or disapprobation in all places of public amusement."

That was the warm-up act, delivered by the Tammany politician Edward Strahan. When he finished, Rynders spoke, excoriating Macready and claiming that citizens were killed "to please an aristocratic Englishman, backed by a few sycophantic Americans." Mike Walsh, another incendiary speaker, followed. He told the crowd that this was about more than Forrest and Macready: "When the Opera House was opened," he reminded the crowd, "it was restricted to those only who wore white kid gloves, such was the spirit of pride and presumption of the nabobs of the Fifteenth ward, who, led by the Mayor, have brought troops to fire upon the people. Who will take care of the families they have made desolate?" He ended the rally on an inflammatory note, interrupted by loud cries for vengeance from the crowd: "We owe it to ourselves, to our fellow-citizens, and to society, if ever there is a repetition of this shooting, to arm ourselves, and to call upon every man to arm himself."

Stirred by these orations and shouting "To the Opera House" and "Burn the den of the aristocracy," five thousand protesters marched up Broadway toward Astor Place. The militia was ready and waiting. Hussars, dragoons, and artillery moved into position as soldiers cordoned off the area, blocking the march. For an hour or so, the outcome hung in the balance, as the protesters jammed the streets, set up their own barricades, and lit bonfires opposite the line of troops. The police tried forcing their way into the crowd to arrest ringleaders, but were beaten back. Finally, the militia leveled their muskets and the protesters were warned that if the bombardment of cobblestones didn't stop, the troops would open fire. Further bloodshed was averted as the stone throwing ended. The soldiers then cleared the streets with fixed bayonet charges. The rioting was over.

There were no winners in the Astor Place riots, which seem to have tarnished everyone and everything they touched. Macready skipped town, leaving his hotel before a lynch mob arrived, and sailed home from Boston. He would never perform in America

103

again and soon retired from the stage. Though Forrest was careful to say little during the rioting, his reputation was damaged by it. While Rynders managed to avoided arrest, Buntline was jailed for a year for his role in the riots, and after his release resumed his writing career, specializing in dime novels.

The violence at the Opera House brought into sharp relief the growing problem of income inequality in an America that preferred the fiction that it was still a classless society. A few days after the rioting ended, the New York correspondent for the Philadelphia *Public Ledger* wrote that the events at Astor Place left "behind a feeling to which this community has hitherto been a stranger—an opposition of classes—the rich and poor," a "feeling that there is now in our country, in New York City, what every good patriot hitherto has considered it his duty to deny—*a high and a low class.*"

Some saw an upside to the bloodshed, including the Whig newspaper the *Courier and Enquirer.* The willingness of the troops to fire on the protesters, the newspaper argued, was "an excellent advertisement to the capitalists of the old world, that they might send their property to New York and rely upon the certainty that it would be safe from the clutches of red republicanism, or chartists, or communionists of any description." The message to the wealthy in Paris, Vienna, Venice, Berlin, Milan, and other European cities that had recently seen revolutionary violence was: bank here, where we shoot protesters.

Others saw only social corrosion, not benefits. An editorial in the *Tribune* argued that "the evils that follow such a conflict do not end with the repairing of the damages, nor even with the sorrow of the dead. They penetrate into all the relations of industry and citizenship. They appear in the diminution of confidence in the silent and peaceful force of the law, in the weakening of neighborly feeling among the different classes of society." Decades later, Henry James, who was a 6-year-old living on Fourteenth Street at the time, called Forrest's willingness to "suffer his followers to organize the disgraceful scenes" at Astor Place "the instinctive response of barbarism to culture."

Historians have pointed to a number of other consequences, including the reorganization of the New York police force. Some have traced the fallout from the Astor Place riots to such reforms as the end of child labor, the institution of a ten-hour workday, better public education, and unionization. There was certainly a greater recognition of the need for shared public space: two years after the riots, in early May 1851, Woodhull's successor as mayor, Ambrose Kingsland, proposed building a large park suited for "the wants of our citizens." Though still conceived from the top down, Central Park would be carved out by the end of that decade. The bloody events of May 1849 had a sobering effect: there would not be another major outbreak of violence in the streets of New York City until the draft riots of 1863.

When the historian Lawrence Levine reflected on the Astor Place riots in *Highbrow/Lowbrow: The Emergence of Cultural Hierarchy in America*, in what remains the most influential account of Shakespeare in America, he reached two conclusions. The first is surely right: that what happened at the Opera House "was a struggle for power and cultural authority within theatrical space," and "simultaneously an indication of and a catalyst for the cultural changes that came to characterize the United States at the end of the century." But his other conclusion is unwarranted: that after Astor Place, theater "no longer functioned as an expressive form that embodied all classes with a shared public space, nor did Shakespeare much longer remain the common property of all Americans." If anything, the story of these riots spoke, rather, to an intense desire by the middle and lower classes to continue sharing that space, and to oppose, violently if necessary, efforts to exclude them from it. Shakespeare continued to matter and would remain common cultural property in America. The transformations Levine describes would come, but not because of the riots, and not until after a Civil War in which Shakespeare would matter, to both sides, more than ever. What did change in the aftermath of Astor Place was that violent protests in theaters were no longer tolerated. When competing claims over freedom of speech collided, the right of actors to be heard would prevail over the right of protesters to shout them down. Forrest's supporters lost that battle. Theatergoing in America would henceforth be a quieter and more passive experience.

One of the most astute contemporary commentators on what the riots were ultimately about was Nathaniel Parker Willis, a popular writer who published his "After-Lesson of the Astor-Place Riot" two weeks after the events. While accepting that "the law is supreme," he also believed that "wealth, in a republic, should be mindful where its luxuries offend." He located the roots of the Astor Place riots not in a quarrel between actors, or between nations, but rather in the fatal decision by wealthy New Yorkers to change the rules: by "aristocratizing" the pit they had overstepped the "most jealously guarded line of human distinction."

The "Massacre Place Opera House" or "Dis-Astor Place," as some now mockingly called it, did not survive as a theater for long. In 1852 the managers tried renaming it to avoid the lingering stigma, but that change was merely cosmetic. It took a few years, but the wealthy subscribers finally learned their lesson; when in 1854 they relocated farther uptown and built the Academy of Music on the corner of Fourteenth Street and Irving Place, they did away with the offending "cockloft" where the lower classes had been shunted and ensured that there would be inexpensive seats for sale. The Opera House was auctioned off that same year to the Mercantile Library Association, and for the next few decades (before the building was torn down in 1891) its library there, serving city clerks, was known as Clinton Hall. The building that now stands on the site went up in 1904. A ghostly trace of the original can be found at the southbound Astor Place subway station, where over a bricked-off staircase is a lintel that reads: "Clinton Hall."

Astor Place remains a contentious site, straddling the cultural divide of New York's West and East Village. Joe Papp understood its significance when he established the Public Theater—providing free Shakespeare for all—in an Astor Place building a stone's throw from where the Opera House had stood. The wealthy still claim this real estate as their own; Jared Kushner owned a multi-million-dollar apartment on the site (at 21 Astor Place) and Ivanka Trump moved in there briefly when they married. Rumblings of dissent are still felt on the site from time to time, as protesters push back against perceived incursions by wealthy capitalists and the forces of "law and order" that protect their interests. In April 2012 there was a fresh riot when those attending an anarchist book fair nearby, chanting "cops are murderers," scuffled with police and tried to smash the windows of the Starbucks now located on the site where the Opera House once stood "during a wild, hours-long spree." The Opera House may be gone, but the divisions remain.

John Wilkes Booth (*left*), Edwin Thomas Booth, and
Junius Brutus Booth Jr. in *Julius Caesar*, 1864.

CHAPTER 4

1865: Assassination

On April 26, 1865, twelve days after he assassinated Abraham Lincoln, the fugitive John Wilkes Booth was caught and killed by Union soldiers. A letter was found in his possession addressed to Dr. Richard Stuart, a Confederate sympathizer. Booth had written it two days earlier, on a page of an appointment book he used as a diary. Hobbled by a broken ankle, running out of cash, and demoralized by how even Southern newspapers were vilifying him for murdering Lincoln, Booth arrived at Stuart's house in King George County, Virginia, along with three companions, late in the afternoon of April 23—Shakespeare's birthday—having been directed there by Confederate agents. But Stuart refused to treat Booth's injury, denied the men shelter, and only grudgingly provided a meal before sending them on their way. Booth saw in Stuart's chilly reception a mirror of how his act was being received in the South. Though he knew that his capture or death was imminent, Booth paused to draft this biting letter, before sending a slightly revised copy of it, in which the money he enclosed was halved:

> I was sick and tired, with a broken leg, in need of medical advice. I would not have turned a dog from my door in such a condition. However, you were kind enough to give me something to eat, for which I not only thank you, but on account of the reluctant manner in which it was bestowed, I feel bound to pay for it. It is not the substance, but the manner in which kindness is extended, that makes one happy in the acceptance thereof. The sauce in meat is ceremony; meeting were bare

without it. Be kind enough to accept the enclosed two dollars and a half (though hard to spare) for what we have received.

The letter is straightforward enough (once past the glancing allusion to *King Lear*—"Mine enemy's dog, / Though he had bit me, should have stood that night / Against my fire" [4.7.37–39])—until its next-to-last sentence, which is lifted from the scene in *Macbeth* in which Lady Macbeth upbraids her husband for his lack of hospitality:

> My royal lord,
> You do not give the cheer. The feast is sold
> That is not often vouched, while 'tis a-making,
> 'Tis given with welcome. To feed were best at home;
> From thence, *the sauce to meat is ceremony;*
> *Meeting were bare without it.* (3.4.32–37)

It's one of the more impenetrable speeches in Shakespeare, so dense that Booth has to supply his own paraphrase in the preceding sentence. Shamed by how Stuart had treated him, Booth offers a Shakespearean rebuke—yet the words he quotes were themselves a rebuke of an assassin. Pride, self-justification, self-doubt, and suppressed guilt commingle in this complicated allusion.

Booth's thoughts kept returning to Shakespeare during these desperate days. A diary entry written soon after he shot Lincoln invokes *Julius Caesar*: "After being hunted like a dog through swamps, woods . . . with every man's hand against me, I am here in despair. And why? For doing what Brutus was honored for." Like Shakespeare's conspirators "groaning underneath this age's yoke" (1.2.61), Booth laments finding himself in a "country that groaned beneath this tyranny." The same diary entry closes with another quotation from *Macbeth*, one that valorizes courage in the face of inevitable defeat: "I do not wish to shed a drop of blood, but I must fight the course," Booth concludes, likening himself to a doomed Shakespearean hero fighting against the odds, a role that had been the hallmark of his theatrical career. He lifts these words from one of Macbeth's last speeches, spoken when hemmed in by his enemies: "They have tied me to a stake. I cannot fly, / But, bearlike, *I must fight the course*" (5.7.1–2). Having performed these words for years, he found himself enacting them for real. That the reviews were already in, and dismissive ("I struck boldly, and not as the papers say," he insisted in his diary), must have been crushing. The part he was playing aligned with what would soon be labeled the "Lost Cause" of the Confederacy, a catchphrase he anticipates when he writes in his diary of how, "our cause being almost lost, something decisive and great must be done."

ABRAHAM LINCOLN HAD SEEN Booth act and knew Shakespeare's plays as intimately as his murderer did. Lincoln didn't have much formal education; he told an interviewer in 1861 that "I never went to school more than six months in my life." Even the brief time that he spent in rural schoolhouses was broken up, a few weeks here, a few months there, usually in the winter when the never-ending demands of farm life—planting and harvesting, clearing land, caring for livestock—slackened a bit. There weren't many books around either, other than a Bible. His father was illiterate; his mother could read but not write. Lincoln was born in 1809 and spent his first seven years in Kentucky before his family moved west to Indiana, where they cleared a plot of land and built a one-room log cabin in which Lincoln would live for the next fourteen years. His mother fell ill and died two years after the move, and a year after that his father remarried. Lincoln's stepmother remembered young Abe as "diligent for knowledge," a boy who "read all the books he could lay his hands on," including the handful she had brought with her.

One of these—William Scott's popular *Lessons in Elocution*—was likely his first introduction to Shakespeare. In Scott's anthology of famous speeches, Shakespeare's plays figure largely—thirty-three passages are excerpted. Some of these don't seem to have left much of a mark on Lincoln, including the "Queen Mab" speech from *Romeo and Juliet*, the "Seven Ages of Man" from *As You Like It*, and four long excerpts from *Julius Caesar*. And he didn't much care for the martial rhetoric of Henry V at Agincourt. But what caught his imagination stuck. While he loved *Henry IV*, he hated the arrogant rebel Hotspur, and decades later was still complaining that Hotspur's "dying speech" (which Lincoln encountered in Scott) was "an unnatural and unworthy thing" in privileging honor above self-knowledge. Lincoln had little patience for heroic figures who, dying by the sword, pontificate, and near the end of his life he confessed that he had "only one reproach to make of Shakespeare's heroes—that they make long speeches when they are killed."

Lincoln preferred poetry to prose, old writing to new, and only slightly exaggerated when he told a White House visitor, "I never read an entire novel in my life. . . . I once commenced *Ivanhoe*, but never finished it." In his most revealing comments about his interest in Shakespeare, in a letter to the actor James Hackett, Lincoln wrote, "Some of Shakespeare's plays I have never read, while others I have gone over perhaps as frequently as any unprofessional reader." He goes on to list the plays he kept returning to: "*Lear, Richard III, Henry VIII, Hamlet* and especially *Macbeth*." Lincoln had encountered all of them (except *Macbeth*) in Scott's anthology. And while he undoubtedly read the plays from beginning to end, his interest tended to be narrowly focused on a few key speeches, a habit no doubt shaped by *Lessons in Elocution*. Some of the passages he first read in Scott's collection almost seem tattooed inside his skull, and would remain at the center of his imaginative and emotional worlds.

Hamlet offers a case in point. *Lessons in Elocution* printed on facing pages the most famous soliloquy in the language—Hamlet's "To be, or not to be" (3.1.57)—and the one spoken later in the play by Claudius, tortured by guilt over having killed his brother and seized his wife and crown. Defying convention, Lincoln thought Claudius's speech was far superior and wasn't afraid to say so. It was a topic Lincoln warmed to in March 1864 right before going to see Edwin Booth's Hamlet. He spoke about Shakespeare that day with Francis Carpenter, a portrait painter who shadowed him for four months in the White House, telling Carpenter that Claudius's soliloquy had always struck him "as one of the finest touches of nature in the world." To underscore the point, Lincoln threw "himself into the very spirit of the scene," and began reciting "Oh, my offence is rank! It smells to heaven. / It hath the primal eldest curse upon't, / A brother's murder" (3.3.36–38). Claudius's self-recrimination continues for another thirty-eight lines, and Lincoln, Carpenter reports, "repeated this entire passage from memory, with a feeling and appreciation unsurpassed by anything I ever witnessed upon the stage."

Lincoln's insistence on the superiority of Claudius's soliloquy was a hobbyhorse, one for which he was ridiculed after Hackett leaked Lincoln's letter, in which Lincoln also spoke of this, to the press. It says something about America in the 1860s that it was unremarkable that a self-educated president would have such strong opinions about what he liked or disliked in Shakespeare—or even that he read him so attentively. Were Lincoln less revered, we would probably call him a bore for asking friends, family, government employees, and relative strangers to listen to him recite, sometimes for hours on end—and then discuss—the same few passages from Shakespeare again and again. But that's what he liked to do, and at times of great emotional strain needed to do.

From an early age Lincoln's hunger for Shakespeare was extraordinary. We have William Herndon to thank for most of what we know about what young Lincoln read. Herndon was Lincoln's junior partner in his Springfield, Illinois, law firm, and shortly after the assassination began contacting those who had known the president in his youth—testimony vital to Herndon's planned biography of Lincoln. Decades-old recollections of what a young man was like are untrustworthy, especially when, in Lincoln's case, they were reported after his murder, when the deification of the fallen president was well under way. Yet there is a remarkable degree of uniformity in what friends, kin, and neighbors independently reported to Herndon. Lincoln's friend William H. Greene reported that Lincoln "nearly knew Shakespeare by heart." His cousin Dennis Hanks also remembered that Lincoln read Shakespeare, as did James Matheny and Caleb Carmin ("His conversation very often was about books—such as Shakespeare and other histories"). Carmin mentions a shadowy figure in Lincoln's life named John Kelso, who apparently nurtured his love of Shakespeare. Kelso, Carmin recalled, "loved Shakespeare and fishing above all other things. Abe loved Shakespeare but not fishing—still Kelso would draw Abe: they used to sit on the bank of the river and quote Shakespeare— criticize one another." That skillful recitation was an essential part of Lincoln's attraction to Shakespeare is clear from others who corresponded with Herndon. Frances Todd Wallace, mingling recollections of hearing Lincoln recite Shakespeare with a glimpse of the melancholy that seems to have possessed him from an early age, remembered how Lincoln "would read generally aloud," and "with great warmth all funny things—humorous things, etc.: read Shakespeare that way: he was a sad man."

When Lincoln started practicing law, he could finally afford his own copies of the plays. A hint of how he purchased them appeared in the *New York Herald* in 1861, when Lincoln arrived at the Astor

Hotel in New York City the month before his inauguration, was introduced to a number of admirers, and "mistook one old gentleman for a person who formerly used to call on him at Springfield to sell illustrated copies of Shakespeare, but was set right by some person present." The story dovetails with the description of Lincoln in his late twenties offered by the young lawyer's mentor and partner, John Todd Stuart: "Mr. Lincoln commenced carrying around with him on the circuit—to the various courts, books such as Shakespeare."

In May 1862, when the war was going badly for the North and Lincoln was mourning the recent death of his beloved son Willie, he traveled to Fort Monroe with his secretary of war, Edwin Stanton, and General Egbert L. Viele, to consult with his commanders. Several accounts of the trip survive. Viele was impressed with Lincoln's ability to "repeat, almost word for word, whatever he had read," and recalled how the president "would sit for hours during the trip repeating the finest passages of Shakespeare's best plays." Once at Fort Monroe, Lincoln again found himself needing to read Shakespeare, for distraction and comfort. One of the officers there, Le Grand B. Cannon, recounted this many years later to Herndon. During the visit, Lincoln borrowed a copy of Shakespeare's works from him, read it for hours, and then asked if Cannon wouldn't mind if he recited aloud. Lincoln proceeded to "read from *Macbeth*, *Lear*, and finally *King John*"—the passage beginning "Grief fills the room up of my absent child, / Lies in his bed, walks up and down with me" (3.4.93–94), in which "Constance bewails the loss of her child." Cannon was struck by how "deeply moved" the president was:

His voice trembled. Laying the book on the table, he said, "Did you ever dream of a lost friend and feel that you were having a direct communion with that friend, and yet a consciousness that it was not a reality?" My reply was, "Yes, I think all may have had such an experience." He replied, "So do I dream of my boy Willie." He was totally overcome. His great frame shook, and bowing down on the table he wept as only such a man in the breaking down of great sorrow could weep.

In the histories and tragedies that Lincoln found so absorbing, Shakespeare put his protagonists, most of them leaders, under unbearable pressure. Among the most powerful moments in these plays are the speeches in which characters confront moral dilemmas and give voice to the guilt and grief that crushes them. That these characters were often evil—Richard III, Macbeth, Claudius—mattered little to Lincoln; what did was their degree of self-awareness, how fully they understood the difficult choices they faced.

JOHN WILKES BOOTH's early exposure to Shakespeare could not have been more different. His father was Junius Brutus Booth, one of England's leading Shakespeare actors by the age of 21. A few years later, accompanied by a lover, Mary Ann Holmes, he sailed for America, where he quickly established himself as a touring star. Soon after his arrival he purchased a farm with a modest house and 150 acres in rural Harford County, Maryland, near Bel Air. He and Mary Ann had ten children out of wedlock, six of whom survived. The second youngest was John Wilkes Booth, born in 1838.

Junius Brutus Booth, in addition to being an unforgettable and tireless actor, was also an alcoholic who had brushes with insanity. He was also remarkably tolerant, a vegetarian who wouldn't allow animals to be slaughtered on his farm or allow trees to be felled. He was curious about other religions and read the Talmud and Koran. His own father, who joined him in Bel Air, described the secluded farm as "Robinson Crusoe's Island." It would be more accurate to call it "Prospero's Island," for the home was filled with books, including Shakespeare editions and plays in several languages, as well as promptbooks and theatrical costumes and props. Family life on the farm was rich in contradictions. Junius Brutus Booth wouldn't own slaves, though he rented them from a neighbor. A world-class actor, he discouraged his children from entering his grueling profession, "as if he feared," his daughter Asia recalled, "to throw that glamour over its reality which might delude the senses." While he frowned upon their seeing plays, he allowed his children access to his playscripts, and they entertained themselves and neighbors with dramatic performances. For a learned man, able to read many languages, Junius Brutus Booth did not press much formal education on his children.

John Wilkes attended a number of nearby schools but was never a great student. Like his older brothers Junius and Edwin, he began performing Shakespeare at an early age. His sister Asia, with whom he was especially close, and who wrote a warm recollection of him, is the source for most of what we know about his childhood. As a boy, she recalls, he "put on my long-trained dress and walked before the long glass, declaring that he would succeed as Lady Macbeth in the sleep-walking scene." It's an unusual role and a surprising choice of scene for a child—even a precocious one—to aspire to master. His model for a Shakespearean heroine may have been Charlotte Cushman, for Asia goes on to describe how, in another bit of cross-dressing, John Wilkes "secretly 'got himself up' after Charlotte Cushman as Meg Merrilees"—a gypsy in *Guy Mannering*—and of how, in Asia's words, his performance "terrified me and all the darkies." From an early age, then, Booth seems to have been keen on entertaining others—including his sister and the children of the slaves that worked on the farm. His older brother Edwin remembered him as a "rattle-pated fellow, filled with Quixotic notions. While at the farm in Maryland, he would charge on horseback through the woods, 'spouting' heroic speeches with a lance in his hand, a relic of the Mexican war, given to my father." The image of that young man, racing his horse through the countryside, bearing that souvenir of a war fought to extend the reach of slavery while reciting heroic speeches, is as indelible as Asia's recollection of him as a guilt-ridden Lady Macbeth, trying but failing to scrub away the blood she has spilled. Looking back, both his brother and sister saw the child as father to the man; John Wilkes's identity seems to have been fixed at a young age and, as Asia put it, he "did not change much as he matured only his opinions and principles became more riveted."

Asia's first recollection of his performing publicly was at a picnic in Cockeysville, where he thrilled a crowd with one of Shylock's speeches. After their father's death (when John Wilkes was 14) and their grief-stricken mother's withdrawal, Asia and John Wilkes drew even closer, and spent summers on the farm reading aloud. She recalled how he "would recite poems and much of the play of *Julius Caesar*, and some other tragedies," while she "held the book," serving as a prompter. His choices might have been inspired by a performance that Edwin and John Sleeper Clarke (Asia's future husband) had given in nearby Bel Air, in August 1850, when John Wilkes would have been twelve. The two young actors (Edwin was only sixteen) even printed up a playbill for the event, which culminated in "the great Quarrel scene from *Julius Caesar*," in which Edwin played Brutus and John was Cassius.

By his teenage years John Wilkes was already convinced that whites were superior to blacks, and bosses to their employees. Asia recalled the "first evidence of an undemocratic feeling in Wilkes was shown when we were expected to sit down with our hired workmen. It was the custom for members of the family to dine and sup with the white men who did the harvesting." But John Wilkes had trouble with this equality. Even as a teenager, he had, as she put it, that "Southern reservation which jealously kept the white laborer from free association with his employer or his superior." As a result, "we were not," she concludes, "a popular family with our white laborers." And these views were reinforced at clandestine "Know-Nothing" meetings that the teenage John Wilkes attended a few miles from their home, secret gatherings that stoked anti-immigrant hatred and promoted conspiracy theories about the dangers that Catholics posed to America. Booth also came to loathe Northern Irish Catholics. During the Civil War, Asia writes, "Nothing grated this fierce Southern partisan so sorely as beholding the easy enlistment of Irishmen who were wild to free the 'nagur' before they had even looked upon a black face."

Perhaps the most telling of Asia's recollections involved John Wilkes chastising her for failing to forgive a neighbor. Alluding to Shylock, John Wilkes teasingly suggested that she must have "a tinge of Jewish blood." He then added: "Much of the evil of us boys and girls, some of the good as well, must have been engendered by power of those furious plays our father enacts. The Shylock, and Pescara, mad-seeming Hamlet, and love-sick Romeo, et cetera, et cetera." It's an extraordinary thing to say. John Wilkes acknowledges the powerful moral influence that the plays had on forming their character, especially their propensity for evil.

John Wilkes's immersion in Shakespeare deepened considerably once it was clear that the farm, which he had tried to run after his father's death, was failing, and he would have to make a living as an actor. But unlike his older brothers, he didn't see his future out West or up North: according to Asia, he worked "to make himself essentially a Southern actor." To that end, he "applied himself studiously to Shakespeare," and she would listen to him recite the "parts over and over again." Shakespeare was now work, a skill to be mastered, and John Wilkes committed himself to it. He was a perfectionist, and "would not allow a word or syllable to go wrong, and *Julius Caesar*, that test part for the theatrical scholar, was so constantly repeated that even the little darkies, whose privilege was to sit and loll about in the corners of whatever rooms we occupied, were caught repeating after him." She also remembered a time when a young slave girl recited the lines more accurately than he, which provoked John Wilkes to say, "Hark to that thick-skulled darky! She has sharper wits than I."

John Wilkes's gift for reciting Shakespeare—and *Julius Caesar* in particular—is confirmed by Edward M. Alfriend, a friend the 21-year-old Booth met in Richmond when he was acting there. When Booth, though a civilian, joined Alfriend and other soldiers from the First Virginia Regiment to oversee the execution of the abolitionist John Brown in December 1859, he would, Alfriend writes, "entertain us with dramatic recitations from different plays. He was very fond of reciting, which he did in such a fiery, intense, vigorous, brilliant way as to forecast that great genius he subsequently showed on the stage." Alfriend never forgot Booth's "recitation of Brutus' speech in *Julius Caesar* in defense of his share in the assassination and with what force he rolled out the line 'My ancestor did from the streets of Rome the Tarquin drive'" (2.1.53–54).

GIVEN HIS IMMERSION in Shakespeare, it is surprising that Lincoln never littered his speeches and letters with quotations from the plays. Despite the best efforts of admirers to find echoes of Shakespeare in his most magnificent speeches—the Gettysburg Address, or his first or second inaugural addresses—they are almost nonexistent. Lincoln kept a firewall between Shakespeare's words and his own, avoiding the casual quotation of Shakespearean phrases that marked the writing of so many at the time—including that found in the letters home of many soldiers, both Union and Confederate, or in John Wilkes Booth's self-aggrandizing diary.

Lincoln's compulsion to recite Shakespeare never slackened. One of those who frequently heard him recite was his young secretary, John Hay. Hay had met the future president while working next door to Lincoln's law practice in 1858 in Springfield. He was devoted to Lincoln and something of a surrogate son, especially after Willie's death. In the humid summer months, Hay would accompany Lincoln to the more comfortable surroundings of the Soldiers' Home, a presidential retreat three miles north of the White House, where they would work. One evening there, he recalled, Lincoln "read Shakespeare to me, the end of *Henry VI* and the beginning of *Richard III* . . . till my heavy eye-lids caught his considerate notice and he sent me to bed." Hay helpfully recorded Lincoln's favorites: "The plays he most affected were *Hamlet*, *Macbeth*, and the series of Histories; among the latter, he never tired of *Richard the Second*," including the deposed Richard's speech on the "hollow crown" and the unhappy fate of rulers:

> For God's sake, let us sit upon the ground
> And tell sad stories of the death of kings—
> How some have been deposed, some slain in war,
> Some haunted by the ghosts they have deposed,
> Some poisoned by their wives, some sleeping killed,
> All murdered. For within the hollow crown
> That rounds the mortal temples of a king,
> Keeps Death his court. (3.2.155–62)

Hay notes that he had heard Lincoln recite these words "at Springfield, at the White House and the Soldiers' Home." How often Lincoln returned to these poignant words and how their meaning may have deepened for him over the years is lost to us.

Francis Carpenter records similar experiences, including a long sitting when he sketched the president in which the conversation turned to the opening of *Richard III*—"Now is the winter of our discontent" (1.1.1). Lincoln complained that modern-day actors "often entirely misapprehended" the speech, delivering it in a "sophomoric style." Lincoln believed he had a better understanding of Richard's "repressed hate and jealousy," and to demonstrate this, "unconsciously assuming the character," he recited it "with a degree of force and power that made it seem like a new creation." Carpenter shared his experience with the journalist Samuel Sinclair, who had sat through a similar performance, and who agreed that "he never heard these choice passages of Shakespeare rendered with more effect by the most famous of modern actors."

Lincoln relied on a few dependable listeners, including the young men who worked in the War Department's telegraph office, which he visited on a daily basis to keep up with news from the front and convey instructions to his generals. While awaiting news, Lincoln recited Shakespeare from copies of the plays he brought with him. David Homer Bates, who worked there for the duration of the war, remembered a time in late 1863 (after Lincoln saw James Hackett play Falstaff), when the president carried with him "a well-worn copy in small compass of *Macbeth*, and one of *The Merry Wives of Windsor*, selections from both of which he read aloud to us in the telegraph office." Bates remembered one visit in particular, when "I was his only auditor, and he recited several passages to me with as much interest apparently as if there had been a full house."

So far as we know, until the last two years of his life, Lincoln had never seen Shakespeare staged. In his youth he hadn't had many opportunities to see productions, and during his first two years in office he had avoided the theater because of the demands of the wartime presidency, concern with the optics of a president frequenting a place many Americans still associated with sinfulness (especially when so many were fighting and dying), and perhaps because of an extended mourning period for his son Willie. But from March 1863, when he first saw Hackett's Falstaff, until the night he was shot in

April 1865 during a performance of an English farce, *Our American Cousin*, where Booth knew where to find him, Lincoln became a devoted playgoer, witnessing many of his favorite Shakespeare plays, along with other works, performed by the greatest stars of the day, whose company and conversation he sought out. As Carpenter's and Hay's accounts confirm, his trips to the theater in the last two years of his life didn't replace his readings; if anything, they intensified them, as Lincoln measured his own performance and interpretation against those of leading actors.

A pair of Washington playhouses that booked the leading Shakespeare actors of the day made this possible: the New National Theatre, just three blocks from the White House, on Pennsylvania Avenue, better known as Grover's Theatre; and John T. Ford's Theatre on Tenth Street, a half mile away. There was a third playhouse which Lincoln frequented far less often, the Washington Theatre, at the corner of Eleventh and O Streets, a mile distant. It's hard to know precisely how often Lincoln went to see plays during the last two years of his life. What evidence we have comes from newspaper accounts of sightings of him at Ford's or Grover's or from contemporary diaries. But since he often slipped into the theater late and unnoticed, many of his visits went unrecorded. Four decades after the assassination, Leonard Grover claimed that the president had visited his theater "probably more than a hundred times," which sounds like a wild exaggeration. But if he attended even half that number of productions at Grover's, and roughly the same number at Ford's, that would work out to an average of one performance a week.

In his first few months of intensive theatergoing, Lincoln saw Hackett as Falstaff in both *Henry IV* and *The Merry Wives of Windsor*, Charlotte Cushman and James Wallack in *Macbeth*, and Edward L. Davenport as Hamlet and as an orientalized Othello (a role that Lincoln apparently never discussed or quoted, though he went to see *Othello* twice more when Edwin Forrest—who also avoided appearing black—played the Moor). In early 1864 he saw Edwin Booth seven times (including his Hamlet, Petruchio, Richard II, Brutus, and Shylock) in a three-week span. Though John Wilkes Booth performed often in Washington, Lincoln only went to see him once, at Ford's, on November 9, 1863, in *The Marble Heart*. John Hay, who joined the small party that accompanied the president that evening, noted in his diary that the performance was "rather tame than otherwise."

Leading actors visited the White House and Lincoln enjoyed grilling them about what he thought were unconscionable changes to what Shakespeare wrote. He asked Hackett to justify why he cut the scene in which Hal and Falstaff take turns playing King Henry IV and was unconvinced by Hackett's explanation that it didn't work onstage. This wasn't simply banter or idle curiosity. It mattered to Lincoln in the way a scriptural variant might matter to a believer. He brought up the same passage when the actor John McDonough visited the White House. Lincoln pressed him hard on why actors cut the scene, maintaining that there "is nothing I have read in Shakespeare, certainly nothing in *Henry VI* or the *Merry Wives of Windsor*, that surpasses its wit and humor." McDonough, a Democrat who had previously thought Lincoln a "buffoon," was surprised when the president pulled from the shelf a copy of the play and recited the passage. McDonough tried justifying the cut on the grounds that if included, other lines "which might be objectionable" would have to be as well. Lincoln told him that his defense was better than Hackett's, but not good enough, and to prove his point read aloud another potentially offensive passage that wasn't cut, and with a lawyer's flourish concluded: "This is not withheld, and where it passes current there can be no reason for withholding the other." Pressing his advantage, Lincoln then demanded to know why versions of the plays that "people crowd to hear are not always those planned by their reputed authors," especially the version of *Richard III* that now held the stage, that "was never seen by Shakespeare, but was written, was it not, Mr. McDonough, after his death, by Colley Cibber?"

Lincoln understood that just as he could criticize the actors' choices in the White House, he was subject to criticism of his decisions when on their turf. One of those who opposed his policies was Forrest, who frequently performed in Washington during Lincoln's late theatergoing years, including an extended Shakespeare run on the tercentenary of Shakespeare's birth. Lincoln went to see his *Lear* that month, and during intermission invited John McCullough, who played Edgar, to visit the presidential box. He may have invited Forrest too, but if he had, Forrest declined the invitation. When Forrest returned to Washington and was performing at Ford's on January 4, 1865, Lincoln went to see him in *Richelieu*, a modern play familiar to the president, who had previously seen Edwin Booth play the lead. The war was by this time nearly over, a Union victory ever more assured, though the cost—as General Sherman continued his savage, scorched-earth march through the South—was hard for many to stomach.

A young actor, William J. Ferguson, was holding the prompt-book that night and is the source of what happened at that performance. Decades later, Ferguson recalled that "sentiment among stage folk during the war was sharply divided," and among "those who strongly disapproved of the President's war policy was Edwin Forrest":

> I was standing at the "prompt stand" following the manuscript, when Forrest came to the line: "Take away the sword. States *may* be saved without it." Turning to look directly at the President, he declaimed intensely: "Take away the sword. States *must* be saved without it." By the alteration of a single

word the tragedian was able to give voice to the bitterness of his own feelings.

A more thin-skinned president would not have taken a public rebuke so kindly; yet Lincoln reportedly gave a "patient smile" to the "glaring tragedian," and returned to Ford's later that month to see Forrest perform as Lear—the last Shakespeare production he would ever see. A young French writer, Auguste Laugel, a friend of Senator Charles Sumner's, was invited to join Lincoln, Mrs. Lincoln, their young son Tad, and Sumner at that performance. Laugel seems to have spent as much time watching Lincoln as he did the play, and his closely observed account captures Lincoln's unshakable habit of measuring what he was hearing against Shakespeare's original: Lincoln "seemed extremely familiar with Shakespeare, and in several places remarked on the changes made in performance." The president "listened attentively, although he knew the play by heart." Laugel also allows us a glimpse of what led Lincoln to watch the great actors of his day perform Shakespeare. The performances touched him deeply, spoke to the loss and guilt that were nearly overwhelming. Laugel writes that "his boy of eleven was beside him, and the father often clasped him very tenderly, as the child leaned his head upon his shoulder; and when the little fellow, as he often did, asked for explanations, Lincoln invariably made answer, 'My child, it is in the play.'" Laugel also saw how "certain allusions made by King Lear to parental grief brought a cloud over the President's forehead."

THE THREE HUNDREDTH anniversary of Shakespeare's birth—April 23, 1864—fell shortly before the Battle of the Wilderness, where Ulysses S. Grant and Robert E. Lee would square off in a grinding war of attrition. That day, up in Boston, Ralph Waldo

Emerson hosted thirty or so men of letters at Revere House to honor Shakespeare. In New York City, plans for the anniversary celebration centered on laying the cornerstone for the statue of Shakespeare that now stands at the south end of the mall in Central Park; actors, not writers, took the lead, offering benefit performances that day at the Winter Garden, Niblo's Garden, and the Brooklyn Academy of Music to help pay for the statue.

Edwin Booth may have hoped that his brothers—Junius, who had returned from California, and John Wilkes, who had finished an engagement in New Orleans and was on his way to Boston—would join him onstage for the benefit at the Winter Garden. But Edwin acted without them that night, as Romeo, and his sold-out benefit, along with Hackett's performance as Falstaff at Niblo's, raised roughly a tenth of the cost of the $30,000 statue. Edwin tried enlisting his brothers for a follow-up benefit in July, writing to a friend, "My brother W[ilkes] is here for the summer, and we intend taking advantage of our thus being brought together, with nothing to do, and will, in the course of a week or two, give a performance of *Julius Caesar* . . . for the benefit of the statue we wish to erect in Central Park." Edwin added that he would "take the part of Brutus instead of Cassius," inviting all sorts of now unanswerable questions about how the leading roles were assigned. Not long after, Edwin wrote that "*Julius Caesar* did not take place on account of J. Wilkes' absence" and "is now postponed until the 9th of August when I hope it will be cool enough to proceed with it."

But the joint performance was postponed yet again. It wasn't until November 25, 1864, that the three Booth brothers shared the stage for the first and only time in a benefit performance of *Julius Caesar* at the Winter Garden. Edwin was cast as Brutus, Junius as Cassius, and John Wilkes as Antony. The repeated delays sharpened the topical edge of the play now that Lincoln had been reelected in early November, an outcome that had been in doubt

127

over the summer. Lincoln's enemies were now accusing him of aspiring to be "President for Life," and Edwin recalled arguing with his brother over John Wilkes's "belief that Lincoln would be made King of America."

A year earlier the politics of the times were mercurial enough for Lincoln to be depicted as Brutus. In October 1863, the *Southern Illustrated News* reprinted a racist parody from the London *Punch* featuring Lincoln as an American Brutus, wrapped in a toga made of the Stars and Stripes, regretting his decision to free the slaves. But by late 1864 the political winds had shifted, and Lincoln was now imagined more as the tyrannical Caesar. By then, the Albany *Atlas and Argus* had declared that "Caesar had his Brutus, Charles I his Cromwell . . . and we the People recommend Abraham Lincoln to profit by their example." In a similar vein, the *Richmond Dispatch* maintained that to "slay a tyrant is no more assassination than war is murder." Lincoln's exercise of his executive powers was viewed by his opponents as tyrannical in its trampling upon congressional authority and the rights enshrined within the Constitution. By the time of his reelection in 1864 the list of charges against him had grown long. As early as 1861, in calling up the militia and blockading Southern ports after Fort Sumter was fired upon, Lincoln was attacked for declaring war without securing congressional approval. His critics also argued that in allowing the military to arrest civilians, Lincoln had suspended habeas corpus, first locally in 1861 (after Union troops had been attacked in Baltimore), and then again in 1863, on a national scale. The Constitution allows its suspension "in cases of rebellion," so from Lincoln's perspective arresting traitors under arms was legitimate. Lincoln's administration, potentially infringing on First Amendment rights, also closed more than three hundred opposition newspapers deemed treasonous. And, as the war dragged on, Lincoln refused to exchange prisoners (his accusers overlooking his demand that captured black Union soldiers be exchanged as well, which the Confederacy refused to do). Lincoln was also accused of abusing his powers by demanding that the Confederacy remain within the Union, subjecting free people even as he emancipated enslaved ones. All these charges cut to the heart of the basic rights and freedoms of American citizens— and who counted as one. By staging *Julius Caesar* in the immediate aftermath of Lincoln's reelection in November 1864, the Booth brothers inevitably foregrounded the issue of how defenders of liberty should best respond.

Between the initial plans for a joint performance and the staging of *Julius Caesar* in November 1864, John Wilkes had become radicalized. His tour earlier that year of slave states now occupied by Union forces undoubtedly contributed to this. It's likely, either while performing in New Orleans in March (where he narrowly avoided arrest for singing a banned rebel song in public) or in Boston in July, that Booth met with and was recruited by Confederate agents. In October 1864, a month before he performed in *Julius Caesar* in New York, he traveled to Montreal, where he consulted with Confederate officials and received funds to help cover the costs of a plot in which he and his fellow conspirators would kidnap the president while he was riding with only a small guard in Washington's streets, or subdue and bind him while he was seeing a play at Ford's Theatre, then smuggle him across the Potomac to the Confederacy. The kidnapping was to take place in late January. After abducting Lincoln, Booth's acting career in the North would be over, so while in Canada, he arranged for his wardrobe and scripts to be put aboard a ship that would attempt to run the Union blockade. It never made it.

Booth was not the only desperate supporter of the Confederacy undertaking violent acts long considered beyond the pale. A group of Confederate agents lit multiple phosphorus fires throughout New York City the very evening that the Booth brothers were performing *Julius Caesar*, hoping to terrorize the city or burn it to the ground, just as General Sherman had recently put Atlanta to the torch. One of the buildings set on fire was the Lafarge Hotel, which abutted the Winter Garden. While the plot is barely remembered today, the *New York Times* then called it "one of the most fiendish and inhuman acts known in modern times." Only the arsonists' poor training—they closed the doors and windows in the rooms which they had set alight, cutting off the oxygen needed for the flames to rage out of control—prevented the two thousand playgoers gathered to see *Julius Caesar* from burning to death or being crushed in a stampede in what might well have been remembered as the greatest theatrical disaster in the nation's history. The following morning, when the brothers met for breakfast, an argument broke out over the attack; when Junius said that the perpetrators should be strung up, and Edwin reiterated his support for Lincoln, John Wilkes responded by justifying the arson as a legitimate act of retaliation for Union atrocities.

It had been an unusually fraught performance, but also a critical and box-office success. Sam Chester, who acted in the production, thought that John Wilkes's Antony "completely electrified the audience." After the assassination, the *New York World* reported that "many who witnessed" the benefit recalled that John Wilkes "interpolated, at some inappropriate point in the oration over Caesar's body, the words '*sic semper tyrannis*'"—'thus always with tyrants'—words he would reportedly repeat after shooting Lincoln (and which in his fugitive diary he falsely claimed to have cried out *before* he fired that fatal shot). Even as he was watching his brothers, as Brutus and Cassius, recruit conspirators, he was busily assembling a real conspiracy of his own, one that he failed to persuade Sam Chester to join. A seemingly oblivious Edwin hoped to get his brothers to participate in yet another benefit for the Shakespeare statue, this time with a performance of *Romeo and Juliet*; he would play Mercutio alongside Junius's Friar Lawrence and John Wilkes's Romeo, and he wanted it to coincide with Shakespeare's next birthday, April 23, 1865. Aside from a pair of benefits for friends, the performance of *Julius Caesar* was the last time that John Wilkes Booth appeared onstage.

After the November benefit, Booth focused his energies on kidnapping or killing the president. He spent his days drinking, pursuing women, meeting with confederates to establish safe houses and escape routes between Washington and Virginia, procuring horses and weapons, and practicing shooting. When in New York City he liked to do so at Charles Ottignon's shooting gallery on Broadway, where he used Lincoln's photograph for a target. While plans to kidnap the president were still in the works, Booth went to hear Lincoln deliver his second inaugural address, on March 4. Lincoln didn't flinch from placing responsibility for the costly war on the Confederacy: "Both parties deprecated war, but one of them would *make* war rather than let the nation survive, and the other would *accept* war rather than let it perish." He could not have been clearer about the cause of so much bloodshed: "Slaves constituted a peculiar and powerful interest. All knew that this interest was somehow the cause of the war. To strengthen, perpetuate, and extend this interest was the object for which the insurgents would rend the Union even by war." Photographs of that event show John Wilkes Booth standing above and to the left of Lincoln. Later, while drunk, Booth bragged to Sam Chester, "What an excellent chance I had to kill the President, if I had wished, on Inauguration Day." It was a fantasy he had harbored since at least January 1863, when Lincoln's Emancipation Proclamation had declared slaves in Confederate states "then, thenceforward, and forever free"— anathema to a white supremacist like Booth. Booth had been performing in St Louis at this time, and according to the wife of actor Con T. Murphy, during rehearsals, "Booth suddenly seized this big pistol and forced it against my husband's breast, saying 'By God, Murphy, if you were only Lincoln! What a chance I'd have.'" When her husband told her about the incident that evening, he added, "I do believe John Wilkes Booth is losing his mind over slavery and the President.'"

Booth hated Lincoln, a man he preferred not to name. When told that the president admired his acting, Booth reportedly said that he would have "preferred the applause of a nigger." His sister Asia recalled him complaining of voting irregularities: Lincoln "should never have been President, the votes were *doubled* to seat him . . . *He* is made the tool of the North, to crush out, or try to crush out slavery, by robbery, rapine, slaughter and bought armies." Booth's amateurish plot to kidnap Lincoln began unraveling, and by early April, with the fall of Richmond to Union troops, it had been abandoned, and most of his accomplices quietly slipped away. The script was hurriedly rewritten: the plot now turned on killing the president and others. On April 11 Booth went to the White House to hear Lincoln give an address promising limited suffrage for black men. Booth declared afterward that this was the last speech Lincoln would ever make. The next day he visited Ford's Theatre and told Henry Clay Ford: "We are all slaves now. If a man were to go out and insult a nigger now he would be knocked down by the nigger and nothing would be done to the nigger." The theater's ticket seller, Tom Raybold, suggested to Booth that "He should not insult a nigger then." Two days later, on Good Friday, April 14, 1865, Booth urged clerks at a local hotel to go see the play at Ford's that evening, saying that there "is going to be some splendid acting tonight."

It's impossible to know whether performing in *Julius Caesar* for the first and only time in his life fueled John Wilkes Booth's violent intentions. Perhaps his identification with Brutus grew stronger after that or perhaps he recognized that likening himself to Brutus was useful in justifying his actions. Before shooting the president, Booth wrote a long letter defending his actions, one that he expected to have published in the *National Intelligencer*. On the day of the assassination, he gave that letter to a fellow actor, John Matthews, and asked him to deliver it. But Matthews, terrified of being punished as an accomplice after hearing that Booth had shot Lincoln, burned it after reading it through a few times. Many years later, his reconstructed version of it was published. In it, Booth appeals to the precedent of Shakespeare's Brutus: "When Caesar had conquered the enemies of Rome and the power that was his menaced the liberties of the people, Brutus arose and slew him. The stroke of his dagger was guided by his love of Rome. It was the spirit and ambition of Caesar that Brutus struck at." Booth ends the letter quoting from Shakespeare's play: "Oh, that we could come by Caesar's spirit / And not dismember Caesar! But, alas! / Caesar must bleed for it" (2.1.170–72).

THOUGH JOHN WILKES Booth tried to portray himself as an American Brutus, the role suited him—as Shakespeare put it in *Macbeth*—"like a giant's robe / Upon a dwarfish thief." In the course of his career, Booth performed a surprisingly narrow range of Shakespearean roles, even for a touring star dependent on the repertory of resident companies in cities and towns across the land. He seems to have identified fully with the character he played. He told a friend, Louise Wooster, that while performing "he forgot his own identity completely and for a time would feel that he was really the character." Rather than playing introspective or noble parts (as his father and brother Edwin had), the only roles in which he distinguished himself were dark and often villainous heroes, men of action who die fighting. If a character wasn't scripted that way, he didn't hesitate to exaggerate these traits.

He may have greatly admired *King Lear*, but Booth never acted in it, nor did he ever attempt to play Coriolanus, Richard II, Henry V, Orlando, Falstaff, Benedick, Orsino, Prospero, or Leontes. And he gave Shakespeare's romantic comedies a wide berth. Though he acted the parts of Romeo, Shylock, and Othello twenty or so times each in his years as a touring star, the three Shakespeare roles that secured his reputation were Richard III, Macbeth, and Hamlet. Even here, though, he avoided introspection: his Macbeth was a man of action and his Hamlet was less a melancholy prince than a maddened avenger with blood on his hands, more soldier than scholar. His tragic heroes were more alike than different: athletic, combative, intent on a memorable death. And in the two modern tragedies that fleshed out his mostly Shakespearean repertory, Booth played to these familiar strengths—as Pescara, the vengeful and scheming villain stabbed to death at the end of Richard Shiel's *The Apostate*, and as Raphael, the spurned lover who dies at the end of Charles Selby's *The Marble Heart*—shallow and flashy roles that registered more with the eye than with the mind.

In his few short years as a star, Booth played the title role in *Richard III* more than a hundred times—not counting the three occasions in which he performed only the final Act, so that audiences could see what they had come for, his ferocious fight to the death against Richmond. A reviewer for the *New York Clipper* offers a glimpse of what it was like to watch Booth's Richard confront his end: he "appears, 'seeking for Richmond in the throat of death,' and looks like a butcher just come from the slaughter house . . . His face is covered in blood," and he "actually seems 'eager for the fray.'" Booth's next-most celebrated Shakespeare role was Macbeth, in which he played the lead more than thirty times (and again, on a couple of occasions, staged only the final scenes and fight to the death). He clearly enjoyed displaying his physical prowess. A close friend of Edwin's, Adam Badeau, remembered Booth leaping from rocks in his first entrance. And John T. Ford recalled how he would repeat this daring leap later in the play: upon entering "the den of the witches, Booth . . . had a ledge of rocks some ten or twelve feet high erected in their stead, down which he sprang upon the stage." It was a stage trick that Booth would employ one last time when he made his escape after shooting Lincoln.

Booth could not replicate his brother Edwin's success as Hamlet, though he himself starred in the part nearly fifty times. Charles Wyndham, who acted alongside John Wilkes, helpfully distinguished between the brothers' different approaches to the part: "As John Wilkes played it the Danish prince was unmistakably mad throughout. Edwin's conception of the part was that of uneven and unbalanced genius . . . But John Wilkes leaned toward the other view of the character, as was in keeping with his own bent of mind. His Hamlet was insane, and his interpretation was fiery, convincing, and artistic." William R. Taylor's groundbreaking study, *Cavalier and Yankee: The Old South and American National Character* (1961), includes a chapter "From Hotspur to Hamlet" that explores how the ideal of the white gentleman in the antebellum South gravitated to these polar Shakespearean models. The Southern Hotspurs came "to symbolize honorable failure and the lost cause," while the Southern Hamlets lacked the "vitality and masculinity" needed to act: they are "the consciousness and the conscience of the South" who are "are paralyzed by their knowledge." John Wilkes Booth shared the racial and social values of the Confederacy. In turning Hamlet into Hotspur—a mad, masculine, fiery rebel—he managed to combine these two popular types, recasting the Danish prince as yet another one of Shakespeare's heroic but doomed "Lost Cause" types who dies by the sword and pleads at the end for Horatio to tell his story right.

Historians trace the origins of the Confederacy's "Lost Cause" back to Edward A. Pollard's *The Lost Cause: A New Southern History of the War of the Confederates*, published in 1866. Pollard never names Booth, and writes of "the tragical death of President Lincoln, in a public theatre, at the hands of one of the most indefensible but courageous assassins that history had ever produced." The final pages of Pollard's book neatly encapsulate his message: "The war did not decide negro equality; it did not decide negro suffrage . . . it did not decide the right of a people to show dignity in misfortune, and to maintain self-respect in the face of adversity. And these things which the war did not decide, the Southern people will still cling to, still claim, and still assert in them their rights and views." The "Lost Cause" movement tapped into the desire to recover past greatness even as it stoked Southern anxieties about black equality, and it took root in the rich soil tilled by Southern writers, including those who found support for their convictions in Shakespeare.

As early as 1863, with the opening of the New Theatre in Richmond, Virginia (*As You Like It* was the first play staged there), Shakespeare had been mobilized in such an effort. Henry Timrod, the "poet laureate of the South," wrote a poem for that occasion, reprinted in newspapers throughout the Confederacy. The poem, written "Amid the night of war and death," conjures up a visitation of Shakespearean characters, culminating in a doomed Hamlet whose words "cut so deep / Into the core of life!" For Timrod, the "charms of Art" go hand in hand with "the dear rights for which we fight and pray." And, in the end, in life, as in drama, "all at last shall vindicate the right."

The defense of the South made its way into Shakespeare criticism, still in its infancy in America. One of the most remarkable books on Shakespeare written in nineteenth-century America was by a woman with Confederate sympathies, Mary Preston, whose *Studies in Shakspeare* was published in 1869. Little is known about Preston, almost all of it from the pages of her book, where we learn that she lived at a home named "Oaklands" in Bel Air, Maryland—

a few miles from where John Wilkes Booth was born and raised. It would strain belief that someone so invested in Shakespeare would not have known that the most famous Shakespeare family in America lived nearby. Preston wrote on occasion for the local newspaper, the *Aegis and Intelligencer*, and her views of slavery, the Confederacy, and the Lost Cause were close to Booth's own, perhaps even her unshakable conviction that "Othello *was* a *white* man!" (a "dogmatical assertion" that the reviewer of her book in the *Aegis and Intelligencer* was "pleased to accept"). Most of Preston's chapters on major Shakespeare plays were likely written during the war and repeatedly connect those plays to current events. Preston's ambivalent reflections on *Julius Caesar* are among the most fascinating in her book. She reserves some sympathy for Brutus's misguided patriotism and might as well be speaking of John Wilkes Booth when she concludes that such men are capable "of persuading themselves, when they desire to do so, that wrong is right, though they still retain a *lingering suspicion* that they are deceiving themselves."

By the time that Union troops from the 16th Regiment New York Voluntary Cavalry trapped him in a barn on April 26, 1865, Booth had spent years rehearsing what would be his final scene. He understood exits as well as anyone, and desperately wanted to make one befitting a tragic and heroic figure. To his chagrin, the soldiers had no desire to play along. The dialogue from his final hours was later reconstructed. Lieutenant Luther Byron Baker, part of the force that cornered Booth in the barn on the property of John Garrett, called in to Booth demanding that he come out and surrender—"You are surrounded by fifty armed men. We know who you are. If you don't come out in five minutes, we will set the barn on fire." Booth replied, "Be fair and give me a show . . . Draw your men back a hundred yards and I will fight you all. Give me a fair fight." But the troops had no interest in such a scenario, and Booth was given two minutes to surrender. Booth once again begged of them a chance to die fighting, as he had so often as Macbeth and Richard III: "Give me a chance for my life, and I will come out and fight you." When told that his time was up, and they were setting fire to the barn, Booth said: "Well my brave boys, you can prepare a stretcher for me. One more stain upon the old banner." One of the soldiers, Sergeant Boston Corbett, without orders, fired into the barn and hit Booth, severing his spinal cord and paralyzing him from the neck down. Booth was denied the chance to die heroically. His final words, after realizing that he could not even raise his hands, were: "Useless, useless."

LINCOLN SPENT APRIL 9, 1865—five days before he was assassinated—aboard the steamboat *River Queen*, sailing back to Washington after a risky visit to the front, including a tour of the now liberated capital of the Confederacy, Richmond, where fires were still burning. Lightly guarded and accompanied by his son Tad as he entered Richmond, Lincoln was mobbed by newly freed slaves. Lincoln then proceeded to the "Confederate White House" and sat in the office of Jefferson Davis, who had fled the city. It was a gesture that sat poorly with those embittered by its symbolism; John Wilkes Booth was maddened by it, having heard rumors that Lincoln had spat tobacco juice while lounging on Davis's chair. After leaving Richmond, Lincoln made his way to City Point, Virginia, where, awaiting news from General Grant, he visited wounded Union soldiers for five hours, shaking hands with thousands of them. Though Lincoln did not yet know it, as he was sailing back to Washington, Robert E. Lee surrendered at Appomattox, all but bringing the war to an end.

One of those who journeyed home with him on the *River Queen* was Senator Charles Sumner, who recalled how Lincoln's thoughts at this moment turned to Shakespeare, and to *Macbeth* in particular, as the president pulled out a handsome quarto of the play that he had brought with him and twice read aloud "the tribute to the murdered Duncan." Sumner was accompanied by a young Frenchman, the Marquis de Chambrun, whose diary entry for that day offers a fuller account of what took place: "Mr. Lincoln read to us for several hours passages taken from Shakespeare. Most of these were from *Macbeth*, and in particular the verses which follow Duncan's assassination. I cannot recall this reading without being awed at the remembrance, when Macbeth became king after the murder of Duncan, he falls a prey to the most horrible torments of mind." In his usual way, "Lincoln paused here while reading and began to explain to us how true a description of the murderer that one was, when, the dark deed achieved, its tortured perpetrator came to envy the sleep of his victim; and he read over again the same scene":

> Methought I heard a voice cry "Sleep no more!
> Macbeth does murder sleep," the innocent sleep,
> Sleep that knits up the raveled sleave of care,
> The death of each day's life, sore labor's bath,
> Balm of hurt minds, great nature's second course,
> Chief nourisher in life's feast— (2.2.39–44)

A more arrogant leader might have quoted Malcolm's victorious lines at play's end, having triumphed on the battlefield: "and what needful else / That calls upon us, by the grace of Grace / We will perform in measure, time, and place" (5.8.72–74). But Lincoln chose instead to dwell upon how perfectly Shakespeare had captured the unrelieved guilt of the "tortured perpetrator."

It's not surprising that Lincoln had brought along a copy of *Macbeth*. He had told Charlotte Cushman that it was his "favorite play," and in his letter to James Hackett wrote that "I think nothing equals *Macbeth*; I think it is wonderful." Lincoln seems to have found comfort reciting from this dark tragedy. That at least was the impression of John W. Forney, editor of the *Philadelphia Press*, and, during the war years, secretary of the senate, in which capacity he met with Lincoln regularly. Forney writes that "Lincoln had his periods of depression" and that "one evening I found him in such a mood. He was ghastly pale, the dark rings were round his caverned eyes, his hair was brushed back from his temples, and he was reading Shakespeare as I came in. 'Let me read you this from *Macbeth*' . . . :

> Tomorrow, and tomorrow, and tomorrow
> Creeps in this petty pace from day to day
> To the last syllable of recorded time,
> And all our yesterdays have lighted fools
> The way to dusty death. Out, out, brief candle!
> Life's but a walking shadow, a poor player
> That struts and frets his hour upon the stage
> And then is heard no more. It is a tale
> Told by an idiot, full of sound and fury,
> Signifying nothing. (5.5.19–28)

"I cannot read it like Forrest," Lincoln added, "but it comes to me tonight like a consolation." If any American reader of Shakespeare has truly felt—through meditating on the tormented words of guilt-ridden characters like Macbeth and Claudius—the deep connection between the nation's own primal sin, slavery, and the terrible cost, both collective and personal, exacted by it, it was Lincoln.

There was another reason he might have been brooding about *Macbeth* on that trip to Richmond. Lincoln's friend and self-appointed bodyguard, Ward Hill Lamon, recalled that "a few days" before he was assassinated an unusually somber Lincoln had told a small group (that included his wife and Lamon) about a nightmare he had had ten days earlier, while awaiting "important dispatches from the front." It was a dream, Lincoln said, that had "haunted" him "ever since." Lincoln was loath to mention this disturbing premonition to his wife, but the compulsion to share it was too great. Likening himself to a Macbeth rattled by visions, Lincoln said that "somehow the thing has got possession of me, and, like Banquo's ghost, it will not down." In his dream, Lincoln recalled how "I thought I left my bed and wandered downstairs." Calling to mind the sleepwalking Lady Macbeth, Lincoln saw himself entering the East Room of the White House, where he was met with "a sickening surprise": a corpse guarded by soldiers and surrounded by a throng of mourners, some "weeping pitifully." When he asked, "Who is dead in the White House?" a soldier replied, "The President." He "was killed by an assassin." A "loud burst of grief" from the mourners woke Lincoln from his nightmare. The experience was so unnerving that for the rest of the night, Lincoln said, "he slept no more." Lamon (who writes that he jotted down at the time what Lincoln said "as nearly in his own words" as he could recall), adds that Lincoln was "profoundly disturbed" by this nightmare, and continued to dwell on it: in "conversations with me he referred to it afterward, closing with this quotation from *Hamlet*: 'To sleep, perchance to dream! Ay, *there's the rub*,' with a strong accent on the last three words."

LINCOLN'S ASSASSINATION MARKED a beginning as much as an end—of Reconstruction, of the Lost Cause, of a battle for equality for the freed slaves and their descendants, and of the struggle to define the legacies of both Lincoln and Booth, in which Shakespeare, unsurprisingly, figured. Taking the hint from Booth himself, his few and scattered supporters defended the assassination on the grounds that, like Brutus, Booth had killed a tyrant. An editorial that ran in the Warsaw, Kentucky, *Sign of the Times*, praised him as a "lover of liberty, the great American Brutus . . . whose name will go down to future generations as the American Liberator—as the man who had the daring courage to destroy the first American tyrant." The *Texas Republican* similarly maintained that Booth slew Lincoln "as a tyrant, and the enemy of his country." The poem "Our Brutus" (likely written in 1866 but which didn't appear in print until 1913, in the *Confederate Veteran Magazine*) offers another example of how Booth was celebrated by his admirers as an American Brutus: "It was Liberty slain / That so maddened his brain." It was easier to claim this heroic status for Booth, to hide behind the conspirators' cry that "Tyranny is dead" (3.1.79) than to admit that Booth, a white supremacist, did what he did out of hatred for Lincoln and a deep-seated loathing of emancipation and racial equality.

Some of those who knew John Wilkes saw Shakespeare's hand behind his act. In 1878, the theater manager John T. Ford told a journalist that "John Wilkes Booth was trained from earliest infancy to consider the almost deified assassin Brutus, just as Shakespeare immortalized him." Ford imagined Booth thinking, "If I failed to serve the South in my conspiracy to abduct, I can now be her Brutus." Booth's mind, Ford believed, "was turned by the poetic and dramatic glamour which transmitted the story of the Roman assassination." Others who knew Booth shared this view, including George Alfred Townsend, a harsh critic of the South, who published the first popular book about Lincoln's murderer in 1865. Townsend had seen Booth perform and spoke with him not long before the assassination. He too subscribed to the belief that Shakespeare was somehow behind it all, that Booth "had rolled under his tongue the sweet paragraphs of Shakespeare referring to Brutus . . . until it became his ambition . . . to stake his life upon one stroke for fame, the murder of a ruler obnoxious to the South." Townsend also believed that Booth "burned to make his name a part of history, cried into fame by the applauses of the South," and "that whatever minor parts might be enacted—Casca, Cassius, or what not—he was to be the dramatic Brutus."

Thirty-six years after the assassination, when it was safer to say such things, Edward M. Alfriend recalled that Booth had told him: "Of all Shakespeare's characters I like Brutus the best, excepting only Lear." Alfriend also implicated Shakespeare in the assassination. He had "no doubt" that Booth's "study of and meditation upon those characters had much to do with shaping that mental condition which induced his murder of President Lincoln," and "that if the truth could be known, John Wilkes Booth, in his insanity, lost his identity in the delirious fancy that he was enacting the role of 'Brutus,' and that Lincoln was his 'Julius Caesar.'"

But efforts to recast the assassination of Lincoln as a reenactment of *Julius Caesar* found little purchase among the vast majority of Americans, even in the defeated South. The play that the nation settled on to give voice to what had happened, and define how Lincoln was to be remembered, turned out to be *Macbeth*. As news of the president's murder swept through the land and Americans struggled to put their feeling into words, lines from Act 2, scene 3 of *Macbeth* came immediately to mind: "O horror, horror, horror! / Tongue nor heart cannot conceive nor name thee," wrote Benjamin Brown French, who would be responsible for planning Lincoln's funeral, adding, "We have supped full of horrors." The same words echoed in the mind of Fanny Seward, whose father had been stabbed as part of the larger plot to eliminate the nation's leaders, and who recorded the line in her diary as well. There was even an attempt to implicate Jefferson Davis in the conspiracy to assassinate Lincoln by claiming that he quoted from *Macbeth* upon hearing that the president had been shot; John A. Bingham, who served as the assistant judge advocate at the trial of Booth's coconspirators, quoted sources in those proceedings who had heard Davis say, upon learning from a telegram that Lincoln was shot, "If it were to be done, it were *better* it were well done."

While lines from other plays were tried out, including passages from *Hamlet* and *King John*, it was *Macbeth* to which those mourning Lincoln found themselves turning time and again, especially those likening him to the slain Duncan, who

> Hath borne his faculties so meek, hath been
> So clear in his great office, that his virtues
> Will plead like angels, trumpet-tongued, against
> The deep damnation of his taking-off. (1.7.17–20)

These four lines were repeatedly recited in eulogies. They appeared on banners strung from storefronts. They were printed on illustrations, such as *The Martyr of Liberty*, in which they offer a commentary on the moment of the assassination. And they formed the centerpiece of the black-bordered funeral broadside that circulated: "Shakespeare Applied to Our National Bereavement." The words became, as Richard Wightman Fox puts it in *Lincoln's Body*, "virtually the official slogan of the mourning period."

To mourn Lincoln as another Duncan was to move away from Booth's violent understanding of *Macbeth* as much as from Lincoln's introspective one. True, the play was about an assassination, but, unlike the one in *Julius Caesar*, not ideologically driven, so better suited to the story that America preferred to tell itself now that the war was over but what was to follow unclear. Some wanted to celebrate Lincoln as a radical who gave his life to free the slaves; others chose to memorialize him as a moderate who fought to save the Union, and whose death was a setback for Reconstruction and the reconciliation of North and South. Likening Lincoln to Duncan papered over the vast gap between these positions, for Duncan was something of a cipher in *Macbeth*. He may be the only ruler in all of Shakespeare's works whose limitations are overlooked, one of those rare instances where Shakespeare did not build on the hints provided in his source, Holinshed's *Chronicles*, where a "soft and gentle" Duncan is criticized for having been "negligent . . . in punishing offenders," leading "many misruled persons" to "trouble the peace and quiet state of the commonwealth, by seditious commotions." In aspiring to die like Macbeth (though not to reflect on his crime, as Macbeth himself had done), John Wilkes Booth had failed to anticipate that the man he cold-bloodedly murdered would be revered like Duncan, his faults forgotten. For a divided America, the universal currency of Shakespeare's words offered a collective catharsis—once the story of Lincoln's assassination was successfully recast as a national tragedy of Shakespearean dimensions—permitting a blood-soaked nation to defer confronting once again what Booth declared had driven him to act: the conviction that America "was formed for the *white* not for the black man."

Shakespeare Tercentenary Celebration, *Caliban by the Yellow Sands*, by Percy MacKaye, 1916.

CHAPTER 5

1916: Immigration

The Tempest is staged so often nowadays in America that it's hard to imagine a time when it wasn't. Yet for a very long stretch—from before the Civil War until the end of World War II—American productions were few and far between, and mostly forgettable. When William Davidge staged it in New York in 1869 it hadn't been seen there for fifteen years, and nearly thirty more years would pass before Augustin Daly—America's first great theater director—would stage it in New York in 1897. Two *Tempest*-less decades later a local theater critic complained that for "the present generation" the play "is virtually unknown on the stage."

It didn't fare much better elsewhere across the land, didn't yet speak to the concerns of American audiences in the ways that plays like *Macbeth, Hamlet, Julius Caesar,* or *Othello* seemed to. Not a line from it appeared in either Scott's *Lessons in Elocution* or McGuffey's *Reader.* When James McVicker staged *The Tempest* in Chicago in 1889 the *Chicago Times* noted that until now it "had never been tried in this country west of New York." A San Francisco company undertook a western tour in 1902, and the British actor Ben Greet toured the eastern seaboard with his imported production a few years later. Otherwise, with the exception of a few scattered and amateur performances and a brief revival in Boston in 1928, that seems to have been it until 1945. In that year, first in Boston, then in New York, Margaret Webster, fresh from her success directing Paul Robeson in a Broadway production of *Othello*, cast Canada Lee, another leading black actor, as Caliban—a first. It wasn't until after World War II, then, that American productions began engaging the darker side of authority and global power that British ones had been wrestling with since Victorian days, and not until the 1970s that *The Tempest* joined the mini-canon of Shakespeare's plays frequently taught and staged in America.

In contrast, in modern Britain, the play never lost its popularity; from the mid-nineteenth to the mid-twentieth century alone more than twenty-five productions were staged there, including major ones by Frank Benson, William Poel, Herbert Beerbohm Tree, and Tyrone Guthrie. British critics and biographers wrote extensively about the play, and two years after Charles Darwin's *The Descent of Man* appeared in 1871, Daniel Wilson published *Caliban: The Missing Link*, suggesting that Shakespeare in *The Tempest* had more or less anticipated Darwin. Wilson's Caliban "seems indeed the half-human link between the brute and man," the "ideal anthropoid in the highest stage of Simian evolution." The book would have an oversize influence on productions on both sides of the Atlantic, including that of Frank Benson, who spent hours at the zoo studying monkeys and baboons in the 1890s to prepare for what many now saw as the play's most challenging role.

But before the 1970s there was a brief moment when *The Tempest* really mattered in America: 1916. That year, in addition to a "doublet-and-hose" revival by New York's Drama Society, there was a large-scale adaptation by Percy MacKaye, *Caliban by the Yellow Sands*, the centerpiece of both national and metropolitan celebrations of the three-hundredth anniversary of Shakespeare's death. A broad range of ethnic groups participated in this community drama, which came to be called simply *Caliban*. With a total of seven thousand local performers in New York and Boston, these were the largest theatrical performances of all time in either city; more than three hundred thousand spectators went to see it staged. It was hoped that a national tour as well as public recitations would follow. The story of Prospero's attempts to educate Caliban rose to prominence that year for a reason few explicitly acknowledged. Through its portrayal of Caliban, and in its reliance on large groups of performers from different ethnicities, the production spoke to one of the most divisive issues of the day—immigration—a concern that was being fiercely debated in Congress, discussions that would lead to the passage of groundbreaking legislation shortly after the tercentenary ended, redefining who could be an American.

Until the 1880s, America had welcomed successive waves of immigrants and saw itself as a haven for those seeking religious, economic, and political freedom. But attitudes began to shift by the end of that decade, in which 5.2 million foreigners arrived, raising the percentage of those who were born abroad to nearly 15 percent of the population. Anxieties about foreigners intensified in the 1890s, when the number of those arriving from eastern and southern Europe surpassed that of those from northern European lands. By 1907 these "new" immigrants constituted 85 percent of all those entering the country, and efforts to curb their influx intensified (Asian, African, and Central and South American immigrants remained a small fraction of those admitted, and a Chinese Exclusion Act had been in place since 1882). Between 1880 and 1920 an unprecedented number of those seeking opportunity or refuge—nearly 24 million—landed on America's shores.

Immigration authorities began to distinguish not only between what they deemed the "white, black, yellow, brown, and red" races but also between what were imagined to be over a score of white European races as well. At the turn of the century, national census reports very nearly adopted, as immigration officials at Ellis Island had, a table of "Races and Nations" to categorize new arrivals. Until the early 1890s those seeking admission to America had been asked about their nationality, mental and physical health, occupation, where they had come from, where they were heading, if they had any relatives in the US, and whether they had been imprisoned or in a poor house. The scope of such questions would change in 1898, when a supplemental list was added that reflected the emerging scientific racism of the day. Potential immigrants were now required to answer additional questions about their color, place of birth, mother tongue, and religion—which, taken together, spelled race. This in turn led to Jews (of whatever nationality) being categorized as Hebrews, and Italians from Naples or Sicily were racially demarcated from their "Teutonic" fellow countrymen from Milan or Venice. The shift in questions and categories was subtle, but significant: potential Americans were no longer judged on their character but on their lineage.

As one polemicist at that time (of "old," "Anglo-Saxon," "Teutonic," or "Nordic" stock—the terms were used more or less interchangeably) declared: "Our immigration has, until lately, been chiefly made up of the most intelligent and of the most desirable races of Europe, but recently the numbers have greatly increased of those who are without question the most illiterate and the most depraved people of that continent." Those words were written by Robert DeCourcy Ward, one of three recent Harvard graduates who in 1894 founded the Immigration Restriction League, an influential lobbying group committed to preserving the nation's Anglo-Saxon identity. As that organization's first president, John Fiske, put it: a community of people "have a perfect right to build a wall around it and exclude such people as they do not wish to have among them."

How Shakespeare and especially *The Tempest* were conscripted by those opposed to the immigration of those deemed undesirable is a lesser-known part of this story. In retrospect, it is unsurprising that a Shakespearean comedy would be appropriated in this way, since his comedies almost always end with the creation of a new social order defined by who is included and who is kept out. The wrong skin color, religion, or sexual orientation, or simply the unwillingness to act and sound like everyone else is enough to warrant exclusion. The pattern is repeated in one comedy after another. The sexually rapacious Falstaff cannot be accommodated into the domestic world of suburban Windsor. A melancholy Jacques refuses to join the rest as they make their way from the Forest of Arden back to court at the end of *As You Like It*. Though he has agreed to convert, Shylock is repudiated at the end of *The Merchant of Venice*, while Portia's unsuccessful wooer, that dark-skinned Muslim, the Prince of Morocco, is rejected as well. Community in Shakespeare's comedies depends—much like immigration policy—on who is barred admission as much as on who is accepted. So too in *The Tempest*, although here the geography of inclusion is reversed: Prospero, Miranda, and the courtiers, clowns, and sailors all abandon the island and sail home to Italy. Even the traitorous and unrepentant Antonio, because of ties of blood, is included in the group. Ariel flies off to freedom. At masque's end it is only Caliban, eager for companionship, who is excluded, left alone on the island. The hint of cruelty in all this, the self-justification of those who do the excluding, even our own complicity in watching this unfold, is overshadowed by the feel-good ending. But make no mistake: a more hopeful community at the end of a Shakespeare comedy typically depends on somebody's exclusion.

Despite this, the role assigned to Shakespeare in the debate over immigration in early twentieth-century America is surprising. Few would have been more amused than Shakespeare to learn that he was "Anglo-Saxon" (let alone a "white man," another term that doesn't appear in his works and was only beginning to enter the vocabulary during his lifetime). He would have known that the first advocate of Anglo-Saxonism as a racial and political category was his contemporary, the London-born Richard Rowlands, a Catholic apologist who was himself of immigrant stock (his Dutch grandfather had sought refuge in England around 1500). Shakespeare likely knew that Rowlands became a refugee; he fled religious persecution in England, settled in Antwerp, took the name Verstegen, and in 1605 published the wildly influential *Restitution of Decayed Intelligence*, which argued for Teutonic racial purity and superiority. Rowlands's case for England's Germanic-Saxon roots—which was essentially a Catholic's thinly disguised attack on King James's claim to lead a British and Protestant nation—would be appropriated three centuries later by American Protestants bent on excluding Catholic immigrants.

Positioning Shakespeare as a foe of immigrants is all the more surprising given what he himself had written about refugees. Victorian scholars first identified the playwright's handwriting, "Hand D," in a collaborative manuscript of a play called *Sir Thomas More*. Shakespeare's likely contribution concerned More's reaction to the violent anti-immigrant riots in London in 1517. He wrote a powerful scene in which More admonishes nativists who would "put down strangers, / Kill them, cut their throats, possess their houses" (including, perhaps, the throats of Richard Rowlands's immigrant ancestors). "Imagine," More says, "that you see the wretched strangers,"

> Their babies at their backs and their poor luggage,
> Plodding to the ports and coasts for transportation,
> And that you sit as kings in your desires,
> Authority quite silent by your brawl,
> And you in ruff of your opinions clothed. (2.4)

It is an extraordinarily empathic speech, all the more so given the xenophobia of Shakespeare's own day. By the 1880s Shakespeare could have been seen as a pioneering advocate for refugees, especially those who had fled religious and political persecution on the Continent. But that never happened. Instead, Shakespeare's reputed Anglo-Saxon identity, along with his plays, were marshaled by influential scholars and politicians frightened by the threat that unrestricted immigration posed to America's identity.

NONE WAS MORE instrumental in this effort than Henry Cabot Lodge, for more than a quarter century the leading voice in Congress for curbing immigration. Lodge was born in Massachusetts in 1850 and traced his family's roots on both sides back to English ancestry. Lodge attended Harvard, where he received a doctorate in history, one of the first to be awarded there. His thesis was on Anglo-Saxon law, part of a collaborative effort to show that racial traits were behind the transmission of ancient laws and liberties. He briefly taught history at Harvard before embarking on a political career, first serving in the House of Representatives from 1886 to 1893, then in the Senate until his death in 1924.

Lodge's love of Shakespeare was lifelong. When memorializing him, Bishop William Lawrence vividly recalled seeing Lodge "taking out his little volume of Shakespeare which was always with him." Lodge himself acknowledged that he was "brought up to a blind devotion to Shakespeare." Before the age of 10 he was taken to see Edwin Booth's *Julius Caesar*. His father helped found the Boston Theater and was president of its board, so the young Lodge had free run of the place and saw some of the great Shakespearean performers of the day. Lodge acted while an undergraduate, and a striking photograph of him survives from these years, cross-dressed as Lady Macbeth. One of his good friends was Brander Matthews, a Shakespearean who taught at Columbia, to whom Lodge confessed that he had "always wanted to write a book about Shakespeare's plays." While he never wrote that book, he invoked Shakespeare in speeches and essays in his decades-long effort to change America's immigration policy.

Like many others in the Republican Party, Lodge had supported open immigration before denouncing it. A recent revisionist

153

explanation attributes this shift to pragmatism, not racism: the demand for cheap industrial labor had slackened and Republicans were
losing working-class voters, so in the 1890s the party decided that
targeting more-recent immigrants was the way to win those voters
back. That argument may well be true of others in his party, but
not of Lodge, one of the most intellectually gifted individuals of his
generation, whose views on race went beyond political calculation.

Lodge published three linked essays on this subject in 1891. In
the first, "Restriction of Immigration," his argument was twofold:
the recent wave of newcomers was both an economic threat to
working-class Americans and "an infusion which seems to threaten
deterioration." Lodge then published an uglier piece—"Lynch Law
and Unrestricted Immigration"—in which he responds to news that
a mob broke into a jail in New Orleans and lynched eleven Italian
immigrants. Rather than condemn this hate crime, Lodge argues
that "such action, if not justified, is predictable," given "America's
open borders to unwanted immigrants," and warns that if "we do
not act, and act intelligently, we must be prepared for just such
events as that at New Orleans, not merely bringing in their train
murder and sudden death, but breeding race antagonisms and national hostilities." Having blamed the victims, he pivoted in a third
essay to praise those responsible for American greatness—in "The
Distribution of Ability in the United States"—a statistical analysis
of fifteen thousand individuals who contributed to American society. Predictably, men of Northern European ancestry take the
prize. This same year he gave his first speech urging Congress to
revisit immigration policy and introduced the first of several bills
requiring that adults entering the country be literate. Heads of
households and single adult immigrants would be presented upon
landing with a short passage from the Constitution in their own
language; if they could not read and transcribe it they would be
sent back to where they came from.

Such a test for immigrants might appear modest, and if you consider how little impact it would have on Eastern European Jews (most of whom could read and write Hebrew or Yiddish), largely ineffective, as it proved to be, for only a few thousand immigrants were ultimately denied admission on these grounds after the legislation finally passed in 1917. But the only alternatives considered at the time were raising the head tax paid on entry into the United States or vetting potential immigrants before they set sail. The idea of establishing racial or national quotas as yet remained unthinkable, or unspoken, and even getting Congress to pass a literacy requirement was an uphill battle. The real aim of restrictionists was to harden American hearts against an open-door policy, to no longer think of their country as a refuge. The restrictionists were playing a long game, and their focus on literacy appealed to the elites, whose support they needed; it was easy enough riling working-class whites fearful of losing their jobs to foreigners.

In 1896, Lodge, by now a senator, delivered a major speech on immigration reform. But before doing so he published a piece on "Shakespeare's Americanisms" in *Harper's Magazine*. In it, he made the counterintuitive argument that Americans had a better claim to Shakespeare's linguistic heritage than modern-day British subjects did because the language that the founders of America "brought with them to Virginia and Massachusetts was . . . the language of Shakespeare, who lived and wrote and died just at the period when these countrymen of his were taking their way to the New World." And while initially "common to the English on both sides of the Atlantic," a surprising amount of Shakespeare's vocabulary had only survived in America. Lodge's essay pushes back against British claims that the English language has degenerated in America and takes exception to how "words used by Shakespeare himself, should have lived to be disdainfully called 'Americanisms' by people now living in Shakespeare's own country." For Lodge, "English speech is too great an inheritance to be trifled with or wrangled over. It is much better for all who speak it to give their best strength to defending it and keeping it pure and vigorous, so that it many go on spreading and conquering." In one stroke, Lodge declares America's superiority to England and its greater proximity to pure Shakespeare, while implicitly supporting the position that in order to retain its imperial vigor, American immigration policy must be literacy based.

His speech to the Senate on March 16, 1896, was a tour de force. It was covered widely in newspapers and subsequently published, and shaped the national conversation on immigration for years to come. In order to justify imposing a literacy test, Lodge had to reinvent a past that explained the present crisis. The decisive moment in that past was when Shakespeare lived. At this pivotal juncture, the "work of race making had been all done and the achievements of the race so made were about to begin." The defining features of what would emerge as American greatness—its anti-despotic ideology, its Teutonic roots, its Protestant faith—can be traced back to this extraordinary Elizabethan moment. In support of this claim, Lodge quotes at length from Thomas Carlyle: "Ideas of innumerable kinds were circulating among these men; witness one Shakespeare . . . the finest human figure, as I apprehend, that nature has hitherto seen fit to make of our widely diffused Teutonic clay."

Immediately after this work of race making was complete, the heirs of this legacy carried it with them to Jamestown and Plymouth Rock. Soon, others from northern Europe began settling in America as well. Happily, this did nothing to diminish homogeneity, since "the people of the thirteen colonies were all of the same original race stock. The Dutch, the Swedes, and the Germans simply blended again with the English-speaking people, who like them were descended from the Germanic tribes," and who had "been welded together by more than a thousand years of wars, conquests, migrations, and struggles, both at home and abroad" through which they "attained a fixity and definiteness of national character." In Lodge's elaborate racial fantasy, America's uniformity (African Americans, Native Americans, Asians, Mexicans, and early Jewish and southern European immigrants don't figure) continued undiluted until 1875. That's when things took a sharp turn for the worse: "Russians, Hungarians, Poles, Bohemians, Italians, Greeks, and even Asiatics, whose immigration to America was almost unknown twenty years ago, have during the last twenty years poured in in steadily increasing numbers." This had to be stopped, for "when you begin to pour in in unlimited numbers people of alien or lower races of less social efficiency and less moral force, you are running the most frightful risk that a people can run. The lowering of a great race means not only its own decline, but that of civilization."

Lodge's bill requiring that new arrivals be able to both read and write—crafted in collaboration with the Immigration Restriction League—carried the majority in both the House and Senate, but was vetoed by President Grover Cleveland. A disappointed Lodge wrote to his friend and future president Teddy Roosevelt that he "was disappointed because I wanted this great piece of legislation upon the statute books." In 1907 Roosevelt, now President, appointed an Immigration Commission that included Lodge among its nine members. They held no hearings and heard little testimony before producing a forty-one-volume report in 1911 strongly urging that immigration be restricted, and recommended a literacy test. A bill to impose one was passed, then once again vetoed, this time by President William Howard Taft in 1913, and then again by President Woodrow Wilson in 1915, who, in his letter to the House explaining why he rejected the bill, made the stakes perfectly clear: Lodge and his supporters were advocating a "radical change in the policy of the nation," for the "new tests here embodied are not tests of quality or of character," and their object "is restriction, not selection." This set the stage for yet another showdown, when it appeared as if there was finally enough will, and votes, to overrule yet another expected presidential veto in 1916, the same year that Americans were gearing up for a nationwide celebration of Shakespeare's tercentenary.

To CONSIDER SHAKESPEARE an American hero is a strange idea. Joseph Watson was among the first to make such a claim, in 1877, in a column in the *New York Herald*, "Shakespeare in America," where he argued that the English were "slow to recognize the appalling grandeur of the genius of her immortal bard," while Americans "could read those lessons of the poet and witness his historical plays while untrammeled and uninfluenced by monarchical surroundings." Watson conceded that the English might not agree, and reports a conversation from around the time of the War of 1812 between the English actor George Frederick Cooke, who was performing at the time in New York, and an unnamed American interlocutor. Cooke objected to Americans calling Shakespeare "our great poet," and insisted that "you are not the countrymen of Shakespeare." When the American replied that he had the right to "claim the same share in the heroes, poets and philosophers of former days as any Briton of this day can," Cooke would have none of it: "No, no, that won't do. You are a race of yesterday, mere upstarts. You abandoned Great Britain and gave up your share in her fame." What had changed in the course of the nineteenth century was the notion of racial inheritance: for Cooke, Americans were a newly forged race—"a race of yesterday"—but by the close of the century it had become increasingly accepted that America had been, since its founding, racially Anglo-Saxon, and so the Shakespearean inheritance was a shared one.

As late as 1892, with the publication of Howard H. Furness's comprehensive Variorum edition of *The Tempest*, no critic had explicitly tied the play to the future United States. It had long been understood as a European dynastic play that was indebted, among its various sources, to recent New World narratives. Yes, as far back as 1797, Richard Sill noted that Shakespeare's sources included "narratives of discovery of the New World," and in 1808 Edmond Malone elaborated on these connections at length. But it was quite a leap to associate Caliban with the natives of North America or the play with American political values.

By the close of the nineteenth century, critics were increasingly willing to make that leap. In 1898 Frank M. Bristol published *Shakespeare and America*, in which he argued that *The Tempest* "has an entirely American basis and character," and that Caliban "is an American." Four years later the Massachusetts native Edward Everett Hale pressed the case for a New England rather than a Virginian interest on Shakespeare's part. He gave a talk to the American Antiquarian Society arguing that the setting of *The Tempest* was Cuttyhunk Island, off Cape Cod, on which an English explorer had landed in 1602. In 1916, Henry Cabot Lodge, who had heard Hale's talk and thought it "very convincing," persuaded his old friend Brander Matthews to publish it, along with a long introduction by Lodge himself. In this introduction Lodge speaks of Caliban as "distinctly human, and yet wholly unlike the humanity we know," in whose character "we find Shakespeare's intimation of the evolution of man and the missing link," and he concurs with the British scholar Walter Raleigh's conclusion that "Shakespeare, almost alone, saw the problem of American settlement in a detached light."

Much of the credit for popularizing the belief that *The Tempest* was preoccupied with America goes to the English scholar Sidney Lee and his 1898 biography of Shakespeare. Lee's argument reached an even wider audience when he published an extended version of his thesis, "The Call of the West: America and Elizabethan England," in *Scribner's Magazine* in 1907. What Lee had to say about Caliban sounded a lot like what restrictionists were saying about undesirable immigrants: Caliban's "life is passed in that stage of evolutionary development which precedes the birth of moral sentiment, of intellectual perception, and social culture. He is a creature stumbling over the first stepping-stones which lead from savagery to civilization." In Caliban, Lee declares, Shakespeare "propounded an answer to the greatest of American enigmas," and *The Tempest* was "a veritable document of early Anglo-American history." By 1916 a critic for the *New-York Tribune* could confidently write that *The Tempest* "was mainly inspired by Shakespeare's interest in America"; the latest revival was now being touted as "Shakespeare's One American Play."

Along with Lodge, Charles Mills Gayley, who taught at the University of California, Berkeley, did the most to popularize the connections between Shakespeare, America, race, and restricted immigration. Gayley was a charismatic professor who wrote for a national audience. In 1914, as war broke out in Europe, he embarked on a sabbatical in England in which he researched a popular book, *Shakespeare and the Founders of Liberty in America*, published in 1917. The xenophobic version of America's past that Lodge had been telling in Congress, and that the Immigration Restriction League had been promoting to journalists, lawyers, and policy makers, was now authorized by literary scholarship. If anything, Gayley's version was even harsher toward new immigrants, berating them as at best superstitious and grasping, and at worst, as seditious anarchists:

> If it be true that, during the past generation, we have with too light scrutiny admitted to our large freedom and easy fatness tens of thousands whose hands grasp our privileges, but whose heirs still cherish the superstitions of the political inhumanity from which we thought they had escaped, who is to blame? If it be true that we have admitted tens of thousands who, crazed with license, leap to the torch and bomb and in the name of liberty flaunt the rag of anarchy, who is to blame?

Gayley is at pains to make clear that America was and must remain Anglo-Saxon. Until the 1870s, others who sought refuge in America had "gloried in identifying themselves with the inheritors of Anglo-Saxon blood and speech, common law, individual freedom and national responsibility." But now, thanks to the crush of undesirable new immigrants, that was no longer so. Since for Gayley our "American heritage is of the revolutionary fathers, of the colonial fathers, of the English fathers of colonial liberty," the primary aim of his book was to show that these early settlers were "the contemporaries and friends" of Shakespeare, who was both "the poet and prophet of the race."

Gayley pressed this political link very hard, in a syllogistic argument that runs something like this: Shakespeare was close to a patriotic "liberal faction" of Elizabethan notables who helped bankroll the early colonial voyage to Virginia, a source of *The Tempest*. Shakespeare shared their dislike of monarchy and their promotion of individual freedom and "equality before the law"—not pro-democracy exactly, but close enough. Shakespeare should therefore be considered one of the founders of liberty in America. Scholarly reviewers pointed out that there was no solid evidence for any of this. One of Gayley's harshest critics, E. E. Stoll, took special exception to Gayley's suggestion that *The Tempest* was about the Virginia colony: "There is not a word in the *Tempest* about America or Virginia, colonies or colonizing, Indians or tomahawks, maize, mocking-birds, or tobacco"; Shakespeare, he insisted, knew "exceedingly little" of America, and "said nothing of it as American." But Stoll and others were publishing their critiques in obscure academic journals; Gayley's book was a popular one. In 1916 Gayley pressed his racial claims in a poem—"The Heart of the Race"—that reached a wide readership when published in newspapers in America and abroad:

Poet, thou, of the Blood: of states and of nations
Passing thy utmost dream, in the uttermost corners of space!
　Poet, thou, of my countrymen born to the speech,
　　O Brother,
　Born to the law and freedom, proud of the old embrace,
　Born of the Mayflower, born of Virginia—born of the
　　Mother!
　Poet, thou of the Mother! the blood of America,
　Turning in tribute to thee, revisits the Heart of the Race.

By 1916 the line between speaking of Caliban in Shakespearean and immigration contexts was increasingly blurred. In the early years of the century, the sociologist Edward Alsworth Ross conducted a bit of field work in New York City's Union Square. He watched hundreds of recent immigrants employed as garment workers trudge home from grueling labor in nearby sweatshops. Ross studied their faces as they passed, and of the 368 he counted, only 38 looked American to him, that is, "had the type of face one would find at a country fair in the West or South." "To one accustomed to the aspect of the normal American population," he noted, "the Caliban type shows up with a frequency that is startling." Even when these immigrants appear in their "Sunday best" one "is struck by the fact that from ten to twenty per cent are hirsute, low-browed, big-faced persons of obviously low mentality."

Ross made a similar claim in another jeremiad published in 1914, *The Old World in the New*, in which he argues that, like Caliban, these new immigrants are "sub-common," and admitting them into the country is committing racial suicide: "In every face there was something wrong—lips thick, mouth coarse, upper lip too long, cheek-bones too high, chin poorly formed, the bridge of the nose hollowed." Earlier in his career, in 1900, while teaching in California, Ross had opposed Asian immigration, saying that "should the worst come to the worst it would be better for us if we were to turn our guns upon every vessel bringing Japanese to our shores rather than to permit them to land." The jibe had cost him tenure at Stanford. By now, thanks to the effectiveness of anti-immigration campaigners, espousing such views was increasingly acceptable. By 1915 the *Los Angeles Times* could publish an opinion piece by a physician, John Madison Taylor, on the danger of "The Race Peril at Our Doors," that shared this set of assumptions and linked Caliban to recent immigrants imagined to be "defective": "Already our almshouses, jails, homes for feeble-minded, insane, deformed, blind and chronically diseased are filled with the foreign-born and their second generation." Dr. Taylor warns that "mixing old and new American stock" risks producing offspring that "become alternately one fairly sound, the other a monster, a Caliban."

In 1915, at the height of his fame, the 40-year-old playwright Percy MacKaye was commissioned to write and produce *Caliban*. MacKaye espoused a new kind of national theater, a noncommercial one by and for the American people. This in turn demanded a new dramatic form, large-scale outdoor community pageants he called masques. MacKaye had recently staged one in St Louis, where, remarkably, roughly 100,000 spectators attended each of the four performances celebrating that city's history.

MacKaye's success was enabled by and in many ways tied to the immigration debate, and when that died down in the mid-1920s, so did his career. In the years leading up to *Caliban*, MacKaye wrote tirelessly on the subject and served on the advisory editorial board of the short-lived journal the *Immigrants in America Review*. He wrote a play called *The Immigrants* (1912), and followed that up with a commissioned drama, *The New Citizenship* (1915). When the time came to seek out a leading playwright to contribute something major for Shakespeare's tercentenary, one involving the large-scale participation of immigrant groups, he was the obvious choice.

MacKaye's views on immigration resist easy categorization. The one thing he did believe was that if anything was going to break down the barriers separating "new" and "old" Americans it was participatory theater. In *A Substitute for War* (1915), MacKaye quotes an admirer of his *Saint Louis: A Civic Masque* who spoke of how, at the end of its final performance, when everyone in the cast and audience sang *The Star-Spangled Banner*, it "was like a transfiguration": "There was no race or national antipathy then. It was destroyed, not by logic or reason, but by playing together, working together."

Yet his works undermined their ostensibly progressive position on immigration. Take *The New Citizenship* for example, that enacts an initiation ceremony in which groups of newly naturalized foreigners listen to the Founding Fathers speak, then sing religious hymns and perform folk dances to show how their "distinctive national cultures contributed to our country as the common heritage of Americans." But becoming American requires them to renounce what those powerful symbols of their identity stood for. And while MacKaye insists that he is committed to the "welcoming of all world cultures to create an American excellence," he nonetheless introduces a "representative" American who reminds the foreign-born citizens (whom MacKaye identifies by nations—Russian, Italian, Greek, etc.) that "you cannot become thorough Americans if you think of yourselves in groups." When he published *The New Citizenship* MacKaye admitted how troubled he was that the "vast majority" of America's "15,000,000 foreign-born white persons" are "essentially out of touch with the basic traditions of liberty and democracy." And he added an appendix that drew on the overheated rhetoric of the Immigration Restriction League, noting that more "than one-sixth of the American population" is "not yet Americanized," and observing as well that three million adult immigrants (half of whom are illiterate) can't speak English.

MacKaye records that Percival Chubb, president of the recently formed Drama League of America, first suggested that he write a "Memorial Masque to Shakespeare." At much the same time, the Players Club decided to raise money through a celebratory masque that would pay for a statue of Shakespeare as well as contribute to the Actors' Fund of America. Both organizations were likely behind his commission. *Caliban* would serve, in MacKaye's words, "as the central popular expression of some hundreds of supplementary Shakespeare celebrations" from coast to coast, and the text was rushed into print "to give communities, societies, colleges, and Drama League centers throughout the country an opportunity to read the text and thus arrange their celebrations in harmony with the Masque."

MacKaye worked fast, and in early January 1916 read from his draft to three hundred distinguished guests, invited to hear him at the Metropolitan Opera House by the banker Otto Kahn, who chaired the Shakespeare Tercentenary Celebration Committee. MacKaye announced that *Caliban* would be performed in late May in the Sheep Meadow in Central Park. But that immediately ran into a buzz saw of local opposition. He had planned to charge a modest admission fee to pay for the massive enterprise, with the profits, as in St Louis, used to fund future efforts, but such fees were forbidden in Central Park. Popular resistance to holding the Shakespeare masque there intensified, and in the end a disappointed MacKaye agreed to relocate it uptown to a smaller and more obscure venue, Lewisohn Stadium, at New York's City College. His overreliance on the support of cultural elites, coupled with his reluctance to make use of grassroots organizations and local actors (as he had done in St Louis) for what was heavily promoted as a community effort, hobbled the production from the outset.

*

THE TEMPEST PERFECTLY suited MacKaye's didactic, top-down approach to art. Its four main characters—Prospero, Miranda, Caliban, and Ariel—offered a framework for celebrating not only literary culture from ancient to modern times, but also Shakespeare's greatest hits, all in the service of Caliban's education. Like many at the time, MacKaye believed that Prospero was Shakespeare's autobiographical stand-in, pronouncing on his own art, and at the end of *Caliban* Shakespeare himself enters and replaces Prospero, as Caliban crouches at his true master's feet. When MacKaye speaks of Prospero's art, then, he is also speaking of that of a benevolent Shakespeare, whose goal, like his own, or so he imagined, was to "liberate the imprisoned imagination of mankind from the fetters of brute force and ignorance." What he took to be Shakespeare's central theme—"Caliban seeking to learn the art of Prospero"—anticipated his own mission: "the slow education of mankind through the influences of co-operative art." When elaborating on this in a long interview in the *New York Times*, MacKaye adds that he saw in Caliban "that passionate child-curious part of us all, groveling close to his origin, yet groping up toward that serener plane of pity and love, reason and disciplined will." But it remains unclear whether his Caliban is quite so universal or whether MacKaye, when speaking of "us," is referring to only that segment of his audience and cast who, like Caliban, were of inferior racial and national origin.

While *The Tempest* as a story of the moral education of a brutish and illiterate creature clearly appealed to MacKaye, Shakespeare's plot brought with it potential obstacles, the most glaring of which was that, however much progress Caliban makes, it is never enough; he remains a sexual and political threat, having sought to rape Miranda and conspire in Prospero's overthrow. Prospero, in Shakespeare's original, is clear about this, declaring that Caliban is one on "whose nature / Nurture never sticks." It didn't help that MacKaye had himself thought of Caliban as irredeemable; in October 1914 he published an antiwar poem in the *New York Times*, "A Prayer of the Peoples," in which Caliban, along with the wolf, serves as a shorthand for those who are irredeemably bloody-minded:

> God of us, who kill our kind!
> Master of the blood-tracked Mind
> Which from the wolf and Caliban
> Staggers toward the star of Man—
> Now on thy cathedral stair,
> God, we cry to thee in prayer!

His Caliban didn't stand much of a chance of redemption once MacKaye chose to represent him as a bestial Missing Link. The popular British actor Lionel Braham was given the part. Braham stood six feet four inches and weighed more than two hundred pounds, and in production photographs he appears fanged and sub-human, his body and feet covered in thick hair, his skin blackened, and his long fingers claw-like. His hulking image adorned the official program. MacKaye's depiction of Caliban did not take place in a political vacuum. The moment was fraught: the Immigration Act that overwhelmingly passed the House of Representatives in late March 1916, two months before the masque opened, was awaiting a Senate vote that would bar entry not only to illiterate migrants but also to those who in other respects resembled Caliban: drunks, anarchists, and those deemed mentally and physically defective.

While more than 1,500 locals were included in the New York production, the starring roles went to 47 professional actors—a sharp departure from MacKaye's earlier work. Isadora Duncan even took a star turn, dancing across the titular yellow sands one evening during the run. All key aspects of the production—including costuming, scenic design, and choreography—were overseen by established professionals, not recent immigrants. And most of the community groups that acted or sang tended to be from upscale organizations, such as the Hellenic Union, the German University League, the Alliance Française, and the New York Oratorio Society. The reality, then, fell far short of Otto Kahn's assurances at the tercentenary dinner that MacKaye's masque was neither a "'high-brow' affair" nor "a benevolent up-lift movement backed by a few men and women of wealth," but rather "stands upon a deep and popular base it enlists and has significance for Avenue A no less than for Fifth Avenue."

The recollections of Cecil Sharp, an English folklorist employed by MacKaye to help with the masque's Elizabethan interlude, reveal how deep the chasm ran between the creative team and the locals who were involved, as well as how momentary the transformative nature of the performance turned out to be for "them": "the spirit of the tunes and dances was such that all participants became infected by it and for the moment they became English, every Jew, German, French, Italian, Slav of them." While MacKaye recognized "the problem of carrying its community meaning to the still polyglot population," his provisional solution, translating *Caliban* "into Italian, German, and Yiddish," didn't stretch nearly far enough (and was never done). He showed no interest in traffic flowing in the opposite direction. No effort was made to involve those who had long been staging Shakespeare's plays in Yiddish on the Lower East Side, or include the African American community, which had recently packed the Lafayette Theater in Harlem, where *Othello* was performed by an all-black cast; Edward Sterling Wright, who played the lead, felt it necessary to remind the crowd of 1,500 or so before a performance, a bit defensively, that the "Negro people are Americans in the highest sense of the word . . . they are law-abiding, patriotic and as capable of being inspired by the plays of Shakespeare as any race in the world."

*

ON MAY 24, 1916, ten thousand New Yorkers filled City College's Lewisohn Stadium to witness Caliban's long journey "toward that serener plane of pity and love," a number that swelled to more than eighteen thousand the following evening. We don't know what proportion of these playgoers were immigrants, but it's a safe assumption that it was a considerable one, as roughly 40 percent of the 5 million or so inhabitants of New York City at this time were foreign-born. In his first entrance, Caliban is seen crawling on his belly, barely able to speak, hissing and stuttering. He is bedazzled when he first catches sight of Miranda, sniffing her, dancing around her, excited by the prospect of impregnating her. The threat of rape is repeated throughout the masque. Prospero enters and protects his daughter, announcing that Caliban must be "transformed," a process that will require his exposure to great cultural landmarks, including Shakespeare's plays. But this approach initially backfires, as Caliban is overstimulated by the seduction scenes in *Troilus and Cressida* and attacks Miranda; she is saved once again from sexual assault by the arrival of her father, who wonders aloud, "How shall mine art reclaim this lapsing ape / From his own bondage?"

The answer: more culture, including works from Germany, France, Spain, and Italy, entertainment interrupted by Miranda's abduction by (and subsequent rescue from) Caliban. Slowly, however, progress is made in Caliban's education. Watching the scene from *As You Like It* in which Old Adam is saved makes a deep impression on him, and he grasps that Miranda has likewise pitied him. By now, Caliban speaks English far more fluently and has learned empathy and gratitude. But sadly, he is now in love with Miranda, who just wants to be friends, something he has trouble understanding. There is one more relapse, as Caliban misreads *Henry V* to justify his attempt to kill Prospero and rape Miranda: "Ho, God for Caliban and Setebos! / War, War for Prosper's throne!" Yet again Prospero must intercede and curb Caliban's desires, explaining that Miranda "is charmed

169

against thy body's rape / By chastity of soul." It is at this point, as the long pageant approaches its end, that Shakespeare replaces Prospero onstage. "Out of the dimness" Caliban approaches the poet, and "in a voice hoarse with feeling" announces, with new self-awareness: "A little have I crawled, a little only / Out of mine ancient cave. All that I build / I botch; all that I do destroyeth my dream." He begs for help, prostrating himself at the feet of Shakespeare, who gazes on him "with tenderness" and recites Prospero's valedictory speech from Act 4, scene 1, "Our revels now are ended."

In the program summary we learn that Caliban then stepped forward and addressed the crowd directly, urging everyone to join him in bowing down to Shakespeare. The distance between the aspiring Caliban and the thousands of spectators who have witnessed his incomplete journey collapses:

> You, you my fellow dreamers in the dark,
> We which are one, you millions that are me,
> Like as our dreams shall we ourselves become!
> My brothers, now with me! To yonder Spirit
> Bow down, bow down, and on this bed of clay
> Together let us dream another world.

Caliban then raised "his arms toward Shakespeare with a great gesture of aspiration," and the orchestra broke into "the strains of the national anthem." MacKaye had stolen a trick here from the ending of his St Louis masque, and the shift here from bardolatry to patriotism is seamless. Or so we may assume. It is worth noting that the playing of the *Star-Spangled Banner* was both new and controversial. It was only in this year that President Wilson had ordered that it be performed at military events, and recent efforts in Baltimore (where its lyrics were written) to impose a fine on anyone who refused to stand when it was played were met by resistance to "the folly of trying to instill patriotism by law, to create reverence by statute."

Toward the end of the extended run, the *New York Times* published a poem, "Caliban at the Stadium," by Florence Ripley Mastin, an American-born poet and teacher of immigrants (including the future novelist Bernard Malamud). In her poem, Mastin connects the dots, making explicit what MacKaye had gestured at: "The audience itself is Caliban!" she writes. "Monstrous and murmuring beneath the stars," and in the end it "roars and crawls away." If MacKaye's goal was to use theater to break down the boundaries that divided new and old Americans, Mastin's admiring poem suggests how profoundly he had failed. Anti-immigrant assumptions, in circulation now for twenty years, had clouded MacKaye's vision and undermined his best intentions. If the restrictionists needed more evidence for why a literacy test was warranted, and for the folly of imagining that the Caliban-type could ever be fully assimilated, they didn't need to look further than this masque. The brief New York run of *Caliban* was well attended and was extended for a few nights, as the Boston one that followed in 1917 would be. But by the time it was restaged there, Congress had already overridden a presidential veto and voted the literacy requirement into law. Few who witnessed MacKaye's depiction of Caliban's struggle and ultimate failure to acculturate would have been surprised when seven years later the anti-immigration forces achieved their ultimate goal: the institution of racially driven quotas in 1921, and even more restrictive ones in 1924, that would be the law of the land until overturned in 1965.

SHAKESPEARE WOULD CONTINUE to be implicated in the story of American immigration. On April 23, 1932, President Herbert Hoover and three hundred or so other luminaries, including members of

Congress and foreign ambassadors, crammed into a small theater across from the United States Capitol, for the opening of the Folger Shakespeare Library, an unsurpassed collection of Shakespeare materials as well as a stunning building in which to house them. Not many Shakespeare scholars get to lecture a sitting president; that task fell to Joseph Quincy Adams, the Folger's first director of research.

Adams chose to offer those gathered there a historical overview of "Shakespeare and American Culture." He was interested in Shakespeare's racial origins and had published an essay suggesting that Shakespeare may well have had both French and Anglo-Saxon blood; if so, Adams argued, the fusion of "two important race elements" helps us grasp "the versatility of Shakespeare's genius." A child of the South (Adams was born in South Carolina, not far from where his grandfather had owned a slave plantation), he was drawn to the notion that *The Tempest* was "more closely allied with the founding of Virginia than has been generally realized." His take on Shakespeare's view of the natives that early colonists encountered (in the conclusion of an unpublished essay he wrote about "Shakespeare and Virginia") is chilling: "in the person of Caliban, Shakespeare represented the treacherous nature of the natives, as reported by the colonists," and Shakespeare "agreed" with the Elizabethan travel writer Richard Hakluyt "that it would be fatal to show them any leniency. In Hakluyt's advice as to how to treat them," Adams writes, Shakespeare "foresaw their ultimate extermination."

Adams began his inaugural lecture by declaring that with the opening of the Folger Shakespeare Library, the nation's capital now had three great monuments to those who had "molded the political, the spiritual, and the intellectual life of our nation": George Washington, Abraham Lincoln, and William Shakespeare. Shakespeare had earned that status by helping to preserve the great "Anglo-Saxon" racial legacy of America's founders, serving as a bulwark against a sea of immigrants that had recently threatened it. Adams recalled for his audience how in the "middle of the nineteenth century" the "first great wave of immigration" brought thousands upon thousands to our land, "mainly from Germany, Norway, Sweden, and other north-European countries." Though "honest, thrifty, and altogether admirable as citizens," they nonetheless began "to alter the solid Anglo-Saxon character of the people." That danger paled in comparison with the dilution posed by those who came after: "Italians, Poles, Slavs, Hungarians, Czechs, Greeks, Lithuanians, Rumanians, Armenians," who "swarmed into the land like the locust in Egypt." These newcomers were "foreign in their background and alien in their outlook upon life" and "exhibited varied racial characteristics, varied ideals, and varied types of civilization." Things looked grim, as America "seemed destined to become a babel of tongues and cultures."

"Fortunately," Adams explained, "about the time that the forces of immigration became a menace to the preservation of our long-established English civilization," compulsory education for the young was instituted, and the study of Shakespeare's plays required. The dissemination of his plays in new editions, in amateur and professional performances, in women's reading groups, in university courses, and by book collectors like the Folgers further stemmed the effects of the wrong sort of immigration. With immigration quotas now imposed and Shakespeare deemed essential to the nation's cultural life, the tide had been turned. By 1932, the racist fantasies that forty years earlier had first enlisted Shakespeare in opposition to a culturally diverse America were now enshrined: "If out of America," Adams concluded, "commonly called the melting-pot of races, there has been evolved a homogenous nation, with a culture that is still essentially English, we must acknowledge that in the process Shakespeare has played a major part."

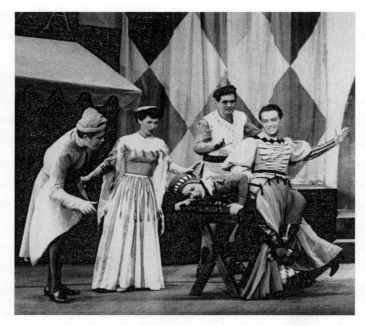

Alfred Drake spanking Patricia Morison in *Kiss Me, Kate*, 1948.

CHAPTER 6

1948: Marriage

Even in its own day, *The Taming of the Shrew*—a play that delivers on the promise of its title, regaling us with how Petruchio breaks the will of his headstrong wife Katherine, declaring, "She is my goods, my chattels . . . my ox, my ass, my anything" (3.2.230–32)— seems to have troubled theatergoers. Shakespeare's fellow dramatist John Fletcher, tapping into this unease, responded with *The Tamer Tamed*; in this sequel, Petruchio, now a widower, gets his comeuppance when he marries a woman who tames *him*. What's notable about Shakespeare's handling of the story is how Katherine is broken: though she may strike him, Petruchio never hits back. Long before our modern-day black sites and their enhanced interrogation techniques, Shakespeare understood that the surest way to break people was first to disorient them, then to deprive them of food and sleep ("She ate no meat today, nor none shall eat," Petruchio brags. "Last night she slept not, nor tonight she shall not" [4.2.185–86]). What happens in the play differs from what some unruly women actually endured in Elizabethan England, where punishments included wearing a "scold's bridle," or, in a precursor to waterboarding, being dunked in a pond while strapped into "a cucking stool." It's no surprise that *The Taming of the Shrew* fell out of favor, replaced by less disturbing adaptations; more than two centuries passed before the original version finally rejoined the repertory in 1844 in Britain—the very last of Shakespeare's plays to do so.

It took even longer in the United States. It wasn't until 1887, at a time when American women were organizing in their struggle against discrimination and fighting for the right to vote that would not be won for another thirty-three years, that American playgoers had a chance to see something approaching Shakespeare's original, in the socially conservative production directed by Augustin Daly, starring Ada Rehan. The nation's leading critic, William Winter, considered Daly's interpretation "one of the few really great and perfect dramatic creations of its time" and heaped praise on Rehan's transformation as Katherine from "shrewishness to loveliness." As her resistance to Petruchio wilts and she submits to him as her "master," Rehan's Katherine was, for Winter, "unmistakably the same woman, only now her actual self." When, after the turn of the century, Margaret Anglin, the first woman director to tackle (and star in) the play, brought her production to New York, a deeply offended Winter savaged it for treating Katherine's final speech (in which she urges wives to abase themselves and "place your hands below your husband's foot," then does so herself) "as if it were mere mockery . . . a jest, secretly understood between Petruchio and his wife." The world was changing and men like Winter weren't happy about it.

A half century would pass between Daly's production and the next groundbreaking American one, by Alfred Lunt and Lynn Fontanne in 1935. Lunt and Fontanne were at this time the leading stars of the American theater, and since 1924, not long after they married, had insisted on performing together. Plays with strong roles for both of them were not easy to find, and *The Taming of the Shrew*, which proved to be one of them, was a hit, opening on Broadway to rave reviews, then touring across the country. They went all in on the farcical, bringing onstage acrobats, "dwarfs," and horses, distracting audiences from the ugliness of the plot. The celebrity of the leads also meant, as another reviewer put it, that "at least half the fun comes in watching them enact Mr. and Mrs. Alfred Lunt." Shakespeare didn't often write about married life, focusing instead on courtship. Having a power couple play the leads in *The Taming of the Shrew* gave audiences the rare pleasure of responding to the comedy as one that was also about the push and pull of a real (or at least an imagined) marriage.

Lunt and Fontanne restored the usually cut Induction of *The Taming of the Shrew,* in which a lord commands a troupe of traveling players to perform at his behest in order to fool a drunkard who has fallen asleep. Their performance creates for spectators a sense that they are watching a play-within-a-play. In Lunt and Fontanne's production, these players were an irritable troupe worn down by endless touring. They fake-coughed loudly when anyone in the house failed to suppress a cough, repeated cues, and shouted out lines from offstage. It got violent. Fontanne's Katherine broke a lute over Lunt's head, ground her heel into his foot, and bit him; Lunt's Petruchio retaliated by smacking her on her bottom, kicking her, and dragging her around. For one reviewer, Fontanne accepted "defeat not sweetly and softly as many Katherines do, but with a mental reservation that she still may have something to say about this business of being tamed." And when at the end she declares that she is ready to place her hand beneath her husband's foot in token of her submission, the promptbook indicates that "as she swings her hand to punctuate her meaning," she (accidentally?) smacks him in the face. "You were left to wonder at the finish," the reviewer for the *Boston Globe* wrote, "whether her humility was not more mock than real." In a final gesture meant to puncture (in the very act of staging) the fantasy of eternal marital bliss, the production ended with the lovers departing in a chariot drawn by a unicorn. *Esquire*'s critic was convinced that once "the curtain fell," Fontanne's Katherine "would get revenge for hardships and humiliations by beating the hell out of her spouse." Katherine, having lost the battle, may well win the war; but if so, that victory is deferred, Petruchio the victor, and patriarchal norms left battered but still standing.

In February 1940, Lunt and Fontanne returned to Broadway for a one-week, standing-room-only revival of their production, a benefit for the Finnish War Relief Fund, staged as the world slid toward war. One of those involved in mounting it was Arnold Saint Subber, who would go on to a long career as a Broadway producer. At the time, though, he was just an ambitious 21-year-old trying to make his way in the theater. Thirty years later Saint Subber told an interviewer for the BBC that "one of the jobs I had had was as a play reader in the Alvin Theatre where Alfred Lunt and Lynn Fontanne were performing *Taming of the Shrew*. I was constantly backstage and would listen to Mr. Lunt and Miss Fontanne screaming at each other, in rage, 'If you ever do that again I will never go on stage with you ever again in my life.' And then, both appearing onstage cuddly, sweetly, and I thought to myself—that's quite a sketch." Saint Subber, convinced that this frontstage/backstage drama would make for a great show, "went about peddling the idea of turning *Taming of the Shrew* into a musical."

Eight years and a world war would pass before Saint Subber assembled a creative team that transformed the seed of his idea into one of the most enduring and successful American musicals, *Kiss Me, Kate*. Typically, popular attitudes toward marriage, divorce, and women in the workplace evolve at a glacial pace. But the war changed that. The draft had left industries desperate for workers, and the number of women who for patriotic or economic reasons joined the workforce exploded during the war, going from 11.9 million in 1940 to 18.6 million by the war's end. In 1940 a little over a third of white-collar workers were women; by 1945 they accounted for half. Even in blue-collar jobs—typically associated with the kind of labor it was assumed that only men could really handle— the percentage of women rose, from roughly a quarter to a third of all workers. Those gains were almost entirely wiped out at war's end, when women came under enormous pressure to step aside and let returning veterans take over. After 1945, the percentage of white-collar jobs held by women returned to near prewar level, and blue-collar ones plummeted to below that. Most of the women who continued to work saw their paychecks shrink. "We Can Do It" posters that had exhorted women in the workplace were discarded, replaced by a drumbeat message from the federal government that "a mother's primary duty is to her home and children." Making sense of these conflicting directives wasn't easy, and it was to imaginative works like *Kiss Me, Kate* that whipsawed Americans flocked to make sense of the marital state of the nation.

The government's patronizing guidance was reinforced by academic experts, such as Barnard College professor Willard Waller, who warned in his book *The Veteran Comes Back* that after "a war, women do not easily give up their newfound freedom, and since men are scarce and morality in general relaxed, the post-war period tends to be a time of experimentation and new family customs and forms." As the military campaigns in the European and Pacific theaters were ending in victory, Waller warned that a new war was imminent for America's men—and it wasn't against the Russians. He wrote about it in an op-ed that ran in the *New York Herald Tribune* in February 1945 (and appeared in many other leading newspapers as well) titled "The Coming War on Women." Waller takes as a given that "the two halves of the human race have struggled for supremacy," and that in the immediate aftermath of a major war "men and women [are] at loggerheads," and "one might say the women get out of hand." He has little doubt that when the troops come home, "women will probably put up a stronger fight for supremacy because this war's changes have merely climaxed generations of feministic progress." He anticipates conflict on three fronts: "the battle for jobs, the battle of the birth rate, and the battle of personal ascendancy." Victory will only be achieved when the "patriarchal family" is "restored and strengthened" and "millions of women" surrender "their jobs." The "young men who have fought a war," he warns, "are not likely to accept petticoat domination." A deeper problem for Waller is that "the woman of today is so constituted that she cannot help trying to dominate her husband, and if she fails she will resent that, but if she succeeds she will be forever embittered."

Waller's conclusion reads like a gloss on the increasingly ana-chronistic take on *The Taming of the Shrew*, with men sounding tough and women playacting furious resistance but secretly enjoy-ing male dominance: "It is better just to tell her plainly that he is going to be the boss, and then she will be very angry and will threaten to leave him and will love him to distraction." Newspapers across the country were flooded with responses when his op-ed ran, and even Eleanor Roosevelt was moved to respond to it, urging women not to leave their jobs.

Yet Waller's view was moderate when compared with that es-poused in the controversial bestseller *Modern Woman: The Lost Sex*. Its authors, the psychiatrist Marynia F. Farnham and the historian Ferdinand Lundberg, had first tried out their pseudoscientific attack on feminism in November 1944 in the pages of *Ladies' Home Journal*, to which millions of American women subscribed. Farnham and Lundberg's argument boiled down to this: women were unhappy because they wanted to act like men. But biological determinism (including the "fact" that only men achieve sexual satisfaction in casual relationships) confirmed that such a pursuit was doomed to failure. Modern women, they concluded, were "sick, unhappy, neurotic, [and] wholly or partly incapable of dealing with life," be-cause the working woman is "in the dangerous position of having to live one part of her life on the masculine level, another on the feminine." This self-destructive resistance to patriarchal authori-ty must end: "Women's rivalry with men today, and the need to 'equal' their accomplishments, engenders all too often anger and resentfulness toward men. Men, challenged, frequently respond in kind." The moral of their story was much the same as the one that

William Winter had taken away from *The Taming of the Shrew* in the previous century: a "woman who is to find true gratification must love and accept her own womanhood as she loves and accepts her husband's manhood."

There was one more turn to their argument: all this unhappiness is a *modern* phenomenon. Things had only changed for the worse in the seventeenth century; back in Shakespeare's day things had been different, and better. All this would be grist to the mill for those fashioning *Kiss Me, Kate* at the very time that Farnham and Lundberg's book was making such a splash. *Modern Woman* spoke to a nostalgia for a lost (and imaginary) world, where things were simpler, and where all—especially women and minorities—knew their place. But the war had punctured that fantasy. African American and Japanese American soldiers had served heroically in combat. Women had held down blue-collar jobs and didn't have to rely on men to put food on the table.

Because working women were less dependent on men for support, the loss of jobs, especially well-paying ones, for women after the war ought to have led to a lower divorce rate, as more wives now had to depend upon their husbands for financial support. Yet the opposite occurred, with the divorce rate in America skyrocketing in the aftermath of the war. The unraveling of many hasty wartime marriages had something to do with it, but the epidemic of divorces at the time went far beyond that, reflecting a deeper crisis about cultural expectations for married life. The figures were sobering: in 1940, one marriage in six had ended in divorce; by 1946, the figure was one in four. And with the return of millions of American husbands from the front, that rate continued to soar. A headline in the *New York Times* in April 1944 warned that "7 of 10 War Marriages Held Headed for Trouble." Two years later *U.S. News & World Report* announced that the country's divorce rate had reached an all-time high in 1945, with more than a half million divorces projected for the following year. A battle between the sexes was now replacing the one between the Axis and Allied powers; the time was ripe for a Broadway show that enacted it.

In 1947, Arnold Saint Subber persuaded Lemuel Ayers, a talented young designer, to coproduce his as yet unnamed musical. They tried to get the playwright Thornton Wilder to write the book, but he turned them down. They then approached Bella Spewack, one of only a few women at the time writing for Broadway. Spewack told the young producers that she had read *The Taming of the Shrew* in school and thought it "a lousy play," one "of the worst Shakespeare wrote." She also told them that if they were "thinking—you know—of just musicalizing Shakespeare, that's for high school." She left them with the promise that she would "think about it and if I get a notion how to make it a Broadway show I'll call you and tell you." By the autumn of 1947 she had found a way, and committed to writing the book.

A lyricist was now needed, and despite his reputation, Cole Porter was not the first to whom the producers turned. Porter, who had produced a string of hits in the 1930s, had been eclipsed by Richard Rodgers and Oscar Hammerstein, whose wartime musicals—*Oklahoma!* and *Carousel*—had deftly integrated songs and story line in a way that other lyricists, including Porter, had failed to do. Because of that, many considered Porter past his prime. Yet Spewack, who along with her husband, Sam, had worked with Porter a decade earlier, urged her producers to approach him. When they did, though offers were scarce, Porter was ambivalent. He thought a Shakespeare musical "was too esoteric, too high-brow for the commercial stage" and wondered "how he could expect audiences to understand something that he didn't." That might have been the case with a more complicated Shakespearean plot, but Spewack was able to pare down Shakespeare's contribution to the accessible story line of its title: Petruchio meets then tames Katherine, who in the end submits; Porter's lyrics would work like soliloquies, providing insight into the characters' inner experience. A breakthrough for him came shortly before Christmas 1947, and by May 1948 an inspired Porter had written twenty-five songs for the show, a third of which were never used.

There were good reasons for both Spewack and Porter to be wary of investing so deeply in the project. The modern Shakespeare musical only dated back a decade to the 1938 show *The Boys from Syracuse*, based on *The Comedy of Errors*. The genre was distinctly American, ultimately tracing its roots back through vaudeville to the raucous and racist minstrel shows that had freely adapted Shakespeare in the mid-nineteenth century and had combined (somewhat haphazardly) text, song, and dance. The defining feature of the Shakespeare musical was its hybridity—mixing musical styles, mixing Shakespeare's language with contemporary American idiom, mixing races, and mixing highbrow, middlebrow, and at times lowbrow. Getting the mix right was no easy task.

On the heels of its modest success—*The Boys from Syracuse* ran for more than two hundred performances—a second Shakespeare musical, *Swingin' the Dream*, based on *A Midsummer Night's Dream*, opened on Broadway the following year. It starred mostly black performers and featured some of the most popular musicians of the day. Count Basie wrote music for it, and Louis Armstrong played Bottom. Benny Goodman's band played on one side of the stage and Bud Freeman's on the other. There were star performers center stage, including the Dandridge Sisters, Maxine Sullivan, and a hundred African American jitterbug dancers, choreographed by Agnes de Mille. Set designs by Walt Disney were used. Talent rich, it should have been a huge hit, but it turned out to be a box-office disaster, closing after only thirteen performances and losing its investors a whopping $100,000. Because the show was never recorded—only traces of it survive—it is difficult, in hindsight, to explain precisely why it failed. Perhaps Broadway audiences weren't ready for so racially integrated a production. Whatever the explanation, the Shakespeare musical was no longer seen as a ticket to success. Nearly a decade passed before the next one, *Kiss Me, Kate*, would be attempted. It struggled to find backers, and had to be done on the cheap, under a budgeted $180,000. It was initially booked into a second-tier theater. Even the producers expected it to fail.

By her own reckoning, it took Spewack six weeks to hit upon a story line with box-office potential. She decided to set it on the "opening night of the tryout of a musical version of Shakespeare's *Taming of the Shrew* at Ford's Theatre in Baltimore." Her working title for the musical was "Backstage," which is where most of her interest was focused: a contest over women's autonomy taking place in a messy and modern backstage world. This half of the story involved a recently divorced couple, Lilli Vanessi ("a star in musical films") and Fred Graham ("the Orson Welles of musicals"). Backstage, the women in the musical make choices—about their careers and about the men they want in their lives. At the outset of the play, Lilli, still drawn to Fred, considers leaving show business to marry the wealthy if boring Harrison Howell. Fred also has a love interest, Lois Lane ("a night club singer and Fred's 'discovery'"), while a sexually liberated Lois has also had a fling with Howell, and has her eye on Bill Calhoun (a "dancer to whom Lois is faithful in her fashion"). Elements of Saint Subber's original idea remained, hinted at in the names of the leads, Fred and Lilli, derived from Al*fred* Lunt and *Lilli*e Louise Fontanne. Spewack, who consulted a copy of their 1935 playscript of *The Taming of the Shrew*, even penciled Lunt's and Fontanne's names into an early scene before thinking better of it.

Backstage, people bicker, quarrel, gamble, drink, and listen to jazz; relationships are hard to maintain; people have affairs and regrets, and men worry about sexual dysfunction; there are hints of same-sex relationships. It's also a violent world in which gunmen pack pistols and an ex-wife complains of being beaten "black and blue." The backstage plot is set in motion when Bill Calhoun, who gambles, runs up a $10,000 debt (under Fred's name) that he owes to a mobster, who sends a couple of thugs to the theater to collect the money. Fred, confronted by the gunmen, sees them as a means to keep Lilli in the production of *The Taming of the Shrew*, and tells them he will pay them out of the show's profits if they keep her from quitting. Fred's effort to pursue both his ex-wife and his new fling backfires when a bouquet he sends to Lois is mistakenly delivered to Lilli; after Lilli reads a card Fred enclosed to her rival, she storms onstage to confront him—conveniently for the show, at the very moment that her Katherine attacks his Petruchio. In the second Act, this backstage plot is resolved when news arrives that the mobster to whom the money is owed has been killed and the debt canceled—allowing Lilli the freedom to leave. The gunmen, for their part, deliver a vaudevillian song and dance number before Lilli, who has walked out on both Fred and Howell, rejoins *The Taming of the Shrew* just in time to deliver Katherine's submission speech.

The frontstage world of the Shakespeare play they perform couldn't be more different. It is the traditional premodern world of *The Taming of the Shrew*, in which daughters are expected to obey their fathers and husbands, only men are free to do what they please, women are sold off in marriage, and shrewish women who challenge these norms are tamed. Its very first words are a daughter's declaration of submission to her father's will, as Bianca tells Baptista: "Father, to your pleasure humbly I subscribe." (It's enough that she says the right thing and acts dutiful.) It's a nostalgic and brightly colored world, and unlike the backstage one, has an all-white cast. In this Renaissance world, Lilli plays Katherine; Fred her tamer, Petruchio; Lois is Bianca, Katherine's obedient sister, who cannot marry until her older sister does; and Bill plays Lucentio, Bianca's successful wooer. The scenes in which the plot of *The Taming of the Shrew* is reenacted are carefully spaced through the show and, enlivened by Porter's lyrics, take up roughly a third of it. Spewack understood that the proportions had to be right; by her rough calculation, Shakespeare was responsible for twenty-two pages of the script, Porter for sixty, and she herself for the remaining seventy-two. Competing narratives about marriage, women's independence, and domesticity are held up to each other, with the frontstage Shakespearean world standing in for old-fashioned values while the backstage world depicts more modern and liberal ones. *Kiss Me, Kate* offered, then, rival visions of the choices women faced in postwar America—one in which women are urged to capitulate and their obedience to men is the norm, and one in which independence and unconventionality hold sway.

The tension between frontstage and backstage worlds was heightened by a third, offstage, level of contention, as the artistic team squabbled. This creative tension, invisible to audiences, was a byproduct of the different temperaments and identities of the lead producer, writer, and lyricist. Saint Subber, Spewack, and Porter were outsiders who were keenly aware of cultural norms in 1940s America, the terrain on which the war between men and women in their musical was waged. Like many in the American theater of his day, Saint Subber was gay at a time when those who weren't heterosexual had to mask their sexual orientation if they had any hope of thriving professionally. Saint Subber also likely knew that neither Lunt nor Fontanne were exclusively heterosexual; they even shared the friendship of the young and gay star Montgomery Clift, who reportedly encouraged Saint Subber to create the show, and who had been more or less adopted by Lunt and Fontanne, who took him in, invited him to act in their shows, and urged him to marry as well, for the sake of appearance, to protect his career. Lunt and Fontanne had perfected the role of a married if childless couple—even modeling what that behavior should be for many millions of admirers—while keeping out of the tabloids any trace of scandal, so that nowadays biographers struggle to find conclusive evidence that they were gay. Their successful performance as an ideal heterosexual American couple may have been their finest, and a necessary one, as hostility to gay culture intensified in the 1930s. No doubt Saint Subber's initial idea for the show, in which a couple acts one way frontstage and more honestly backstage, was shaped by the split between the star couple's public and private lives.

Bella Spewack was also an outsider, as a woman playwright and an immigrant, one of those Eastern European Jews who entered America before its doors were barred. Born Bella Cohen, and brought as a child to America by a mother whose husband had abandoned her, she was raised in harsh circumstances on the Lower East Side, and had a tough, at times violent, childhood. Sexual assault was no abstraction for Spewack, who recalls in a diary of her formative years how she repelled the advances of a neighborhood boy who pinned her against a wall and tried to assault her; she had to kick him repeatedly to make her escape. For the previous decade or so Spewack had thrived as part of a playwriting team with her husband, Sam, whom she married in 1922 in her early twenties. But at the time she was approached by Saint Subber, her long marriage was unraveling (Sam wrote to her that while he hoped they could continue collaborating professionally, he "would not be seduced, cajoled, bribed or frightened into a relationship that just won't work"). Saint Subber later claimed that "Bella was in a state of desperation" while "composing the libretto," for Sam "had walked out on her and was living with a ballerina."

On top of that, Spewack was treated with a disrespect that her collaborators would never have shown to a similarly accomplished man. In August 1948 she wrote—though perhaps never sent—a letter to the coproducer Lemuel Ayers, letting him know how greatly she resented his claim that "I will never apply my full creative powers to the further improvement of *Kiss Me, Kate*, and that I have been confused, evasive, and mentally distraught and will continue to be so." The irony that they were reproducing the very double standard against which Lilli rebels in the musical (while employing Petruchio's trick of asserting that Katherine is confused and distraught) seems utterly lost on the men behind the show. Three months later Spewack had to ask her lawyer to intervene when ads for the show put her name in smaller typeface than the director's. Though she wrote the book, Saint Subber insisted that the story was really his, and would tell Porter's biographer, William McBrien, that her early efforts—contrary to the archival evidence—were "complete failures," and that all the drafts "were terrible." The writing contract for *Kiss Me, Kate* was drawn up exclusively between Cole Porter and Bella Spewack. Sam Spewack was brought in late in the game to contribute, mostly on the gunmen scenes. Though Sam's contributions to the book were limited, Porter asked that he not only be named but get top billing, and sent a telegram to Sam explaining that it "will make our public much happier to read 'Book by Sam and Bella Spewack.' Will you do this great favor for me?" Bella Spewack agreed to the arrangement.

Porter too was an outsider: gay, but closeted and married, and extremely self-protective. He was also disabled, though he did his best to hide his crippling and excruciating injuries, sustained when a horse-riding accident had crushed his legs a decade earlier. He too knew the rules governing how one appeared in public. Privately, he could be cutting. When he grew irritated with Spewack he would mock her as "Russian" and address her as "Madame Spewack." In "A

Woman's Career"—one of the backstage songs he wrote for *Kiss Me, Kate*—Porter couldn't resist adding a stanza alluding to Spewack's marital woes, underscoring how professional success would never be enough: a woman may write prize-winning Broadway plays, but if she can't satisfy her husband she'll end up bored and lonely.

Their sniping notwithstanding, each of the principals nudged the musical in a daring, crucial, and quietly subversive direction. It would take a group of exceptionally talented artists, who all stood outside of the ideal of an American family of the 1940s, to fully grasp the contradictions of their society and create of one of America's most enduring musicals, one that turned on a woman's ability to perform the pliant role demanded of her. They managed to do so by juxtaposing a frontstage Shakespearean world that mirrored the fantasy of a patriarchal, all-white America—with a backstage one in which black and white performers mingled and that was forthright about a woman's say over her desires and her career. If this was Bella Spewack's brilliant twist on Saint Subber's initial conceit, Cole Porter's contribution was to infuse both worlds of the play with hints of transgressive behavior. The provocative Kinsey Report—*Sexual Behavior in the Human Male*—had just been published, offering a long-hidden view of American sexual practices. It was so topical that Porter even name-drops "the Kinsey report" in his racy song "Too Darn Hot," then alludes to Kinsey's revelations about what American men were really up to: infidelity, masturbation ("pillow, you'll be my baby tonight"), and homosexual activity ("A marine / For his queen").

It's staggering what Porter got away with in *Kiss Me, Kate*, especially in the repressive frontstage world. So, for example, when Lois Lane's Bianca sings about her desire to wed (because she is so eager to have sex), her seemingly clueless language is almost beyond the pale, as her willingness to marry any Tom, Dick, or Harry turns into a desire for what sounds like any "hairy Dick"—and then to a longing for what sounds identical to the words "a Dick, a Dick, a Dick, a Dick, a Dick, a Dick, a Dick, a Dick, a Dick, a Dick, a Dick, a Dick." While it may have passed under the radar of more naïve playgoers, such lyrics, underscoring how much is repressed in the frontstage world, couldn't have been more sexually explicit—and this and other songs from the show were banned from radio and television. Many theater historians attribute Porter's comeback to his willingness to imitate the success of Rodgers and Hammerstein's integrated musicals. I'm more convinced by the counterclaim made by Dan Rebellato, that Porter was more himself here than he had been in previous musicals, and that his contribution was "more of a manifesto of resistance than a sign of someone placing their talents beneath the master's foot." Lilli isn't tamed, and Porter wouldn't be either, though many assume otherwise.

Spewack later claimed that her initial conception of *Kiss Me, Kate* turned out to be "exactly the show as it was," but her successive drafts indicate that this wasn't so. Spewack's first impulse had been to tamper with the Shakespeare story, introducing into the scenes borrowed from *The Taming of the Shrew* a more feminist dynamic, featuring a Katherine who was creative and bookish, who chafes at being locked up, and who decides to go about dressed as a man. In an early draft we first encounter Katherine wearing men's clothing, disguising herself so effectively that she fools her own sister. In this version, when Petruchio first meets her, they banter on equal terms, and even share a tongue-in-cheek song that Katherine has written, "Were Thine That Special Face." Spewack, who had read a lot of Shakespeare in high school, recognized that many of his greatest heroines had to cross-dress to achieve their desires or to be taken seriously by men. Yet the idea was rejected by her collaborators, after Porter wrote to the director, John Wilson, agreeing that it was best "cutting out Bella's scenes, where Kate is dressed as a boy," unless "a lot of comedy" was lost by doing so.

Their responses may have been yet another encroachment on Spewack's contribution, but also turned out to be savvy, for embedding so obvious a critique of patriarchy in the frontstage plot would have muddied the sharp contrast between what was happening in the conservative *Taming of the Shrew* scenes and what was occurring in the transgressive backstage ones. For that contrast to work, Katherine needed to be seen from the start as trapped and, from the men's perspective, shrewish. So, in the final version of the musical there would be no cross-dressing; and it is Petruchio, not Katherine, who is credited with writing, and then sings, "Were Thine That Special Face."

Kiss Me, Kate's commercial potential depended on striking the right balance between questioning conventional values and giving the audience the happy ending many expected from Broadway musicals. That meant, in the end, eliminating a good deal that pushed too far. It wouldn't do, at a time when there was terrific pressure for women to have children, for Katherine to say in her song "I Hate Men" that husbands "only give you children and with that I could not bother," so the line was altered to "husbands are a boring lot and only give you bother." Several of Porter's songs had to be scrapped entirely, including a too-gay "What Does Your Servant Dream About" ("wine, men, and song") and Bianca's "If Ever Married I'm" (which landed too squarely on why a woman might want to avoid the potentially homicidal boredom of domestic life). Also jettisoned, for similar reasons, was that backstage song "A Woman's Career." When Lilli declares, "I don't have to marry anyone," adding, "I've a life of my own. I'm a person in my own right. I don't need any man," Fred, echoing *Modern Woman: The Lost Sex*, counters that a careerist woman who walks away from marriage is doomed to unhappiness. Like the extra stanza that Porter had written attacking Spewack's own ambitions, this topical exchange proved too harsh, so was cut as well.

Successive drafts from the spring and summer of 1948 indicate that the creative team struggled with the two key moments when frontstage and backstage worlds collide. In the first, as the opening Act winds down, Petruchio puts Katherine over his knee and administers a spanking. Except he does so as Fred, and administers it to Lilli, after (as Katherine) she has kicked and slapped him: "All right, Miss Vanessi—you asked for this and you're going to get it!" As the spanking gets more and more violent, a shocked Lilli also forgets that they are in character and cries out, "Fred, what are you doing?" before she screams and the stage goes dark. Afterward, backstage, a furious Lilli warns Fred: "That's the last time you'll ever lay your hands on me." He replies: "You asked for it. May I remind you, Miss Vanessi, the name of this piece is *The Taming of the Shrew*, not *He Who Gets Slapped*."

The *New York Times* liked the spanking scene so much it put a photo of it above its admiring review. The image of a woman perched on a man's knee, his palm open, her heels pointed skyward, about to be spanked, became iconic, and figured prominently in advertisements for the musical. The image of this spanking is so ingrained that it is easy to imagine that it must have been part of Shakespeare's original play—or at least part of its long stage history. But it wasn't: there was no precedent for a man putting a woman over his knee and spanking her in any Anglo-American production of *The Taming of the Shrew*; the convention, for more than a century, had been for Petruchio to crack a whip.

Yet it's unlikely to have shocked the playgoers who first saw the musical; Hollywood had of late accustomed them to seeing one woman after another put over a man's knee and spanked. In the decade before *Kiss Me, Kate* was first staged in 1948, at least twenty-eight films included such scenes, five of them in 1945 alone, including one, *Frontier Gal*, in which the spanking went on for a full minute. And it wasn't just the movies: open a magazine and you might come across an ad for Van Heusen shirts in which, in a series of images, a spanking gives way to a kiss, or another by Chase & Sanborn, featuring a spanking, warning wives not to serve their husbands stale coffee. The proliferation of spanking scenes occurs at a postwar moment when domestic violence was on the rise: "That fine old stone-age art of wife-beating," the *Austin Statesman* reported in early 1946, "is having a distressing renaissance among returning servicemen . . . it is estimated that there have been 14,000 wives beaten by veterans in the U.S. since the war, with the number increasing. And that doesn't include the countless minor cuffs, slaps, pokes, smacks and spankings which haven't been reported to a court." A psychiatrist, Dr. Andrew Browne Evans, asked to account for "this peculiar phenomenon," is quoted blaming self-deluding working wives: "Women who don't want to go back to being housewives are bringing a lot of friction into the home. These women may bear a resentment toward their husbands of which they aren't really aware. They've been self-supporting, free, without shackles, and when their husbands return they have to take a secondary position.'"

AT A TIME when women were being pressured (or coerced) to return to the way things were before the war, the ending of *The Taming of the Shrew*—where the two plots of the musical collide for the second time—was always going to be a problem. Should Lilli deliver Katherine's submission speech earnestly? Ironically? With a wink, as Mary Pickford had famously done in a 1929 film of Shakespeare's play? On which side of the cultural divide did the show come down? At first, Spewack tried to dodge this choice by eliminating the toxic speech almost entirely. In one early version, she introduced a new character near the very end, a movie producer who wants to film Fred and Lilli performing Shakespeare's comedy in Padua. When Fred asks Lilli how she feels about this, she replies by recalling a line from Katherine's submission speech: "My husband is my lord, my life, my keeper, my head, my sovereign." The producer, who doesn't get the Shakespeare allusion, is confused, so Fred explains, "My wife is simply saying that she wants what I want, and I want it." After a surprised Lilli interjects—"You said, 'My wife'?"—Fred asks her to seal their reconciliation "with a lovely kiss!" This version offered a comedy of remarriage in which everything is smoothly managed, as Lilli gets to have both the man she has always loved and a new and exciting chapter in their career together.

But this too-easy ending was scrapped. So was another, in which Spewack swung in the other direction, this time having Lilli recite Katherine's *entire* forty-five-line submission speech, before Fred's Petruchio takes her hand and they kiss—though still in character, as actors in Shakespeare's play. Then, after the curtain comes down, Fred and Lilli return in street clothes, sharing a song ("It Was Great Fun The First Time"), so that, as Spewack's stage direction indicates, "we know they're going to try it again." But this version proved unsatisfying. Porter was asked to help to solve the problem, though he too was initially stymied: "I can't, for the life of me, figure out how I can make a number of the 'This is the moon if I say it is the moon' scene." He asked his collaborators for "explicit instructions . . . Do you want the number to be literally Shakespeare's words or do you want me to alter them for the sake of rhyme etc.?" Porter's solution was to frame the submission speech with a new and brilliant number, its music "reminiscent of 'East Side, West Side,' i.e., the typical Bowery song of the 1900s." He added that he was sure that "it will tie up the show into a beautiful knot," and he was right.

"Brush Up Your Shakespeare" is sung by the two gunmen during the brief interlude between the time when Lilli walks out on both Howell and Fred, wearing her street clothes, and when she unexpectedly returns, dressed as Katherine, just in time to deliver her long final speech. The song succeeds not only because its lyrics are memorable and its vaudevillian tune catchy, but also because it ties into that "beautiful knot" so many of the show's competing messages while anticipating Katherine's submission speech that follows. The song reaffirms that Shakespeare's work remains common currency in America, a touchstone that unites highbrow and lowbrow—extending even to a couple of thugs who learned their Shakespeare in prison, and who sing:

> Brush up your Shakespeare,
> Start quoting him now.
> Brush up your Shakespeare
> And the women you will wow.
>
> . . .
>
> Brush up your Shakespeare
> And they'll all kowtow.

But as their song builds from stanza to stanza, it also affirms, with a little help from Shakespeare, that women will eventually kowtow, submit to men, even if a bit of coercion is necessary. What begins with a woman pushing back against unwanted physical advances—"If she fights when her clothes you are mussing, / What are clothes? Much Ado About Nussing"—provokes a sharp and violent reaction: "If she says your behavior is heinous / Kick her right in the Coriolanus." Successive stanzas make it increasingly clear that women have no say: "If she says she won't buy it or like it / Make her tike it, what's more As You Like It." The wit and pleasure of the clever punchlines, the humor of these lowbrow figures promoting Shakespeare, the tug of the old Bowery tune, all work to distract us from what is actually being said.

In its closing stanzas, as the violence and threats escalate, the gunmen make clear that it helps to quote from those of Shakespeare's plays that are themselves suffused with the threat of violence: "Better mention 'The Merchant of Venice' / When her sweet pound o' flesh you would menace." And, in the end, if a woman resists an aroused man, a beating may be necessary: "If because of your heat she gets huffy / Simply play on and 'Lay on, Macduffy!'"—here recalling the bloody strokes at the end of *Macbeth*. The cheery song normalizes domestic violence, and Shakespeare is there to legitimate if not facilitate this. And those of us enjoying the musical are complicit in this. It's a perfect prologue to Katherine's long speech.

We're never told why Lilli decides to return and deliver that submission speech, one that brings the show to an end. Because she's a committed professional? Because she is still in love with Fred? Her speech—now cut to half its length, and sung in a classical style—is taken verbatim from Shakespeare. Lilli plays the scene straight, her Katherine encouraging women to submit to their husbands before doing so to her own. Fred's Petruchio then takes her hand, saying, "Why! There's a wench! Come on and kiss me, Kate." After they kiss, a company finale follows, and as the curtain descends, there is a rousing reprise of "Brush Up Your Shakespeare," the show ending with the words, "Brush up your Shakespeare . . . they'll all kowtow."

There's a small but revealing change from the late draft of this scene to the one that appears in the published version of the musical five years later in 1953, where the original stage direction—"*They kiss*," is replaced with: "*They kiss as Fred and Lilli*." It suggests more than a little anxiety that the scene had failed to signal that the action is resolved in a conventionally satisfying way. But since Fred and Lilli are still in character and costume, still acting in a version of *The Taming of the Shrew*, how could playgoers possibly know that they are kissing as their real-life selves and not as Petruchio and Katherine—especially when in the earlier spanking scene such a shift was telegraphed by Lilli and Fred calling each other by their real names? The best explanation for this difference between the stage script and the published one is that a cultural shift, one registered in this seemingly minor change, had taken place in the intervening five years.

What playgoers saw in 1948 had allowed those who want Lilli and Fred to reconcile and remarry to leave the theater thinking that they do; yet it also permitted more skeptical playgoers to believe that Lilli, who is still in character as Katherine, merely performs the role of the dutiful wife, a role that, by divorcing Fred, Lilli has already walked away from, and may do so again as soon as the final curtain descends. Whatever the differences between Arnold Saint Subber, Bella Spewack, and Cole Porter, the one thing they all understood was what it meant to perform a role in midcentury America, to conform to public expectations while at the same time quietly continuing to do what one needed to do. We don't know—and perhaps neither does Lilli—whether she will return to Fred after the play is over, and if so, on what terms. All we know for sure is that she'll continue working (while Lois, who marries in the play, will still be single and sexually liberated outside of it, and will continued to work as well). The ending satisfied early audiences because it offered the solution urged upon American women in the aftermath of the war: neither walking out nor capitulating solved the problem; pretending to be a submissive wife did, though many would discover—and rising divorce rates confirm—that the act would prove a difficult one to sustain. But the action of the musical, like the Shakespearean story on which it is based, stops before that breaking point is reached.

Four million American playgoers saw *Kiss Me, Kate* during its initial two-and-a-half-year Broadway run and subsequent two-year national tour. The show won the Tony Award for best musical, best composer and lyricist, and best author of a musical. *Kiss Me, Kate* was Cole Porter's last great hit. A decade after the show opened, and after thirty-four operations, he finally had his leg amputated. After that, he was free of pain but apparently never wrote another song. As for Bella Spewack, life mirrored art, for the success of the musical led to her reconciliation with Sam, and they remained married and resumed their collaboration, though never again wrote anything approaching the success of *Kiss Me, Kate*. Less than a month after its opening, the *New York Times* reported that *Kiss Me, Kate* "may very well have set a fashion for future Broadway stage offerings," notably "a modern musical drama, as yet untitled, based on *Romeo and Juliet*," that "will arrive in New York next season." Originally intended as a story about Jewish and Christian intermarriage, by the time the next Shakespeare musical opened on Broadway—eight years later—it had turned into another fundamentally American story, one about race, immigration, and gang violence: *West Side Story*.

Kiss Me, Kate was made into a film in 1953 that nearly another four million Americans would see. But in the five years since it had opened on Broadway, America had quietly changed, changes reflected in the film. Its cast was now all white. The reconciliation of Lilli and Fred is never in doubt. Gender roles are fixed and any allusion to same-sex desire scrubbed. The spanking figured prominently in posters advertising the film. Lyrics are cut, the score censored, and to the relief of the reviewer for the *Christian Science Monitor*, the film "has dispensed with the excessive suggestiveness of the original." As far as loose morals and women's independence went, the backstage world was now more or less indistinguishable from the frontstage one, leading one reviewer to complain that "the cast seems to have no grasp of the temperamental, backstage comedy" of the Broadway hit. Frontstage conventionality—embodied in Shakespeare's taming plot—had won out over what an anxious Willard Waller had in 1945 called "a time of experimentation and new family customs." Playact submission long enough and it is easy to forget that it is just a performance. A door that had briefly opened was firmly shut and mostly stayed that way until the 1960s ushered in civil rights, second-generation feminism, Stonewall, and with those social movements freshly transgressive ways of staging and interpreting Shakespeare. In our own day, the recent clamor to "Make America Great Again" harks back to a fantasy version of this period in the nation's history—though one that more closely resembles the sanitized world of the 1953 film version of *Kiss Me, Kate* rather than the grittier and more honest one of the 1948 musical, which had allowed a fleeting glimpse of the struggle in postwar America for greater sexual freedom, racial integration, and women's choice.

David Parfitt, Donna Gigliotti, Harvey Weinstein, Gwyneth Paltrow,
Edward Zwick, and Marc Norman at the 71st Academy Awards,
March 21, 1999.

CHAPTER 7

1998: Adultery and Same-Sex Love

A month before it was scheduled to open in movie theaters on December 11, 1998, *Shakespeare in Love* still lacked an ending satisfying enough to please American test audiences. Some viewers felt that it was missing an "emotional punch." Others couldn't understand why the heroine "didn't just run off with Shakespeare." That cut of the film had scored a solid 85 out of 100 in test screenings; but if this score had any chance of being nudged past 90, the ending would have to be changed. Director John Madden and screenwriter Tom Stoppard were under intense pressure from Harvey Weinstein and other Miramax executives to find a solution—which, to the producers, meant giving audiences a happier ending. Weinstein, who flew to London and reportedly badgered Stoppard, was nervous enough to consider a limited release that would allow interest in the film to build rather than risk a more ambitious opening. Miramax executives also worried that putting Shakespeare's name in the title would be box-office poison, and had pressed, unsuccessfully, for *Shakespeare in Love* to be replaced by *Thou Art My Girl* or *How Should I Love*.

There wasn't much time left to change the ending, which had long bedeviled Stoppard, nor was it financially feasible to reshoot the final scenes in the replica Elizabethan playhouse that had been built for the film, or reassemble the eight hundred extras who had filled it. If *Shakespeare in Love* was to compete for the upcoming Academy Awards, to be held in March—which it had to do if Miramax hoped to turn a decent profit—its opening couldn't be delayed. Those involved in making the film now found themselves in the same predicament in which they had placed the film's hero, Will Shakespeare, who was struggling to bring the play he was writing to a satisfying conclusion.

The ending of *Shakespeare in Love* continued to be tinkered with until shortly before its December opening. By mid-February 1999, Valentine's Day weekend, the film was playing at close to two thousand movie theaters across America, and the following month would win seven of the thirteen Academy Awards for which it had been nominated, including Best Picture and Best Original Screenplay. It would go on to gross more than $100 million by the end of July in the United States alone, a phenomenal success for a film that lacked car chases, animation, or intergalactic battles, and that had been given an "R" rating, which meant that those under 17, a significant percentage of the moviegoing public who wanted to see it, had to be accompanied by a parent or guardian. A movie ticket cost on the average five dollars in the US in 1999, so roughly 20 million Americans saw the film during its thirty-three-week run in movie theaters. That's roughly 10 percent of the adult population in America. No other film about Shakespeare or of his works has ever come close to that figure. And the film's reach extended further when it became available on DVD. How America imagined Shakespeare at the end of the twentieth century both influenced and was powerfully shaped by *Shakespeare in Love*—and how this Hollywood success story happened, and what was altered or suppressed in the making of the film, would in turn reveal a great deal about the fault lines in American culture at that pre-9/11 moment.

Hollywood had long been in love with Shakespeare, but as far back as Warner Brothers' *A Midsummer Night's Dream* (1935)—directed by Max Reinhardt, and starring Mickey Rooney and James Cagney—American moviegoers had failed to requite that love; that film barely made back the million dollars it cost to make. With few exceptions, movie versions of Shakespeare's plays, even critically acclaimed ones, were box-office disappointments. The decade leading up to the release of *Shakespeare in Love* was typical. Kenneth Branagh's *Henry V* (1989) had cost $9 million to make and earned back in the United States little more than that. A year later, Franco Zeffirelli's *Hamlet* (1990), starring Mel Gibson, grossed only a little more than $20 million domestically, as did Branagh's *Much Ado about Nothing* (1993), despite a glittering cast. A brilliant *Richard III* (1995), starring Ian McKellen, failed to clear even $3 million in America. Hollywood learned the hard way that it didn't matter how talented the director was or how many stars were in the cast; the only truly popular Shakespeare play for American moviegoers in the late twentieth century was the one they knew and loved best from high school: *Romeo and Juliet*. Back in 1968, Zeffirelli's European-produced version of that play (distributed in the US by Paramount) earned close to $40 million dollars domestically, and Baz Luhrmann's 1996 version, *William Shakespeare's Romeo + Juliet*, set in Miami and starring Leonardo DiCaprio and Claire Danes, earned $46 million in America. Part of the genius of *Shakespeare in Love* was embedding familiar highlights from *Romeo and Juliet* (leaving out the unromantic bits) within a suspenseful biopic about the creative and emotional travails of the man who wrote it.

The premise of *Shakespeare in Love* is that *something* had to account for what catapulted Shakespeare from the dodgy author of *Two Gentleman of Verona* to the brilliant creator of *Romeo and Juliet*. The film's fictional answer is to be found in an inspiring extramarital affair Shakespeare has with Viola de Lesseps, a wealthy merchant's daughter who is about to be married off by her parents to a money-hungry and crass aristocrat, the Earl of Wessex. Will can't seem to finish his next play, *Romeo and Ethel the Pirate's Daughter*, though he has already sold it to competing theater managers, Philip Henslowe and Richard Burbage. The year is 1593.

Biographers don't know much about the real Shakespeare's life at this time, leaving the filmmakers an unusual degree of freedom. Will Shakespeare, who begins the film in despair about love and art, ends up finding in Viola his muse. For her part, Viola, who loves theater, falls for Shakespeare's words before falling in love with the playwright himself, after disguising herself as a young man and auditioning for one of Will's plays (at a time when women were forbidden to perform in the public theaters).

How will the uninspired comedy of *Romeo and Ethel the Pirate's Daughter* get transformed into the timeless tragedy *Romeo and Juliet*? Can Will, who is under pressure from his financial backers to give his play a happy resolution (and if possible, toss in a crowd-pleasing clown and a dog), come up with the right ending in time for an opening that cannot be postponed? And will Viola and Will end up as star-crossed lovers, or can they somehow escape their loveless marriages?

As the film progresses, the multiple strands of the plot get woven together ever more tightly. At the film's climactic moment, Viola steps into the role of Juliet and performs her part opposite Will's Romeo, as life and art magically converge—at least until the performance ends with their characters' tragic suicides. This debut performance of *Romeo and Juliet* is so moving that Shakespeare wins a fifty-pound wager with Wessex—the bet overseen by Queen Elizabeth herself—having proved that a play can show the truth of love. But as the story draws to a close, Will and Viola live on, the fate of their own love, unlike that of Romeo and Juliet, as yet unresolved. This was where American test audiences, the studio bosses, the screenwriter, and the director found themselves at odds.

Comedies demarcate what a society considers permissible, and, since they usually end in marriage, turn on who ought to bed whom. Will audiences root for somebody of one race or ethnicity marrying someone from another? A man in love with another man, or a woman with a woman? What about someone who is separated falling in love with one who is engaged to be married? At stake in what sort of union is deemed acceptable is how tolerant a community imagines itself to be. Comedies tend to be more socially conservative than tragedies. Shakespeare's genius in ending his comedies was grounded in his ability to deliver "what you will" while raising larger questions which are then left unresolved. If you want to know what a culture is truly anxious about, look at what kinds of unions make its audiences uncomfortable. That's certainly the case with so accomplished a romantic comedy as *Shakespeare in Love*, confirmed by the ambivalent responses of test audiences to early versions of it. The various endings that were written and discarded in the course of the production provide unusual insight into what sorts of issues had to be quietly suppressed or cleverly evaded.

The origins of the film can be traced back a decade earlier to 1988, when the Hollywood screenwriter Marc Norman was encouraged by his son to write about Shakespeare as a struggling young playwright. It took Norman, who had done postgraduate work in English at Berkeley, a few years to work up a script that would be the basis for what eventually won him, as well as Stoppard, an Oscar for Best Original Screenplay. In 1991 Norman pitched it to his friend and neighbor, the producer Edward Zwick, who planned on directing it himself, and they sold it to Universal. The box-office star Julia Roberts read it, loved it, and was committed to making the film.

Those who have seen the 1998 film will likely be surprised by how much more progressive Norman's 1991 version of the love story had been. The heroine, originally named Belinda, is adventurous, sexually liberated, and fiercely independent. She is discovered by Will Shakespeare while acting for a boys' theater company, passing herself off as a young man named Thomas. Thomas's "dark hair," "adolescent moustache," and "graceful gestures" catch Will's eye, and he invites the young actor to audition for the role of Romeo. They rehearse the shared sonnet—with Will playing Juliet—that the lovers recite when they first meet, and which ends with a kiss. It's love at first sight. As they part, Will's heart is "thumping in his chest," though "he has no idea why."

Will, who considers himself straight, is in a panic, and confides in the theater manager Philip Henslowe that he thinks he is falling in love with a man. When Henslowe suggests it must be brotherly love, Will replies: "It's not brotherly. I have brothers—I don't want to kiss their neck where it joins their shoulder," then blurts out that the attraction is "erotic." Over the course of the first quarter of Norman's screenplay Will's confusion about his sexual orientation intensifies. He walks London's streets at night, talking to himself: "It's a *boy* . . . And if it is? Then you've lived thirty years of your life and never known who you really were. Will Shakespeare? Oh yes—minor playwright, likes boys." Another night, after a few drinks, Will tries killing himself by throwing himself into the Thames—but it turns out to be a comic scene, as the tide is out and he lands in the mud. Will decides at that moment that "It can be. You love him—and you must follow love."

Will summons the courage to declare his love to Thomas, and seeks out the young actor's advice on a romantic scene between two men. The two improvise, Will playing a page's part and Thomas the "master," when Will confesses: "There is no play. It's you. I love you." He chases Thomas around a tree, pins him, and "presses his mouth against the boy." Thomas struggles at first, but "slowly melts—he kisses Will back." It is only after Thomas's fake mustache falls off that Will discovers that Thomas is in fact Belinda de Lesseps, a young woman he had earlier glimpsed at court. They fall into bed, an uninhibited Belinda stripping naked first. When she asks Will whether he would "have still loved me if I were a boy," Will replies that he prefers that she's a girl, "Only because it allows us to make love face to face." Will later goes to a "gay" tavern where he buys a round for all, proposing a toast to "the soul of love."

In challenging heterosexual norms, Norman drew heavily on *As You Like It*, especially the scenes in which Rosalind instructs Orlando about what men don't understand about women. As part of Will's education, Belinda and Will stroll about town both dressed as men and later, as women. The effect on Will's writing is extraordinary, and he acknowledges that Belinda is his "muse." There is lots of unconventional sex, as the pair "made love on rooftops, in cemeteries, always searching for the path to the very soul of love." By now Belinda is carrying Will's child. Will, for his part, never tells her that he is married and fantasizes about running off with her.

But it is not to be. Belinda agrees to marry Wessex if she is allowed to act once in *Romeo and Juliet*, and if he promises not to have Will imprisoned or close the playhouses. And Shakespeare becomes a shareholder in the Chamberlain's Men. The former lovers only catch sight of each other once more, from a distance, at a court performance of one of Will's plays. Henslowe provides a final voice-over, in which we learn that Wessex "died in a duel two years later," and that Belinda, who remarried, raised her son by Will, and the boy "came out fine." The screenplay then ends awkwardly, as if unnerved by its own daring, retreating into a heritage vision of an aging Shakespeare, now in retirement in Stratford, at a picnic with his wife and dutiful daughters, as "grandchildren gambol at their feet."

Even in this last-minute reversal, Norman's screenplay reflects the uncertain moment of its creation. Americans in the early 1990s remained deeply divided when it came to gay and women's rights. The beginning of the decade had witnessed the awful national spectacle in which Anita Hill was publicly vilified in Senate hearings, and her crude sexual harasser, Clarence Thomas, given a seat on the Supreme Court. Books like Susan Faludi's *Backlash: The Undeclared War Against American Women* (1991) captured that contentious era while exposing the ways in which Hollywood couldn't deal with independent women. At the same time, playwright Tony Kushner was bringing gay sexuality mainstream in his *Angels in America*, which premiered in 1991. Norman thought it vital to his story "that Shakespeare made this commitment to follow love wherever it took him." Unfortunately, he added, "there were people involved in the production that were disturbed with that idea," and he "was overruled."

At this point the Czech-born British playwright Tom Stoppard was brought in to take over the screenwriting. After looking over Norman's script, Stoppard wrote to Universal's Barry Isaacson, a producer for whom he had worked before, explaining that "even for a whimsical romantic comedy the present story is just too embarrassingly cavalier about the historical context." Stoppard added that he "had to strip things back to the extent that I am using almost none of the original superstructure, and not much of the foundations either. Be assured, however, that I have not abandoned the true objective here—a romantic comedy for J. R."—that is, Julia Roberts. Stoppard, good as his word, radically overhauled what Norman had written. In successive drafts the storyline became more historically accurate and informed. Stoppard also sharpened the plot and dialogue, and introduced into the plot a pair of playwrights, Christopher Marlowe and the young John Webster. But his Belinda is far more demure, and what Stoppard calls Norman's "gay angle" would almost entirely disappear, replaced by a more traditional heterosexual romance.

Yet Stoppard still couldn't figure out how to bring what was now a far more conventional love story to a close. His first go at it, in which the lovers part amicably and Will contemplates a new play about Cleopatra, was unsuccessful. In his next draft, he tried keeping the lovers together, with Wessex rejecting Belinda on the grounds that he could never be "betrothed to an actor." Will joins the Chamberlain's Men, and, having seen her act, Richard Burbage thinks that Belinda has a future in the entertainment business, telling her, "I think I can make something of you." In this version's final, romantic scene we watch Will and Belinda "being rowed through the summer evening, by London Bridge," as Will describes to her the plot of *Twelfth Night*. But this ending also didn't satisfy Stoppard; it wouldn't do to keep Belinda around as Will's mistress and an occasional actor.

In his next draft, Stoppard tried flipping things around: this time Wessex is so impressed with seeing Belinda act onstage that he happily marries her. As Will watches the love of his life ride off with Wessex, Burbage joins him, "and the two of them go back to the Curtain, like Bogart and Rains at the end of *Casablanca*." At this point Stoppard had the inspired idea of taking Belinda's journey one step further in an epilogue. As we hear Will in voiceover describing a shipwreck and the opening of *Twelfth Night*, we see Belinda "washed ashore" alone in America, where she will "meet her brave New World."

This *Casablanca* ending, coupled with Belinda's arrival in America, was finished by the autumn of 1992 and would be the basis of the film in which Julia Roberts was to star. Costumes were sewn and sets built at Pinewood Studios near London in anticipation of the start of filming, when production was halted in October and the film was shelved. Roberts, who retained the right to choose her costar, only wanted to do it with Daniel Day-Lewis as Will, and he refused, even after she flew over to make the case in person. Universal was out a few million dollars, and put a hefty price tag on the film to prevent another studio from making it. Edward Zwick sent the script to Miramax, where Harvey Weinstein badly wanted it, though it wasn't until 1997 that he was able to wrest the film from Universal for $4.5 million (the most, Weinstein later said, that he'd "ever paid for a script or a project or anything else").

By 1997, Julia Roberts had been replaced by a young actor

groomed for stardom by Miramax, Gwyneth Paltrow. Mirroring the unspoken story of America's love for Shakespeare that under-girded the film, a British actor had to be paired with her as the male lead, and Joseph Fiennes was eventually chosen to play Will. Stoppard was brought back to fine-tune the screenplay, by John Madden, who had replaced Edward Zwick as director. But Stoppard was handed a very different version than the one he had last submitted. It turned out that in the interim, Zwick had given Stoppard's script to a studio writer. Stoppard wrote to Zwick, now one of the producers, telling him that he was "taken aback to find scenes interpolated, re-arranged, edited and omitted; and, of course, a lot of new dialogue." Madden recalled that in this doctored version, "things that might be thought to be questionable for an American audience, such as the fact that the whole movie concerned an affair while this man was married and had children, was sort of swept under the carpet." Stoppard was ready to walk away, making it clear that he would not work from a sanitized script. If they weren't willing to go back to his previous draft, Miramax should stick with their studio screenwriter "from here on, in which case you would have my amicable best wishes—but not, please, my name; at least not in its present authorial presumption."

Stoppard got his way. But times had changed, and the resolution of the version from five years earlier would no longer do. This time around, at least in his early drafts, Stoppard's heroine, now renamed Viola, is much bolder. In one draft she even asks Will to marry her. But Will evasively turns her down, unwilling to admit that he already has a wife. It's only later that Viola learns from others that Will has a family back in Stratford. Will confesses as much to her, a bit defensively: "My love is no lie. I have a wife, yes, and I cannot marry the daughter of Sir Robert de Lesseps. It needed no wife come from Stratford to tell you that. And yet you let me come to your bed." To get past this obstacle, and to make it not feel like a sordid affair, Stoppard then tried something new: a mock wedding in which Viola places on Will's finger a grass ring she has been plaiting. Viola tells Will that she "will go to Wessex as a widow from these vows, as solemn as they are unsanctified." In Norman's version, a deeper understanding of love, stripped of the constraints imposed by gender and convention, releases in Shakespeare a torrent of creativity; in Stoppard's, the love of his life cures Will of "writer's block."

There are two more inventive turns in Stoppard's revision of the script in late 1997. The first is indebted to Norman's earlier draft. As the lovers bid one another farewell and Viola boards ship with Wessex, she whispers to Will, "I'm carrying your child to the new world," leaving him "stunned, in tears," as she "runs aboard." In the second, returning to the contours of his own earlier ending, Viola survives a shipwreck and washes up on shore in America, where she "braces herself and walks on to meet her brave New World." In the next draft Stoppard takes this idea even further—putting a comma after "World" and appending to the typescript a surprising and inspired coda in longhand: "where, beyond the forested foreshore, there rises the ghostly shimmering outline of the skyscrapers of modern Manhattan." Stoppard continued to revise and sharpen the dialogue before submitting his final draft in 1998, and filming began.

But the producers were unhappy with the ending. According to Madden, "after some research screenings, Miramax still had concerns about the film's commercial potential, and a ferocious argument began to develop between myself and Harvey about the way the movie concluded." Weinstein's relentless pressure for a happy ending became a running joke. Madden even included in his DVD outtakes a parodic scene in which Will is asked by Henslowe, who is worried about its appeal, what his new play is about: "What is the story? How does the comedy end? . . . Let us have pirates, clowns, and a happy ending, and you will make Harvey Weinstein a happy man." There's laughter and applause in the background as Madden then steps in front of the camera and says, with a broad smile, "Cut, cut, cut." The clip was sent to Harvey Weinstein.

Weinstein had his own ideas about how to leave the lovers. According to Madden, "Harvey had been hankering for an ending whereby Viola somehow stayed a part of Will's life; the idea seemed to be that we would see her performing in disguise in *Twelfth Night* or something." What Weinstein proposed—essentially relegating Viola to the role of Shakespeare's mistress, one for whom he can occasionally find a role in one of his plays—offended Madden, and he balked at the idea: "I always maintained that this was kind of meaningless and left an odd taste because it meant she was some sort of bit on the side that Shakespeare would have for the rest of his life, and ignored that whole idea that she became his muse in favor of one where she became his mistress." Presumably, Stoppard did not share with Weinstein that early draft from 1992 in which he had mapped out a similar ending, where Burbage, who is in charge of the company, tells a promising young female actor, "I think I can make something of you."

Weinstein's role in shaping the ending of the film, and the fate of Gwyneth Paltrow's Viola, appear a lot differently in hindsight. Three years earlier, he had arranged for the 22-year-old Paltrow to play a lead role in a film version of Jane Austen's *Emma*. At that time, according to Paltrow, Weinstein had invited her to his hotel room for a work meeting, then surprised her by putting his hands on her and suggesting that "she give him a massage." Paltrow, blindsided, refused his advances, and when she told her boyfriend, the actor Brad Pitt, about it, he confronted and physically threatened Weinstein, saying something along the lines of "If you ever make her feel uncomfortable again, I'll kill you." Paltrow also said that Weinstein warned her "not to tell anyone else about his come-on." The incident did not stop Weinstein from reportedly lying to other women he later tried to seduce, allegedly telling them that he had in fact slept with Paltrow and that it was "the best thing you can do for your career now."

A stream of accusations about Weinstein's behavior around the time that *Shakespeare in Love* was being filmed suggests that this was far from an isolated incident. Robert Lindsay, a British actor who had been cast for the film, claimed to have been removed from it by Weinstein after he confronted him about his mistreatment of a fellow actor, Molly Ringwald. Those who subsequently accused Weinstein of sexual assault or misconduct around this time include actors Ashley Judd, Rose McGowan, Asia Argento, Zoe Brock, Angelina Jolie, Uma Thurman, and Tara Subkoff, as well as Weinstein's assistant, Zelda Perkins, who warned him about his conduct and threatened to go public. Lawyers negotiated a settlement with her to buy her silence, as they did when Weinstein assaulted a colleague of hers at the Venice Film Festival in September 1998. In retrospect, it's hard not to conclude that Weinstein's solution to the problem of Will and Viola's relationship was to propose something not unlike what he seems to have imagined for himself and Gwyneth Paltrow and other young women like her: keeping her around as a mistress or plaything who might serve the sexual needs of a married man, in exchange for promoting her career.

A compromise on how to end the film was eventually struck. "After much discussion," Madden recalls, "Harvey conceded to our insistence that the film must end the way it was always intended, but Tom and I agreed to re-examine the final scene." Stoppard then "wrote an amazing scene built on the principle that Viola somehow coaxes out of Will's misery the beginning of his new play . . . becoming in the process both his inspiration, and the model of all the heroines to come." Stoppard himself adds, "I think John protected me from much of the pressure he was being subjected to on the issue of the boy getting the girl and living happily ever after. It seemed obvious to me that if we expunged Will's wife from history we'd look like idiots and be rightly punished for it."

IN THE COURSE of arriving at a final script, the filmmakers kept bumping up against one of the more uncomfortable issues for Americans at the end of the twentieth century: adultery. The United States remained steadfastly puritanical on the issue, at least in theory: in 2001, only 7 percent of Americans polled by Gallup thought that having an extramarital affair was morally acceptable, a percentage that hardly budged—to 8 percent—when the same question was again asked in 2015. To give some sense of Americans' disapproval of infidelity, no other behavior that was polled was considered *less* morally acceptable—not even human cloning, suicide, or abortion. Far more Americans considered gay or lesbian relations morally acceptable: 40 percent in 2001; 63 percent by 2015. Perhaps the most reliable contemporaneous figures are those provided by the National Opinion Research Center at the University of Chicago; in 1994 it concluded that roughly 15 to 18 percent of married partners in America had cheated on their spouses (with 3 to 4 percent doing so in any given year). The data seems to suggest that more than half of those committing adultery disapproved of their own behavior. Those making the film had to decide how far to push the boundaries of what was considered permissible. In the end they played it safe.

However unhappy William Shakespeare's marriage to Anne Hathaway might have been, however powerful the attraction between Viola and Will, and however much test audiences wanted their love to last, it was decided that the story could not end with the lovers still romantically involved. In the film, more than an hour passes before Will tells Viola that he is married, long after they have slept together. Moviegoers, though, have been told about Will's marriage early on, during his therapy session with his astrologer and therapist, Dr. Moth, where Will speaks of his marriage bed as "a cold one" and of his "banishment" from his wife as a "blessing." *Banishment* seems an odd word to use here, but it's one that subliminally echoes the prince's fatal decree exiling Romeo from Verona, and transposing that exile to Will's marital state prompts Dr. Moth to say that Will is therefore "free to love." It's a backstory introduced to clear a path to his love for Viola, but it is a muddy path, with banishment a stand-in for a modern-day separation; and before meeting Viola, Will is promiscuous, having had unrewarding sex, mostly with prostitutes with names like "Black Sue," "Fat Phoebe," and "Aphrodite."

The path was further muddied by current events. The very month that the principal actors had begun rehearsing before filming began in February 1998, a major news story broke in the United States connecting *Romeo and Juliet* with an adulterous affair, one for which Americans would show far less sympathy. On the previous Valentine's Day, an ad had run in the *Washington Post*, addressed to "Handsome" and signed "M":

> HANDSOME
> With love's light wings did
> I o'er perch these walls
> For stony limits cannot hold love out,
> And what love can do that dares love attempt.
> —*Romeo and Juliet* 2:2
>
> Happy Valentine's Day
> M

The famous lines quoted here are spoken by Romeo in Act 2, scene 2 of the play, where he declares to Juliet that true lovers cannot be kept apart. The ad had been placed by Monica Lewinsky, a 23-year-old White House intern, who here assumes the man's part, quoting Romeo's lines. The "Handsome" to whom it was addressed was President Bill Clinton. Their clandestine relationship had begun in November 1995. Lewinsky refused to let the "stony limits" of the White House keep her from the man she desired. Shakespeare's words had their intended effect. Two weeks after the ad ran, the two reunited and had a sexual encounter in the Oval Office, for the first time in nearly a year—a union that resulted in the incriminating stained blue dress. According to Lewinsky, when they met, "the President said he had seen her Valentine's Day message," "talked about his fondness for *Romeo and Juliet*," and gave her a book of poetry. The ongoing drama, and the detailed revelations that came out in the Starr Report in September 1998, preoccupied and distracted the nation, and shadowed the film. Eight days after *Shakespeare in Love* opened, the House of Representatives began impeachment proceedings against President Clinton, the charges grounded in Paula Jones's accusation of sexual harassment. At a time when the Starr-crossed lovers were front-page news, Miramax might well have been anxious about promoting a film that seemed to celebrate an adulterous affair. But the two stories were never linked by critics or journalists.

In the final negotiated version of the script, which appears in the published edition of the screenplay, the affair ends with Viola as Shakespeare's inspiration and collaborator. She is bound for Virginia with Wessex. In the lovers' final minutes together, they map out Shakespeare's next play, *Twelfth Night*, after Viola tells him that "the Queen commands a comedy, Will . . . for Twelfth Night," and Will asks her, "What will my hero be?" Viola proposes that he be a duke, and Shakespeare then imagines that his heroine will be "Sold in marriage—and half-way to America." The contours of *Twelfth Night*—and of Viola's fate—begin to take shape:

> VIOLA: Let's see then: a voyage to a new world.
> WILL: A storm. All are lost.

VIOLA: She lands on a vast and empty shore. She's brought
to the Duke . . . Orsino.

Will then embraces Viola and says, "You will never age for me, nor
fade, nor die." Viola assures him, "Nor you for me," and in her final
words to him, adds: "Write me well."

We then watch Will pen the opening lines of his new play,
Twelfth Night, and hear him in voiceover as we witness onscreen
the tumultuous events he describes, as Stoppard builds on the version of the ending he had first hit on back in 1992: "My story starts
at sea . . . A shipwreck. The wild waters roar and heave. The brave
vessel is dashed all to pieces. And all the helpless souls within her
drowned." But there is one survivor, a "lady whose soul is greater
than the ocean, and her spirit stronger than the sea's embrace." He
imagines for her "a new life beginning on a stranger shore. It will
be a love story. For she will be my heroine for all time. And her
name will be Viola!"

Yet there were still difficulties with how to conclude *this* ending, in which America, and Shakespeare's influence on it, figure
so prominently. What follows is an extended closing shot in which
Viola walks along a windy beach on the American coast toward
the woods in the distance as the film credits begin to roll. But this
screened version replaced yet another, based on Stoppard's draft,
that had been filmed, then cut. In that unused sequence (which can
be viewed as an outtake on the DVD), Viola approaches two men
on the beach. It's shot from a distance, so it's hard to know for sure,
but one appears to be Native American, the other dark-skinned,
perhaps African. It comes as something of a shock, underscoring
that we've only seen white faces for the past two hours. When she
asks them—here quoting the line spoken by the heroine, Viola,
of *Twelfth Night*—"What country, friends, is this?" (1.2.1), one of
the men replies, "This is America." Viola then says in response,

"America . . . oh, good," before resuming her long walk up the beach to the wooded horizon. Stoppard still wanted to end with the final image of the modern Manhattan skyline. Madden was also drawn to this and hoped to film it, but given the mad rush to revise the ending and finish the film they ran out of time to work out what they felt to be this stronger conclusion, with that image of Manhattan's skyscrapers, as Madden memorably put it, "there for those to see who wanted to see it, and not for those who didn't."

At least as early as 1992 Stoppard wanted the story to end in America. Perhaps he sensed that the real trajectory of the story was not toward either union or separation, but toward America. Even so, why conclude an Elizabethan romantic comedy set in 1593 with the heroine striding toward what appears to be the modern Manhattan skyline? Madden offered a hint when he explained that they wanted the closing shot to convey the feeling that "Viola was walking away into history." Marc Norman, now one of the producers, "always had a problem" with what he calls the "bizarre ending in which Viola is shipwrecked and she comes ashore on the coast of America and there is New York City with the Twin Towers and the Empire State Building." He was relieved that, from his perspective, "they finally got the ending right in the cutting room." In the end, the movie's closing sequence left out the larger and implicit frame of the story having to do with Shakespeare and America.

A century earlier, the American novelist Willa Cather had insisted that "Shakespeare belongs to two nations now." She was right, but how he was shared and valued remained up for grabs. This collaborative film—with an American and an English screenwriter, a British director, a cast made up of both British and American stars, and Hollywood money and producers—bears that out. Stoppard's ending offers the fantasy that Shakespeare's influence on America was present from its founding, through the mediating presence of an inspiring Viola.

In suggesting that Viola serves this role, Stoppard was partaking of an old and persistent myth. During the American Civil War an unknown journalist had circulated a "fake news" story that an Englishman who had known Shakespeare personally and subsequently emigrated to America was buried in Virginia. The Englishman's tombstone reportedly told a long and detailed story:

Here lies the body of Edward Heldon, Practitioner in Physics and Chirurgery. Born in Bedfordshire, England, in the year of our Lord, 1542. Was contemporary with and one of the pall-bearers of William Shakespeare of the Avon. After a brief illness his spirit ascended in the year of our Lord 1618—aged 76.

The story was popular enough to inspire a wonderful poem, Frederick Wadsworth Loring's "In the Old Churchyard at Fredericksburg" (1870), as well as, years later, a terrific piece of investigative journalism, Moncure Conway's "Hunting a Mythical Pall-Bearer" (1886), that debunked the legend.

But many, from the 1860s to the 1990s, found a version of this myth attractive; whether Shakespeare and the New World were linked through one of his pallbearers or through his muse and lover, the fantasy spoke to the desire to forge a physical connection between Shakespeare and America, the land, they believed, where his inspiring legacy came to rest and truly thrived. It was a myth that the American entertainment industry embraced and that mirrored the backstory of the film itself: the rough-and-tumble entertainment business, which saw its origins in the Elizabethan playhouses, reached its apogee in America, symbolized by that majestic New York skyline (one that also appears on Miramax's logo, with which *Shakespeare in Love* began).

The ending in which Viola encounters a Native American and what looks like an African man had to be cut. Their appearance introduced associations that threatened to undermine an uplifting ending. Native Americans were to be eradicated or removed to reservations, and the dark-skinned man called to mind the slaves who harvested the tobacco that the Earl of Wessex planned to ship to England, which in turn sent goods to Africa, which completed the triangle by shipping more slaves to the Americas to harvest that tobacco. In his DVD commentary on the film, Madden says of Viola's encounter with these two men that "it seemed to take us somewhere we didn't want to go." He doesn't explain where but it's not hard to guess. It proved easier, and very American, to erase these men and the stories they embodied, leap over time, and look ahead to that iconic Manhattan skyline.

IT WAS ONE thing for *Shakespeare in Love* to flirt with adultery; it was another to raise the possibility, as Marc Norman had so boldly done in the initial draft, that an unhappily married Will would find himself falling in love with another man. Unlike adultery, intimations of same-sex love were hardwired into the circuitry of many of Shakespeare's comedies. Viola's cross-dressed namesake in *Twelfth Night*, the play Shakespeare turns to at the end of the film, is loved by a woman who thinks she is a man at the same time that Viola is in love with a man who seems to be increasingly attracted to her as another man. And in *As You Like It*, Orlando, though professing love for his absent Rosalind in the forest of Arden, falls in love with a youth named Ganymede, only to belatedly discover that Ganymede is Rosalind, disguised as a young man. In both plays, the conservative rules of comedy, in which young men marry young women, prevail. But comedies like *Twelfth Night* and *As You Like It* have long allowed audiences uncomfortable with same-sex relationships to entertain, though fleetingly, the possibility that men can fall in love with men and women with women, or even something more fluid and in-between.

Stoppard's Viola and Will still cross-dress, so a hint of Norman's original idea was kept, but only a hint. All that the final version of the film retains of a cross-dressed Will is a campy comic bit in which he appears as a laundrywoman attending Viola at court. And while we watch Will dash off "Sonnet 18"—"Shall I compare thee to a summer's day?"—any trace of its likely origins as one of the sonnets addressed to a young man, "the Master Mistress of my passion," is erased, as the poem is here inscribed "For Lady Viola de Lesseps." Those creating and marketing *Shakespeare in Love* clearly felt that a gay or bisexual Shakespeare was not something that enough Americans in the late 1990s were ready to accept, even if four hundred years earlier contemporaries who read his sonnets tacitly had been, and even if surveys showed that by the end of the twentieth century 40 percent of Americans didn't think that same-sex relationships were morally wrong. Shakespeare could be an adulterer, but he had to be a heterosexual one in a loveless marriage if the film was to navigate these troubled waters and emerge as a box-office success.

In retrospect, it's easy to see why, at the time, those behind *Shakespeare in Love* recoiled from Norman's openness to Shakespeare's interest in another man. Homosexuality had only been removed from the World Health Organization's International Statistical Classification of Diseases in 1992, and the US military had recently instituted a "Don't Ask, Don't Tell" policy. As the release date of the film in 1998 approached, progress toward greater acceptance of homosexuality went into reverse. In 1997 President Clinton signed the Defense of Marriage Act into law, defining marriage as exclusively a union between a man and a woman. And in October 1998, Matthew Shepard, a 21-year-old gay University of Wyoming student, was beaten, tied to a fence, and left to die, a hate crime that galvanized some and shamed others but failed to shift public attitudes toward gay rights, or lead, in the short term, to any legislative changes. *Shakespeare in Love*, in retreating from the possibility of Shakespeare accepting that he might be in love with another man, proved to be a film of and for its time—and on the wrong side of history.

Of course, when Will first meets Viola when she auditions for one of his plays, she is dressed like a young man, Tom Kent, wearing a doublet and hose and a fake mustache. So the film still had to negotiate the moment when Will discovers that "he" is a she. This brief scene takes place as Will and Tom are rowed across the Thames, and, the script reads, "she kisses him." It happens very quickly, and when the boat lands and Master Kent dashes off, Shakespeare is immediately told by the boatman that Tom is really Viola and rushes after her. Moments later we see them embrace again. But in the few seconds that they were apart, Master Kent is safely transformed: the fake mustache is gone and her long golden tresses have replaced her close-cropped wig.

John Madden, who discussed this scene in his comments on the DVD, was clearly unhappy with the choices he made here, acknowledging that "I would have preferred, and the intention of the scene originally was, that she should be dressed as a boy at this point." The reason he didn't, Madden explains, had "to do with the extraordinary makeup requirements . . . but I wish I hadn't done that." It's a fair excuse, though it certainly sounds like special pleading. Adding another level of complexity, Paltrow herself told an interviewer that in playing Master Kent she thought of herself as a gay man: "I'm not very manly, so when I cross-dressed I tended to think of myself as this gay Elizabethan guy who wants to be an actor."

THE HARSH WORLD of current events and the fantasy one of *Shakespeare in Love* would collide on the eve of the Academy

Awards, at the lavish Miramax party held on March 20, 1999. Tom Stoppard wrote a skit for the event, *Two Gentlemen of Queens*, based on Harvey Weinstein and his brother, Bob, an executive producer of the film. It was not a private performance; the press had been invited, and I draw on George Rush and Joanna Molloy's detailed account of the skit that ran in the *New York Daily News*. Geoffrey Rush—who played Philip Henslowe in the film—slipped on a giant prosthetic stomach to play Harvey Weinstein, while Matt Damon put on a "frizzy black wig" to impersonate Bob Weinstein.

In the skit the Weinstein brothers meet with Tina Brown, editor of the hot new magazine *Talk*, bankrolled by their company, Miramax. "When she gets here," Harvey tells Bob, "let me do the talking." Tina then enters, played by a "plummy-accented" Gwyneth Paltrow, who tells them that she has "this incredible, fantastic idea for the Christmas cover: Monica Lewinsky's baby." When Bob, stunned, asks whether Lewinsky is pregnant, Tina tells him: "This is what I have to talk to you about, Bob. I think Monica will have your baby if Harvey gives her the leading role in *Elizabeth's Loves*." And given *Talk's* publication schedule, Lewinsky needs to give birth no later than November. To which Harvey responds: "We're dead. I already asked her and she won't do it unless I give up my producer's credit." A month after Clinton's impeachment hearings, those attending the Miramax party were making light of it all—Stoppard, Damon, Rush, Paltrow, joking about sex with a producer in exchange for a role in a Miramax film, and of Bob Weinstein impregnating Monica Lewinsky in exchange for Harvey giving her a leading role in *Elizabeth's Loves* and putting a photograph of their baby on the cover of *Talk*. For Frank DiGiacomo, who covered the event for *The Observer*, another "cringe-inducing" moment was when Matt Damon, in his role as Bob Weinstein, said that Ms. Brown was basically into 'English faggots.'" The Weinsteins reportedly loved the skit.

It's as if the shadowy presence of Harvey Weinstein's transgressions and Clinton's affair with Lewinsky had to be invoked, then exorcised. Stoppard is witty and Hollywood stars charming, but twenty years on, in the wake of the #MeToo movement, thinking about the damage done to the lives of so many actors mistreated by Weinstein, to Lewinsky, and to the country, it strikes a dispiriting note. There's even the ghostly return of that illegitimate child that had first been introduced by Marc Norman, then cut by Stoppard, only to be restored and then cut again by him. *Two Gentlemen of Queens* was the doppelganger of *Shakespeare in Love*, fleetingly revealing many of the dark currents suppressed in the making of the film.

The following evening *Shakespeare in Love* went on to win its many Academy Awards, including Best Picture. The film was a success because those who made it had worked hard, were exceptionally talented, and guessed right about the kind of story America wanted to be told about Shakespeare (who never reads a book in the course of the film) and about its values. Had Norman's script been the basis of the film it would never have done this well; Stoppard, whatever his personal beliefs, had a surer finger on the pulse of American audiences. Seven years would pass before the first film to celebrate a gay relationship, *Brokeback Mountain*, would even come close to winning the Academy Award for Best Picture.

Shakespeare in Love was justly celebrated as a very knowing film, one stuffed with allusions that even the most attentive moviegoer or scholar might not catch. Yet there are things, to paraphrase Madden, that those who made the film as well as those who loved it (and I count myself among them) didn't see, or chose not to see, about where America was heading as the century drew to a close. That goes for America's congressional leadership as well, more obsessed with the sex life of Bill Clinton and the bedroom preferences of citizens than with genuine threats to the nation. An astute critic at that time, Stuart Klawans of the *Nation*, thought "the most re-markable feature" of *Shakespeare in Love* and the other nominees that year for Best Picture was "a determination to keep their eyes shut tight against present-day American realities."

Early on in the film, Will, in a therapy session with Dr. Moth, complains about his creative impotence in Freudian terms: "the proud tower of my genius has collapsed." The line, which might have gotten laughs in 1999, would no longer do so two years later, when it would be hard not to cringe when hearing of collapsing towers. The US embassy bombings in East Africa took place on August 7, 1998. And a week before the film opened, on December 4, 1998, the CIA warned President Clinton that al-Qaeda's leaders were preparing for attacks in America and were training its members to hijack airplanes. The 9/11 terrorists also had their sights set on that Manhattan skyline, their plot "there for those to see who wanted to see it, and not for those who didn't."

Cropped screen grab, assassination scene, *Julius Caesar* at the
Delacorte Theater in Central Park, June 2017, YouTube.

2017: Left/Right

The late 1980s and early 1990s were a time of the Culture Wars in America, waged in op-eds, magazine articles, and in books like James Davison Hunter's *Culture Wars: The Struggle to Define America*, Roger Kimball's *Tenured Radicals*, Ivo Kamps's *Shakespeare Left and Right*, and Allan Bloom's best-selling *The Closing of the American Mind*. Shakespeare was dragged into the quarrel, as rival camps fought over his place in the college curriculum. Those at one extreme argued that as a dead white male and agent of imperialism, Shakespeare should no longer be taught; those at the other celebrated him as a pillar of a superior Western civilization and complained that traditional approaches to teaching his plays had been supplanted by a focus on race and gender. But this front in the Culture Wars turned out to be the site of a largely pointless skirmish; the number of students majoring in English had never been that high to begin with (in the single digits since at least the 1970s and currently below 2.5 percent). The real battles were being fought elsewhere.

While the media was preoccupied with what was happening in college classrooms, it largely ignored a far more consequential cultural development: the rise of colorblind casting in American productions of Shakespeare's plays. Shakespeare played a decisive role in dismantling this longstanding barrier, spurring the broader adoption of colorblind casting in mainstream theater, television, and film. Beginning in earnest in the 1960s (and with increasing frequency by the 1970s and 1980s), African American, Latino, and Asian actors in growing numbers were cast in major parts—no longer as just Othello or Caliban. Thanks especially to the New York Shakespeare Festival (where under Joe Papp's leadership more than half of the productions were colorblind cast), playgoers were able to see such emerging stars as James Earl Jones, Gloria Foster, Rosalind Cash, Denzel Washington, Ruby Dee, and Raul Julia in leading Shakespearean roles. While most of those productions were still overseen by white and male directors, that began to change too—though at an even more glacial pace. By the twenty-first century the pace of change accelerated. Nowadays, transgender and disabled actors are being cast as well, and women in increasing numbers invited to play roles long the preserve of men. I cannot recall when I last saw an all-white Shakespeare performance in this country (which was the norm when I was growing up). In the past few years I have found myself working on American productions that have starred a black Hamlet, a transgender Maria in *Twelfth Night*, and a black woman as Prospero, and richly diverse productions of a dozen or so other comedies and tragedies, many directed, designed, and choreographed by nonwhite artists.

The result has been that for the first time in more than two centuries of American history, actors speaking Shakespeare's words have begun to resemble the nation. This wouldn't make much difference if only the coastal elites went to see Shakespeare's plays performed. But it turns out that lots of Americans across the land enjoy seeing them, so much so that in addition to theaters in most cities that regularly stage his plays, there are nearly 150 summer Shakespeare festivals (dwarfing the number held in Britain or anywhere else in the world), spanning all fifty states, quietly acclimatizing many Americans to greater diversity. Two decades ago, when diversity was still valued by compassionate conservatives, President George W. Bush appointed Dana Gioia, in 2002, to run the National Endowment for the Arts, and one of Gioia's first large-scale initiatives was "Shakespeare in American Communities." The program, still in existence, has sent dozens of theater companies touring Shakespeare's most popular plays through the heartland where there are few or no permanent theaters—to schools as well as military bases—foregrounding diversity as one of its primary goals, and reaching several million Americans.

That was then. Diversity, once considered worthy of support by both political parties, would become sharply partisan under Donald Trump, who was swept into office by a base that could barely conceal its hostility to racial and religious others. The face of the nation that Trump's most avid supporters wanted to see reflected back at them from the stage was white, not brown or black. In such a political climate, diverse casting now looked like part of a provocative leftist agenda. It didn't help that the Democratic side of the House of Representatives increasingly resembled the racial and gender mix of these modern-day Shakespeare companies, while the nearly all-white Republican side of the aisle looked like the Shakespeare cast of yore. The Right under Donald Trump—who may be the first American president to express no interest in Shakespeare—now found itself struggling to find anything in the teaching or performance of Shakespeare's plays that aligned with its political and social agenda, and didn't much seem to care.

The future of Shakespeare in America can be predicted with no more accuracy than the future of the nation. But if Shakespeare continues to serve as a canary in the coalmine, one way of reckoning where things are heading is by looking at fresh controversies surrounding his work. It often takes a provocative event to reveal when a tipping point has been reached, signaling that something fundamental in the culture has changed, perhaps irrevocably. This chapter recounts in detail one such event: the right-wing protests against the Delacorte production of *Julius Caesar* in the summer of 2017. Those on the Right, who had counted on able Shakespeare defenders from Henry Cabot Lodge to William F. Buckley Jr., now found themselves ill-equipped to respond to what a progressive director like Oskar Eustis was doing at the Delacorte. And those on the Left found themselves ill-prepared to deal with the force of right-wing media and threats of violence. What ensued may well come to be seen, like the production that triggered the Astor Place riots, as a sign of the times, and of times to come.

ON SATURDAY JUNE 3, 2017, the Delacorte production of *Julius Caesar* was in its eleventh preview, with every show near or at capacity, and standby lines growing longer. That evening Laura Sheaffer went to see it. Sheaffer was a sales manager at Salem Media, a multimedia conglomerate "targeting audiences interested in Christian and family-themed content and conservative values." She was troubled by what she saw and must have mentioned it to someone at work, for she was steered to Joe Piscopo's AM radio show, owned by Salem Media. Piscopo, who had made his name on *Saturday Night Live* in the 1980s, was an early Trump supporter and served as an opening act for him on the campaign trail. By the time the program aired, he had been briefed on Sheaffer's story and couldn't resist asking leading questions about a production that he had not seen but called "dreck." Piscopo assumed that she would confirm that the "audience must have roared with approval" when they saw the Trump-like Caesar "brutally murdered." But Sheaffer refused to, saying only that the crowd "accepted" the assassination, adding that the production "kept the whole script true to William Shakespeare." While she said at the outset that "Julius Caesar was Donald Trump," she later qualified that claim, explaining that "they never actually said this was Donald Trump or this was Melania." Though offended by what she had seen—saying, "This is not OK"—she stayed until the end of the performance.

Sheaffer also compared what she had seen to an incident the

previous week in which the comedian Kathy Griffin had posted an image of herself holding what looked like the severed head of Donald Trump, which drew the attention of the Secret Service. At the end of the interview Piscopo asked: "Imagine if you did it about Barack Obama?" It's likely that without these two frames of reference, the glowing embers of protest would have died out. At this point, only a half dozen or so people had contacted the Public Theater to express their disapproval.

Two days later, kindling was added to the fire when Sheaffer was again interviewed, this time by *Mediaite*, a news and opinion media website, which gave the story an eye-catching headline: "Senators Stab Trump to Death in Central Park Performance of Shakespeare's Julius Caesar." That was enough for the right-wing *Breitbart* to run a similar story later that day: "'Trump' Stabbed to Death in Central Park Performance of 'Julius Caesar.'" *Breitbart* at least kept "Trump" in quotation marks but mostly rehashed the *Mediaite* interview, again relying on Laura Sheaffer as the sole eyewitness.

Then two things happened. First, on June 7, the day after the *Breitbart* story ran, an anonymous spectator at the Delacorte illegally filmed part of the assassination scene and shared it with the syndicated television newsmagazine *Inside Edition*, which quickly uploaded it to YouTube. For a story that didn't have much content, the visuals were crucial. The production was now reduced to a twelve-second clip of the assassination, taken out of context, excising the pained silence and the storm of protest that followed. There has long been something toxic about *Julius Caesar*'s assassination scene on film; it has been controversial as far back as 1908, when the play was first translated from stage to screen. It was censored at that time by the Chicago police, who insisted on excising it from an early nickelodeon film because it so powerfully portrayed the commission of a crime. The clip of the Delacorte assassination was soon distilled in online media into a single off-kilter screen grab that kept white conspirators out of view and showed a pair of anguished white onlookers in the background. It carried a not-so-subliminal message: blacks were out to kill our president.

Next, an unexpected player, the *New York Times*, entered the fray. It's a time-honored practice not to run a theater review until opening night, one that newspapers across the ideological spectrum respect. Yet the *Times* ran its review on June 9, three days before the play's official opening. It reads as if Jesse Green, their new theater reviewer, had been told to rework his review into a culture story. He began by noting other recent plays that take on Trump and warned that "some right-wing commenters are revving up their outrage over what they assume is an incitement to violence against the president." In the online version, Green then linked readers to the inflammatory story in *Breitbart*. Laura Sheaffer's displeasure with what she had seen the previous weekend was now the story of record.

I WAITED FOR conservative critics and reviewers to object to the Delacorte production on grounds more substantial than disrespect for the president. Eustis, after all, had made himself vulnerable to attack by showing that in killing Caesar the conspirators had acted undemocratically in their desire to save democracy. This argument might easily have been pressed further: the production had unwittingly exposed the threat posed to American democracy by leftist agitators like Cassius.

It never happened. Nobody even claimed that what was enacted was criminal (and if the Secret Service had considered it a genuine threat, it would have intervened). There was only anger and the assumption that those on the Left would have reacted the same way had the tables been turned: imagine the outcry from progressives had an Obama look-alike been assassinated. It soon came to light, though, that a well-reviewed 2012 production of *Julius Caesar* directed by Rob Melrose had a lanky Obama stand-in murdered onstage. It had opened at the Guthrie Theater in Minneapolis and then, after a national tour, performed for a month in New York City. At the time, Melrose noted, the "Tea Party was in full effect, the Birther movement well under way, and Mitch McConnell had stated that his main goal was to deny Obama a second term. It wasn't hard to imagine one of these groups pushed to the point where they would consider violence." Yet Melrose's production had not generated any protests, by either the Right or the Left, nor had any corporate sponsors withdrawn their support.

AT LEAST ONE PERSON on the Right knew how to invoke the play to his political advantage. Consider Steve Bannon's "little riff on Plutarch and Shakespeare" when he spoke to a conservative audience at the Values Voter Summit in October 2017: "Up on Capitol Hill, it's like the Ides of March, the only question— and this is just an analogy or metaphor, or whatever you want to call it—they're just looking to find out who's going to be Brutus to your Julius Caesar." As far as Bannon was concerned (he had by now left the White House and returned to *Breitbart*), it was time to topple the old regime and metaphorically (or "whatever you want to call it") assassinate Senate Majority Leader Mitch McConnell. "This is our war," he added. "The establishment started it . . . You all are gonna finish it." There was not a peep of protest after Bannon made this threat. I was surprised that nobody asked Bannon why he would urge his evangelical audience to side with the murderous conspirators of Shakespeare's play. I suspect that in urging that Mitch McConnell be eliminated by some emboldened Brutus, Bannon's unspoken desire was for what would ultimately follow—that the action he was encouraging, in Antony's words, would "let slip the dogs of war," unleash chaos that would overturn the established order.

Support for this conclusion comes from Bannon's own extended reflections on Shakespeare. Earlier in his career he had tried his hand at adapting Shakespeare for the screen, in collaboration with Julia Jones, his long-term screenwriting partner. After a science-fiction version of *Titus Andronicus* failed to attract interest, Bannon tried adapting *Coriolanus*. The screenplay—called *Coriolanus: The Thing I Am*—was given a reading at the Nate Holden Performing Arts Center in Los Angeles in 2006 but was never made into a film. It's not hard to see why. Bannon's adaptation is an incoherent mess, though in retrospect a deeply revealing one.

Coriolanus turns on two conflicts: class warfare within the Roman republic and an ongoing war between the Romans and their enemy, the Volscians. There's very little actual violence in the play until the end; it's mostly a battle of ideas. Yet Bannon wasn't drawn to either the social or international conflicts that Shakespeare had explored. He relocated the story to Los Angeles during the 1992 Rodney King riots and replaced the struggles within Rome, and between Rome and a foreign foe, with inconsequential squabbling between rival street gangs, the Crips and the Bloods. Coriolanus is transformed into a black gang member, a "no bullshit . . . cold killing machine" and enforcer of the Bloods. Though the invitation to the screenplay's reading promises that the script will "shed light on the continuing subversive effects of racial abuse going back centuries" and "show how the culture of greed, elitism, discrimination and inhumanity repeats itself today in a self-defeating replay of atrocities," it does nothing of the sort. It caricatures blacks as lazy, thieving, violent, and untrustworthy. It often reads like a parody, veering between pseudo-Elizabethan dialogue and the sort of imaginary black dialect ("let's unite and don't gangbang") that only a racist white guy could invent.

Bannon briefly flirts with economic populism, introducing from his source a version of an argument against the sort of trickle-down economics long favored by mainstream Republicans: "White folks . . . don't care for us"; Their homes are filled with "nice shit" and they enact laws to help themselves and oppress the poor: "If their wars don't eat us up"—echoing Shakespeare's play here—"they will." But that doesn't go anywhere. Nor does Bannon's initial and gauzy idealization of Coriolanus. We first see the hero as an attractive man in his twenties. Yet Bannon never permits this charismatic African American to become a national hero or aspire to a leadership role politically—both of which are defining features of Coriolanus's role in Shakespeare's play. It's nearly impossible to adapt *Coriolanus* and stray so far from its original premises. Bannon only seems animated when chaos and annihilation threaten. Los Angeles's worst nightmare is not an earthquake but a pack of violent black men on Harley-Davidsons, descending from the desert, bent on destruction—"bad-ass gangstas."

Steve Bannon understood as well as anyone the ideological fault lines that divided Americans. Yet he failed to find any ideological concerns worth projecting onto *Coriolanus*—including those that have long shaped liberal or conservative interpretations of the play—other than his attraction to the idea of a strongman leader who refuses to be hemmed in. All that remained, once he placed the story amid one of the worst race riots in American history, was chaos and the fear of violent minorities. It may not have been enough to get Hollywood to turn his screenplay into a film, but it tells us something crucial about the man who would lead the alt-right and steer Donald Trump to the presidency. Stoking deep-seated anxieties and rage, rather than engaging in a battle of ideas, was key to that victory.

THE AVAILABILITY OF the video clip of a Trump-like Caesar being assassinated (and the fact that the network had been scooped by both *Breitbart* and the *New York Times*) made it inevitable that *Fox News* would weigh in. It did so with a vengeance on that Sunday morning's *Fox & Friends*. The odd headline to the story—"NYC Play Appears to Depict Assassination of Trump"—made it seem that for *Fox*, New York itself rather than William Shakespeare was responsible for this unnamed play. The conclusion to the segment was no less artfully worded, again omitting any mention of Shakespeare or *Julius Caesar*: "At the end of the day, this is a play put on in Central Park in New York City that very obviously depicts the assassination of a US president." The *Fox & Friends* contributors expressed concern that the production might well promote violence against the president and urged viewers to contact the production's corporate sponsors, naming several of them, including Delta Air Lines and Bank of America.

Patrick Willingham, executive director of the Public Theater, was on his way to church at the time this segment ran, to hear his partner preach. He never made it. Tom McCann, the Public's marketing director, called and warned him that threats were pouring in. Corporate sponsors were also being deluged with complaints and warned that they would lose customers if they continued to support the Public Theater. Willingham recalled how he "watched that entire day unspool . . . communicating with Tom, communicating with my board chair, communicating with Bank of America, [and] emailing around Delta." He managed to reassure a number of corporate sponsors, though by day's end Delta Air Lines (which had had no problem backing Rob Melrose's production) had pulled its support. The campaign against the Delacorte production chalked up another victory when the National Endowment for the Arts, fearful of alienating the new president and of having its funding axed by Congress, played it safe. Rather than stand up for freedom of artistic expression, it declared that "no NEA funds have been awarded to support this summer's Shakespeare in the Park production of *Julius Caesar* and there are no NEA funds supporting the New York State Council on the Arts grant to Public Theater or its performances."

These victories were greeted enthusiastically by Trump's supporters. Former Arkansas governor Mike Huckabee took to Twitter, offering "Kudos to @Delta for pulling $$ from 'play' portraying assassination of @POTUS. No one should sponsor crap like that!" Trump's two adult sons tweeted as well, Eric thanking Delta— "This was the right thing to do," and Donald Jr. writing: "I wonder how much of this 'art' is funded by taxpayers? Serious question, when does 'art' become political speech & does that change things?" Tom McCann recalled that the box office at the Public Theater was getting flooded with so many calls, some of them threatening ones, that "we eventually had to stop taking them and just sent people to a voicemail." Angry emails poured in as well. One warned: "If ever a Theater should Burn to the Ground, Its Yours." Another: "I hope the next protests comes with a bang." It was clear where many had received their marching orders: "Heard about it on TV this morning and saw short clip," a third one wrote. "Just another display of how 'low' we have sunk." Quite a few, unaware of Rob Melrose's production, wrote along the lines of: "Imagine the horror & calls to shut down this production if it were an Obama clone being assassinated." Others were obscene: "Why don't you scum bag liberal baby killing piles of shit stop provoking violence through your sick garbage adaptation of Shakespeare? You and your shit director should be in prison for hate crimes and threats against the president!"

The amplification of this campaign through social media led to collateral damage, as staff at other theater companies soon found their inboxes inundated with threats. Stephen Burdman, whose

New York Classical Theatre performed a mile north of the Delacorte in Central Park, reported that "people are Googling 'Shakespeare in the Park,' and we come up on the list even though Shakespeare isn't in our name." The hateful emails he received had to be unnerving:

> Go fuck yourselves! Every last discusting one of you. I curse every one of you. May you each die a more horrible terrifying death!

> How dare you put in that play about Trump Fuck you and hope hell comes to you all who supported this may You be on ISIS list you disgusting scumbags.

Burdman was in touch with other alarmed theater companies around the country and recalled that "'Shakespeare Dallas' received over 40 very violent emails, like 'we're going to come and rape you.'" Threats were being reported in Massachusetts and Washington, DC, and some of the more specific and frightening warnings were passed along to the FBI. It's hard to believe that all of those who were threatening theaters outside of New York City had so badly misconstrued what they had seen or heard. It seems more likely that some were seizing on the controversy to send a message about what would happen if their local theaters performed anything they deemed offensive.

The Public Theater rode out the brunt of this initial and mostly online assault. New sponsors stepped in and civic leaders resisted calls to intervene. Tom Finkelpearl, New York City's Commissioner of Cultural Affairs, made clear that "threatening funding for a group based on an artistic decision amounts to censorship." "We don't interfere," he added, "with the content created by nonprofits that receive public support—period." But it was obvious that the

Public Theater and its supporters had badly underestimated the ways in which they could be targeted through social media, and how little could be done in response.

During June, Tom McCann told me, Facebook reported that the controversy over *Julius Caesar* reached more than two million people. Twitter reported more than 4.6 million organic impressions, and an average of 35,627 impressions per tweet. Instagram counted 167,669 impressions. Anyone Googling "Julius Caesar Public Theater" could scroll through nearly a million hits, while *Inside Edition*'s YouTube clip of the Delacorte assassination scene was viewed more than 300,000 times. The Public Theater's strategy was to maintain a steely silence, letting the production speak for itself and reiterating that it "in no way advocates violence towards anyone." Eustis, not wanting to breathe new life into the controversy, made only a few public statements, turning down close to two hundred media invitations to speak in defense of the production—a decision he would come to regret.

He had underestimated "the right-wing media machine" and how expert it had become in "taking a piece of information, creating a false narrative about it, and riling up the masses of people who feel angry and disenfranchised." He had hoped, he said, for "serious debate over the production, but got instead "a firestorm over 'fake news'" that "liberals were cheering the assassination of President Trump in Central Park. And this was just a complete lie." As McCann, who was closely monitoring the online and social media assault, described the seemingly impossible task of refuting it: "How do you fight the troll without becoming the troll itself?"

WHILE MARSHALING the outrage of Trump supporters and persuading a few sponsors to distance themselves from the production, those angered by Eustis's *Julius Caesar* had failed to stop the show.

They only had a few days left to do so before the run came to an end. On June 16, rumors circulated that a reward had been offered to those willing to disrupt one of the last three performances. And, independently, a notice circulated on Facebook urging protesters to assemble at the "Central Park Theater" to "shut down the Public Theater's offensive production of *Julius Caesar*." There was a Central Park Theater not far from the Delacorte, but it was a marionette theater, currently showing *The Princess, The Emperor, and the Duck*. By the time that crowds gathered to see *Julius Caesar*, only two gray-bearded protesters holding cardboard signs had shown up at the Delacorte, and there were dark jokes by some of the nervous staff expressing concern for those marionettes.

The rumors of protest-for-pay were true. Mike Cernovich, a prominent far-right activist best known for promoting the bizarre Pizzagate conspiracy theory (which claimed that members of Hillary Clinton's campaign ran a child sex ring out of the basement of a DC restaurant), was offering a $1,000 "prize" to each of the first ten people who would disrupt the Delacorte performance "where Trump is assassinated." He urged his followers to all attend the same evening. Ideally, he said, somebody would stand up every minute or so, shouting or displaying a sign that read "CNN is ISIS," or "Bill Clinton is a rapist." "Let them know," he added, "that this play is terrorism." But it was essential to "get it on video . . . We need you Periscoping, videoing and everything." CNN? Clinton? ISIS? Terrorism? It is hard to imagine a more irrelevant list of ideological or moral objections to the show. But Cernovich understood his viewers well; what mattered was recycling slogans familiar to Trump's base. The crucial thing was not what was said but ensuring that the stunt would circulate on social media.

The escalating threats were taken seriously by law enforcement authorities. Behind the scenes the FBI and New York City's Criminal Intelligence Bureau were monitoring the situation and by the end of the run thirty Park Rangers, sixty New York City police officers, a handful of detectives, and sixteen Public Theater security guards were on site for every performance. The Delacorte was an especially vulnerable space—the price paid for being designed as an open-air, communal theater, with no barrier between actors and audience. Those in the house who were determined enough could race from their seats and attack the actors onstage in a few seconds, before security waiting in the wings could intervene. I was told by Jeremy Adams, general manager of the Public Theater, that some of the actors had received death threats. There weren't many exits either—it had been built to 1938 code—so the audience was at risk if something more catastrophic occurred. Security teams scurried through the house when spotting what looked like a potential weapon. For the final nights of the run, the Public decided to break with long-standing policy and not distribute the last free tickets to those waiting on long standby lines. Bag searches were instituted.

Friday, June 16, was especially humid. The actors would have to deal with that, along with the swarms of insects attracted to the stage lights, the distraction of helicopters buzzing overhead, and the random appearance of the raccoons who for several generations had made their home in the Delacorte. But this evening they would also have to cope with people threatening them in a very personal and terrifying way. "If the actors are going to kill trump on stage," one of the emails sent to the Public Theater read, "maybe they should be killed." It took a lot of focus—and a lot of guts—for the actors to expose themselves to that danger.

The show began uneventfully. But at the end of the assassination scene, as the conspirators, holding aloft bloody knives, stood looking at each other, and Casca at last cried out, "Liberty! Freedom! Tyranny is dead!" (3.1.79), a young woman suddenly left her seat and made her way onstage. The play stopped as she filmed herself shouting, "Stop the normalization of political violence against the

Right! This is unacceptable." A playgoer with a thick Brooklyn accent shouted back: "Get off the stage." The disruption turned out to be coordinated, for an accomplice, a man in his thirties, was already standing and filming her.

Nobody knew what she intended to do next. The actor who was closest—Marjan Neshat—moved swiftly to confront the intruder and block her from the rest of the company. Stagehands quickly appeared and interposed themselves. It took another few seconds before a security team took over and escorted her off, as she continued to shout, "Shame on all of you, shame." As she was led away—at this point perhaps thirty seconds had passed—her accomplice started shouting, "You are all Nazis like Joseph Goebbels, you are all Goebbels. You are inciting terrorists." Like many of those who heard him, I was confused, because it sounded like he was saying, "You are all gerbils." It was a very strange moment, as playgoers turned to each other, asking, "gerbils?" He too was led off, now shouting that the blood of Steve Scalise (a Republican congressman who had been shot and badly wounded earlier that week, at a congressional baseball game) was on our hands.

Only a minute or two had passed. But the spell of the drama had been broken, and the actors stood about, unsure what to do. A calm and familiar voice was next heard through the sound system; it belonged to Buzz Cohen, the unassuming stage manager who had been shepherding shows at the Delacorte for decades: "Will the actors pick up from 'Freedom and Liberty'?" It's the kind of prompt the actors had heard from her hundreds of times during the long rehearsal period and they responded to it reflexively. The effect on everyone in the house was electrifying. The audience stood as one and cheered. I've never experienced anything like it in a theater.

The action resumed—only to be interrupted moments later by the dozens of faux protesters, who, on cue, began standing up and shouting at the conspirators, calling their actions into question.

Though I knew that they were actors, it still came as a jolt; for those not in the know, it was unsettling, and for a few (I could see) quite terrifying. The security forces that had gathered in the wings, ready to respond to further threats, began to move on these planted protesters and had to be restrained by those who worked for the Public. (On subsequent nights the actors scattered through the house were told that they could quietly reassure playgoers panicked by their protests that they were only acting.) The performance ran without further interruption until the final ovation.

For a long time, though, the young woman who had disrupted the performance stood outside the Delacorte, yelling loud enough to distract the actors, before she was finally arrested for criminal trespass. It turns out that she badly needed to be taken into custody, having set up in advance a link to which supporters could send her money for her legal defense. She turned a tidy profit. Later that week she appeared on Sean Hannity's show on *Fox*, where she defended her trespass on the grounds that she "was protecting the president's life." Listening to the mock-elitist accent with which Hannity pronounced "Shakespeah in the Park," I began to fear that the Right was now willing to abandon Shakespeare as irredeemably elitist, bringing to an end a vital, two-centuries-long tug of war over his plays in America. The young woman's accomplice was also interviewed on *Fox* and claimed that "this Manhattan Central Park crowd was on their feet cheering—they were cheering as an actor dressed as the president was stabbed to death." They had in fact cheered—but not then and not for that. Ben Shapiro, a free speech advocate, was the only conservative voice to speak out against "these idiots who stormed the stage," calling their actions "snowflakery."

This would be no replay of the Astor Place riots, though tension remained high for the final two nights. During the last performance, first one and then another young man tried rushing the stage, but by now the cast knew the drill and security tackled them and quickly escorted them out. Other potentially dangerous threats were dealt with out of sight. I was told by Ruth Sternberg, who oversaw security at the Delacorte, that a protester who had tried to smuggle in paintballs was caught and denied admission; he left, but not before dripping a long trail of red paint on the ground outside the theater. Had he succeeded in firing paintballs at the actors—or even other playgoers—it could well have ended the show. Someone could have lost an eye. Closing night was extremely tense because of ominous threats on social media that the police took seriously: "Wait till you see what happens tomorrow." "Just wait until the end of the show, the real fireworks are going to come at the end of the show." There was considerable relief as theatergoers headed to the exits after the final curtain call.

Even then the threats didn't stop. Eustis told me about a letter sent to his home address after the run had ended: "It was hand-written and from Harrisburg, Pennsylvania. And the return address just said: 'Othello' . . . The message itself basically said, 'You liberals have not understood the thing called blowback. I would advise you to be more circumspect in your choices in the future. Because you may think of us as crazy gun nuts, but there will be blowback coming.'" Eustis didn't tell me—I only learned about it from reading the *New York Post*—that his wife and daughter had received threatening phone calls at home.

THE DELACORTE PRODUCTION and the angry protests revealed deep connections between the four-hundred-year-old play and Donald Trump's America—just not those Eustis had anticipated. Hillary Clinton, the Democrats, and mainstream Republicans had assumed that the presidential election of 2016 was about differences in policy. And Eustis had assumed that while his production was likely to stir up controversy, the ensuing debate would turn on competing views of how his *Julius Caesar* dealt with contemporary political concerns: the choices confronting those on the losing side, the threats facing our democracy, the ways in which people could be swayed. But, like those who lost in November 2016, he turned out to be wrong. The divisions within America were more visceral and tribal; Trump himself didn't have much investment in any particular ideology and never had. What had provoked those on the Right infuriated by the Delacorte production was much simpler: outrage at how a Trump-like Caesar was portrayed.

Like those who lost in November 2016, the Public Theater had badly underestimated the power of social media in enabling the Right to mobilize this anger. There was also a failure, shared by the FBI, to take seriously enough the extent to which Facebook and Twitter—companies that professed to be advocates of free speech and essential to the preservation of democracy—had allowed themselves to be co-opted. It was only well after the run of *Julius Caesar* had ended that a wave of newspaper stories broke detailing how Russians had exploited social media sites to influence the presidential election and sow division. But anyone who witnessed the concerted attacks on the Delacorte production by the right wing through social media would have seen that this was the new normal and how political battles were now being waged, at least by those willing to play to win.

Julius Caesar had anticipated the times. Even as Brutus cannot bring himself to act as rapaciously in pursuit of victory as Antony and Octavius (or even Cassius), so too, the controversy over the Delacorte production confirmed what was already clear to many: that the Far Right was willing to display a ruthlessness—going so far as to threaten bodily harm to actors, their director and his family, and fellow Americans out to see a play—that those on the Left could rarely match. Everybody knew it, so much so that it was taken as a given, and so went largely unremarked.

The influence of technology on public behavior had also been underestimated. Even a few years earlier, playgoers at the Delacorte would turn off their phones and pocket them when asked to do so. No longer. Many, despite this request, *needed* to leave their smartphones on during the show, as they did everywhere else, and occasionally check them. Which meant that it was next to impossible to prevent the illegal filming of the performance or stop protesters from coordinating disruptions at the Delacorte. During the final, fraught days of the run of *Julius Caesar*, the Public Theater staff—who were now monitoring the posting of video in real time and could even identify where those immediately uploaded links were shot from in the house—still couldn't act fast enough to intervene.

Eustis had challenged his mostly liberal audiences to confront where their desires to rid the country of a potentially autocratic leader might lead. But in doing so, and in inviting them to register both sides of the argument, he had failed to see that while the idea might work inside the playhouse, it no longer had much force beyond that in a deeply divided and angry America. As Eustis ruefully admitted after the run was over, his staging of *Julius Caesar*, and the ensuing controversy, played "exactly into the great cultural divide we have right now":

Part of that divide is between those of us who believe in this democracy and those of us who believe that this democracy has utterly failed. And those that believe that it has failed believe they are victims, they are oppressed by the intellectuals, by the liberals, by the elite, and that that's the source of their problem. And of course it isn't the actual source of their problem, but they are being fed constantly a lie in order to protect the interests of the ultra-rich. And it drives me crazy.

Eustis had wanted a dialogue, even a heated one, while those offended by his memorable production opted for silencing him and his theater company. His production, however inadvertently, had shown how easily democratic norms could crumble.

THE FUTURE OF Shakespeare in America, like the future of the nation itself, would appear secure. No writer's work is read by more Americans. The last time anyone counted was back in the 1980s, when it was determined that 91 percent of American high schools taught his plays. With the establishment of national Common Core standards in 2009, subsequently adopted by almost every state, that percentage has likely risen, for Shakespeare alone among all writers was named as one whose works ought to be studied by every young American. Yet his future also seems as precarious as it has ever been in this nation's history. There has always been a tug-of-war over Shakespeare in America; what happened at the Delacorte suggests that this rope is now frayed. When one side no longer sees value in staging his plays, only a threat, things can unravel quickly.

It has happened before. In the early years of the seventeenth century, playgoers from all walks of life crammed the Globe Theatre, turning to the plays of Shakespeare and his fellow dramatists to understand their fast-changing and unsettling world. A few decades later that great experiment came to an end. The divisions had grown too great. Few of those attending a performance of *Julius Caesar* back then could have predicted that the fault lines in their political culture would lead to civil war and the public beheading of their ruler. In 1642 Parliament declared that "public stage-plays shall cease," and the Globe, along with London's other theaters, was closed, then torn down.

Acknowledgments

I'm deeply indebted to the friends and colleagues who have read early versions of this book and challenged me to make it a better one: James Bednarz, Alvin Snider, Mary Cregan, Richard McCoy, Ross Posnock, Daniel Pollack-Pelzner, Robert Griffin, Daniel Swift, and David Scott Kastan. Michael Shapiro and Harold Aram Veeser have patiently heard out my ideas over the years, and I am grateful for their input. My son Luke Cregan, a better historian than I, has also helped out through many conversations.

I am grateful, once more, for the exceptional advice and support of my friend and literary agent Anne Edelstein. The best thing that has ever happened to me as a writer has been publishing with Faber. I have benefited greatly from the insight and support of my outstanding editor, Alex Bowler, and have been fortunate to work again with the talented Kate Burton and Kate Ward.

A yearlong Public Scholar award from the National Endowment for the Humanities provided the time I needed to conduct much of the research for this book; the NEH asks that I confirm that the views expressed in these pages "do not necessarily reflect those of the NEH." I was also fortunate to have been awarded a Bogliasco Foundation fellowship, which allowed me to write a section of this book in remarkable surroundings, and get feedback from an exceptionally generous group of artists and writers.

Much of what I know about Shakespeare in America I have learned from my extraordinary students—both graduate and undergraduate—at Columbia University. I am no less indebted to the actors, directors, and staff at the Public Theater, and at the

Theatre for a New Audience, from whom I have learned so much about what it means to perform Shakespeare in America.

I am also indebted to the staff at various archives where the research for this book was conducted: the Columbia University Libraries, the New York Public Library (especially the Library for Performing Arts), the Folger Shakespeare Library, the Massachusetts Historical Society, the Library of Congress, and the Harry Ransom Center at the University of Texas at Austin.

My greatest debt is to Mary Cregan, without whose wisdom, insight, and support this book could never have been written.

Bibliographical Essays

What follows is intended to serve the needs of those searching for a particular source as well as those interested in a broader guide to the stories explored in this book. Quotations in the preceding chapters from Shakespeare's plays, unless otherwise noted, are cited from David Bevington, ed., *The Complete Works of Shakespeare*, 6th edition (New York: Pearson, 2008). Except for titles, I have silently modernized spelling throughout.

INTRODUCTION

The best overview of America's Shakespeare is Alden T. Vaughan and Virginia Mason Vaughan's concise survey, *Shakespeare in America* (Oxford: Oxford University Press, 2012), which I draw on for details about the early reception of Shakespeare in America; see as well their edited collection, *Shakespeare in American Life* (Washington, DC: Folger Shakespeare Library, 2007). Charles H. Shattuck's two-volume *Shakespeare on the American Stage*, 2 vols. (Washington, DC: Folger Shakespeare Library, 1976–1987) is another excellent resource. See too: Michael D. Bristol, *Shakespeare's America, America's Shakespeare* (London: Routledge, 1990); Thomas Cartelli, *Repositioning Shakespeare: National Formations, Postcolonial Appropriations* (New York: Routledge: 1999); Kim C. Sturgess, *Shakespeare and the American Nation* (Cambridge: Cambridge University Press, 2004); and Frances Teague, *Shakespeare and the American Popular Stage* (Cambridge: Cambridge University Press, 2006). Also noteworthy is Robert McCrum's two-part BBC radio program, "Shakespeare and the American Dream" (April 2016), https://www.bbc.co.uk/programmes/b077gd52. See as well: Frank M. Bristol, *Shakespeare and America* (Chicago: Hollister, 1898), and Esther Cloudman Dunne, *Shakespeare in America* (New York: Macmillan, 1939).

For appropriations of "To be, or not to be," as well as citations of John Adams, "G.I. *Hamlet*," Jane Addams, Paul Robeson, Mary McCarthy, and Toshio Mori, see my *Shakespeare in America: An Anthology from the Revolution to Now*, foreword by Bill Clinton (New York: Library of America, 2014). For the Bakersville controversy, see https://friendlyatheist.patheos.com/2018/11/11/offended-pastors-and-parents-pray-for-high-schoolers-who-saw-shakespeare-play/. For Alexis de Tocqueville, see *Democracy in America*, Part the Second, transl. Harry Reeve (London: Saunders and Otley, 1840), vol. 3, chapter 19, "Some Observations on the Drama amongst Democratic Nations," pp. 163–73. For Karl Knortz, see Lawrence Levine's important study, *Highbrow/Lowbrow: The Emergence of Cultural Hierarchy in America* (Cambridge, MA: Harvard University Press, 1988).

For Justice Ginsburg on Shylock, see https://www.nytimes.com/2016/07/28/theater/ruth-bader-ginsburg-rbg-venice-merchant-of-venice.html. For Stephen Greenblatt's op-ed, see "Shakespeare Explains the 2016 Election," *New York Times*, October 8, 2016. It formed the basis of his subsequent book, *Tyrant: Shakespeare on Politics* (New York: W. W. Norton, 2018). See too my review of it in the *New York Review of Books*, December 6, 2018.

Much of my information in this introduction about the Delacorte production of *Julius Caesar* in 2017 is based on firsthand observation, information shared with me by the Public Theater, and extended interviews I conducted with Oskar Eustis. Candi Adams—director of communications at the Public Theater—was also exceptionally helpful. For Eustis's remarks in *New York Magazine*, see Boris Kachka, "What Oskar Eustis Has Learned From 30 Years of Friendship With Tony Kushner," *New York Magazine*, October 24, 2017. His speech from opening night is available on YouTube. Eustis's reflections during rehearsals are quoted from the *Leonard Lopate Show*, June 2, 2017, hosted by Jonathan Capehart.

For the history of *Julius Caesar* on the American stage, see John Ripley, *Julius Caesar on Stage in England and America, 1599–1973* (Cambridge: Cambridge University Press, 1980); Maria Wyke, *Caesar in the USA* (Berkeley: University of California Press, 2012); Andrew James Hartley, *Julius Caesar: Shakespeare in Performance* (Manchester: Manchester University Press, 2014); Andrew James Hartley, ed., *Julius Caesar: A Critical Reader* (London:

Bloomsbury, 2016); and Richard Halpern, *Shakespeare among the Moderns* (Ithaca, NY: Cornell University Press, 1997). For Orson Welles's landmark production, see John Houseman, *Run-through* (New York: Simon and Schuster, 1972); Simon Callow, *Orson Welles: Road to Xanadu* (New York: Viking, 1996); the 1974 interview with Richard Marienstras, in *Orson Welles: Interviews*, ed. Mark W. Estrin (Jackson: University Press of Mississippi, 2002); and *The Mercury, A Weekly Bulletin of Information Concerning the Mercury Theatre*, n.d. Most critics believe that Welles was aware of a recent and little-known Delaware Federal Theatre modern-dress production directed by Robert C. Schnitzer.

On the censorship of the early nickelodeon film of the assassination scene, see Roberta E. Pearson and William Uricchio, "How Many Times Shall Caesar Bleed in Sport: Shakespeare and the Cultural Debate about Moving Pictures," *Screen* 31 (Autumn 1990), pp. 246-48; Halpern, *Shakespeare among the Moderns*, p. 67; and *The Nickelodeon* 5 (January 7, 1911). See too: "Is Shakespeare Read?" *Harper's Weekly* 51 (1907), p. 152; and "A School Comment on Shakespeare's *Julius Caesar*," *Atlantic Monthly* 96 (1905), p. 431.

For an illuminating account of how Shakespeare makes an equally strong case for and against the argument that Caesar is a tyrant, see Robert Miola, "*Julius Caesar* and the Tyrannicide Debate," *Renaissance Quarterly* 38 (1985), pp. 271–89. For the Elizabethan training in seeing two sides of every argument, see Joel Altman, *The Tudor Play of Mind* (Berkeley: University of California Press, 1978).

For the Fairness Doctrine, see Federal Communications Commission, *Report on Editorializing by Broadcast Licensees*, 13 FCC 1246 (1949). A useful overview can be found in Steve Rendall, "The Fairness Doctrine: How We Lost It, and Why We Need It Back," http://fair.org/extra/the-fairness-doctrine. See too, on the Obama years: Dan Fletcher, "A Brief History of the Fairness Doctrine," February 20, 2009, http://content.time.com/time/nation/article/0,8599,1880786,00.html.

For Rob Melrose's production (with an Obama look-alike as Caesar) see: "Review: *Julius Caesar* @ The Guthrie Theater," *MplsStPaul*, December 19, 2013. See too Melrose's own valuable reflections on the controversy: http://www.robmel rose.com/julius-caesar.html.

253

CHAPTER 1: 1833

For John Quincy Adams's pair of essays on Shakespeare, see "Misconceptions of Shakspeare Upon the Stage," *The New England Magazine* 9 (December, 1835), pp. 435–440, and "The Character of Desdemona," *American Monthly Magazine* 7 (March, 1836), pp. 209–17. For their subsequent republication, see James Hackett, *Notes and Comments upon Certain Plays and Actors of Shakespeare with Criticisms and Correspondence* (New York: Carleton, 1863). To access John Quincy Adams's voluminous writing in facsimile (as well as the writings of his parents and son) consult the Massachusetts Historical Society digital collection: https://www .masshist.org/jqadiaries/php/. For Adams's correspondence with George Parkman, see especially his letters to Parkman of March 28, 1835; November 19, 1835; December 9, 1835; and December 31, 1835; for Parkman's letters, see those dated March 21, 1835; October 15, 1835; November 23, 1835; December 3, 1835; and January 23, 1836. For the exchange over Cicero and Othello with his son Charles Francis Adams, see Adams's letter of May 13, 1830. I'm grateful to Sabina Beauchard, reproductions coordinator at the Massachusetts Historical Society, for her assistance in providing copies of these materials. For published editions of Adams's diary and letters, see John Quincy Adams, *Memoirs of John Quincy Adams, Comprising of Portions of His Diary from 1795 to 1848*, ed. Charles Francis Adams, 12 vols. (Philadelphia: J. B. Lippincott and Co., 1874–1877); Allan Nevins, ed., *The Diary of John Quincy Adams, 1794–1845* (New York: Charles Scribner's Sons, 1951); and *Diary of John Quincy Adams*, eds. David Grayson Allen, Robert J. Taylor, Marc Friedlaender, and Celeste Walker, 2 vols. (Cambridge, MA: Harvard University Press, 1981); and see too Andrew Delbanco's insightful review of the two-volume *Diaries*, ed. David Waldstreicher (New York: Library of America, 2017), in the *New York Review of Books*, January 17, 2019, pp. 31–33.

For Adams's exchange with Ingersoll on *Othello*, see Charles Jared Ingersoll, *Recollections, Historical, Political, Biographical, and Social, of Charles J. Ingersoll* (Philadelphia: Lippincott and Co., 1861). For what he tells James Kent, see Adams's *Memoirs*, vol. 8, pp. 423–24. For the reviews of his first essay, see *National Gazette* (December 24, 1835) and *Alexandria Gazette* (December 15, 1835). For his "singular" view of *Othello* in his letter to his son Charles in

1829, see *The Diary of Charles Francis Adams*, ed. Marc Friedlaender and L. H. Butterfield, vol. 3 (Cambridge, MA: Harvard University Press, 1968), p. 20. For Adams's Harvard speech of August 28, 1786, on *Othello*, see *Founding Families: Digital Editions of the Papers of the Winthrops and the Adamses*, ed. C. James Taylor (Boston: Massachusetts Historical Society, 2016). For a list of Adams's publications, see Lynn H. Parsons, *John Quincy Adams: A Bibliography* (Westport, CT: Greenwood, 1993).

For studies of John Quincy Adams and race, slavery, and abolition, see: William Jerry MacLean, "Othello Scorned: The Racial Thought of John Quincy Adams," *Journal of the Early Republic* 4 (Summer 1984), pp. 143–60, and David Waldstreicher, ed., *A Companion to John Adams and John Quincy Adams* (Chichester, West Sussex: Wiley-Blackwell, 2013), especially: David Waldstreicher, "John Quincy Adams: The Life, the Diary, and the Biographers," pp. 241–62, and Matthew Mason, "John Quincy Adams and the Tangled Politics of Slavery," pp. 402–21, for Adams as a "sleeping giant." An invaluable resource is David Waldstreicher and Matthew Mason, *John Quincy Adams and the Politics of Slavery: Selections from the Diary* (New York: Oxford University Press, 2017). See too William Lee Miller, *Arguing about Slavery: The Great Battle in the United States Congress* (New York: Knopf, 1996). Several biographies of Adams have been useful: Paul C. Nagel, *John Quincy Adams: A Public Life, a Private Life* (New York: Knopf, 1997); Phyllis Lee Levin, *The Remarkable Education of John Quincy Adams* (New York: Palgrave Macmillan, 2015); James Traub, *John Quincy Adams: Militant Spirit* (New York: Basic Books, 2016); and especially, for the Shakespeare connections, Fred Kaplan, *John Quincy Adams: American Visionary* (New York: HarperCollins, 2014). For laws governing interracial marriage in Massachusetts, see Amber D. Moulton, *The Fight for Interracial Marriage Rights in Antebellum Massachusetts* (Cambridge, MA: Harvard University Press, 2015).

On the N-word: William Faux, *Memorable Days in America* (London, 1823), p. 9; and Lydia Maria Child, *An Appeal in Favor of that Class of Americans Called Africans* (Boston: Allen and Ticknor, 1833), p. 219. Also useful are Randall Kennedy, *Nigger* (New York: Random House, 2002), and John M. Lovejoy, "Racism in Antebellum Vermont," (https://vermonthistory.org/journal/

69/vt69_s05.pdf), which provides additional examples of New Englanders using the N-word in the 1830s.

The standard version of the dinner encounter between Kemble and Adams can be found in *Diary of Charles Francis Adams*, Marc Friedlaender and L. H. Butterfield, eds., vol. 5, January 1833–October 1834 (Cambridge, MA: Harvard University Press, 1974), pp. ix, 84–87. See too: Thomas A. Bogar, *American Presidents Attend the Theatre: The Playgoing Experiences of Each Chief Executive* (Jefferson, N.C.: McFarland and Company, 2006). For Fanny Kemble's American journal, see Frances Anne Butler [Kemble], *Journal*, 2 vols. (Philadelphia: Carey, Lea and Blanchard, 1835). For the publication history and hostile responses, see Clifford Ashby, "Fanny Kemble's 'Vulgar' Journal," *Pennsylvania Magazine of History and Biography* 98 (January, 1974), pp. 58–66. The *North American Review*, run by Alexander Everett, who had been at the original dinner party, said that it was "singularly deficient" in "maturity of judgment." The London *Times* was skeptical that she had even written it herself, and the *Athenaeum* called it "one of the most deplorable exhibitions of vulgar thinking." See too, the excellent: Catherine Clinton, ed., *Fanny Kemble's Journals* (Cambridge, MA: Harvard University Press, 2000), and Catherine Clinton, *Fanny Kemble's Civil Wars* (New York: Simon and Schuster, 2000). For Kemble's experience on the plantation, see her *Journal of a Residence on a Georgian Plantation in 1838–1839* (London, 1863), and for the best scholarly edition, see *Journal of a Residence on a Georgian Plantation in 1838–1839*, ed. John A. Scott (New York: Knopf, 1961; rpt. Athens: University of Georgia Press, 1984). For a history of the Butler plantation, see Malcolm Bell, Jr., *Major Butler's Legacy: Five Generations of a Slaveholding Family* (Athens, Georgia: University of Georgia Press, 1987). For Kemble on playing Desdemona, see: Frances Anne Kemble, *Records of Later Life*, 3 vols. (London: Richard Bentley and Son, 1882), vol. 3, p. 368.

For Abigail Adams on *Othello*, see Charles W. Akers, *Abigail Adams: An American Woman* (Boston: Little, Brown and Co., 1980), pp. 99–100; and Bogar, *American Presidents Attend the Theatre*, pp. 22–23. For a transcript of Abigail Adams's response to seeing *Othello*, and for the letter to her son of September 24, 1785, see *Founding Families: Digital Editions of the Papers of the Winthrops and the Adamses*, ed. C. James Taylor (Boston: Massachusetts

Historical Society, 2016). For John Adams on Shakespeare, see his letter to his son John Quincy Adams, January 20, 1805 (reprinted in my anthology *Shakespeare in America*), as well as his diary entry for January 30, 1768.

For more on *Othello* and race in nineteenth-century America, see Tilden G. Edelstein, "Othello in America: The Drama of Racial Intermarriage," in *Region, Race, and Reconstruction: Essays in Honor of C. Vann Woodward*, ed. James M. McPherson and J. Morgan Kousser (New York: Oxford University Press, 1982), rpt. in Werner Sollors, *Interracialism: Black-White Intermarriage in American History, Literature, and Law* (New York: Oxford University Press, 2000); Heather S. Nathans, *Slavery and Sentiment on the American Stage, 1787–1861: Lifting the Veil of Black* (Cambridge: Cambridge University Press, 2009). For James Hammond on Othello, see: James Henry Hammond, *Remarks of Mr. Hammond, of South Carolina, on the Question of Receiving Petitions for the Abolition of Slavery in the District of Columbia* (Washington City: Duff Green, 1836), p. 13.

For Louisa Adams, see: *Diary and Autobiographical Writings of Louisa Catherine Adams*, eds. Judith S. Graham, Beth Luey, Margaret A. Hogan, C. James Taylor, vol. 2, 1819–1849 (Cambridge, MA: Harvard University Press, 2013). For her remark about Iago, see p. 693. Louisa Thomas, *Louisa: The Extraordinary Life of Mrs. Adams* (New York: Penguin, 2016) is a helpful biography. And for an insightful account of the Adams's marriage, see Gordon S. Wood, "The Strangely Contentious Lives of the Quincy Adamses," *New York Review of Books*, December 8, 2016, pp 55–56.

For studies of amalgamation in antebellum America, see Kyle G. Volk, *Moral Minorities and the Making of American Democracy* (New York: Oxford University Press, 2014), pp. 104–116; Celia R. Daileader, *Racism, Misogyny, and the Othello Myth: Inter-racial Couples from Shakespeare to Spike Lee* (Cambridge: Cambridge University Press, 2005); Elise Lemire, *"Miscegenation": Making Race in America* (Philadelphia: University of Pennsylvania Press, 2002); Tavia Nyong'o, *Amalgamation Waltz: Race, Performance, and the Ruses of Memory* (Minneapolis: University of Minnesota Press, 2009); James Kinney, *Amalgamation!: Race, Sex, and Rhetoric in the Nineteenth Century American Novel* (Westport, CT: Greenwood Press, 1985); Peggy Pascoe, *What Comes Naturally: Miscegenation Law and the Making of Race in America* (Oxford

University Press, 2009); Werner Sollers, ed., *Interracialism*; and Herbert Aptheker, *Anti-Racism in U.S. History: The First Two Hundred Years* (New York: Greenwood Press, 1992). On the threatening sexuality of black men, see Martha Hodes, "The Sexualization of Reconstruction Politics: White Women and Black Men in the South After the Civil War," *Journal of the History of Sexuality* 3 (1993), pp. 402–417.

CHAPTER 2: 1845

For the young Ulysses S. Grant I have drawn on: John Y. Simon, ed., *The Papers of Ulysses S. Grant*, vol. 1, 1837–1861 (Carbondale: Southern Illinois University Press, 1967); Jean Edward Smith, *Grant* (New York: Simon and Schuster, 2001); Roland C. White, *American Ulysses: A Life of Ulysses S. Grant* (New York: Random House, 2016); and Ron Chernow, *Grant* (New York: Penguin Press, 2017). For Grant's reputed girlishness, see William E. Woodward, *Meet General Grant* (New York: H. Liveright, 1928), and "Longstreet's Reminiscences," *New York Times*, July 24, 1885; for Elderkin, see Chernow, p. 42, and White, *American Ulysses*, p. 676 (which cites Emma Dent Casey's typescript, "When Grant Went A-Courtin'").

I have found the following works on the Mexican–American War most helpful: K. Jack Bauer, *The Mexican War 1846–1848* (New York: Macmillan, 1974); Paul W. Foos, *A Short, Offhand, Killing Affair: Soldiers and Social Conflict during the Mexican–American War* (Chapel Hill: University of North Carolina Press, 2002); Frederick Merk, *Slavery and the Annexation of Texas* (New York: Knopf, 1972); Richard Bruce Winders, *Mr. Polk's Army: The American Military Experience in the Mexican War* (College Station: Texas A&M University Press, 1997); Felice Flanery Lewis, *Trailing Clouds of Glory: Zachary Taylor's Mexican War Campaign and His Emerging Civil War Leaders* (Tuscaloosa: University of Alabama Press, 2010); and Martin Dugard, *The Training Ground: Grant, Lee, Sherman, and Davis in the Mexican War, 1846–1848* (New York: Little, Brown, 2008). On the gendering of that war, see Peter Guardino, "Gender, Soldiering, and Citizenship in the Mexican–American War of 1846–1848," *American Historical Review* 119 (2014), pp. 23–46; Harry L. Watson, *Liberty and Power: The Politics of Jacksonian America*, revised ed. (New York: Hill and Wang, 2006), pp. 52–53; Reginald Horsman, *Race and*

Manifest Destiny: The Origins of American Racial Anglo-Saxonism (Cambridge, MA: 1981); and *National Songs, Ballads, and Other Patriotic Poetry Chiefly Relating to the War of 1846*, compiled by William M'Carty (Philadelphia: William M'Carty, 1846), pp. 45–46. For Slidell's words, see Amy S. Greenberg, *A Wicked War: Polk, Clay, Lincoln, and the 1846 U.S. Invasion of Mexico* (New York: Knopf, 2012), p. 86. For Grant on the legacy of this campaign, see his *Memoirs*, vol., 1, chapter 4. And for Porter's fate, see Lewis, *Trailing Clouds of Glory*, p. 62; Lewis notes that before his death, Porter had served as a go-between for Grant and his fiancée (helping to keep their engagement secret, in much the same way that Michael Cassio had for Othello and Desdemona).

On the rich body of work on Manifest Destiny, I am especially indebted to: John O'Sullivan, "Annexation," *United States Magazine and Democratic Review* 17 (July-August 1845), pp. 5–10; Robert D. Sampson, *John L. O'Sullivan and His Times* (Kent, Ohio: Kent State University Press, 2003); Sam W. Haynes and Christopher Morris, eds., *Manifest Destiny and Empire: American Antebellum Expansionism* (College Station: Texas A&M University Press, 1997); Anders Stephanson, *Manifest Destiny: American Expansion and the Empire of the Right* (New York, Hill and Wang, 1995); William Earl Weeks, *Building the Continental Empire: American Expansion from the Revolution to the Civil War* (Chicago: Ivan R. Dee, 1996); Lyon Rathbun, "The Debate over Annexing Texas and the Emergence of Manifest Destiny," *Rhetoric and Public Affairs* 4 (Fall 2001), pp. 459–494; Steven E. Woodworth, *Manifest Destinies: America's Westward Expansion and the Road to the Civil War* (New York: Knopf, 2010); Horsman, *Race and Manifest Destiny*; James M. McCaffrey, *Army of Manifest Destiny: The American Soldier in the Mexican War, 1846–1848* (New York: New York University Press, 1992); and especially Amy S. Greenberg, *Manifest Manhood and the Antebellum American Empire* (New York: Cambridge University Press, 2005), and her *A Wicked War*; Richard Slotkin, *Regeneration through Violence: The Mythology of the American Frontier* (Middletown, CT; Wesleyan University Press, 1973); Albert Weinberg, *Manifest Destiny: A Study of Nationalist Expansion in American History* (Baltimore: The Johns Hopkins Press, 1935); Frederick Merk, *Manifest Destiny and Mission in American History: A Reinterpretation* (New York: Knopf, 1963); Joseph Wheelan, *Invading Mexico: America's Continental Dream and* the Mexican War, 1846–1848 (New York: Carroll and Graf, 2007); Bernard DeVoto, *The Year of Decision: 1846* (Boston: Little, Brown, 1943); Thomas R. Hietala, *Manifest Design: Anxious Aggrandizement in Late Jacksonian America* (Ithaca, NY: Cornell University Press, 1985); William Earl Weeks, *Building the Continental Empire: American Expansion from the Revolution to the Civil War* (Chicago: Ivan R. Dee, 1996); Steven E. Woodworth, *Manifest Destinies: America's Westward Expansion and the Road to the Civil War* (New York: Knopf, 2010); and Richard Bruce Winders, *Crisis in the Southwest: The United States, Mexico, and the Struggle over Texas* (Wilmington, Del.: SR Books, 2002). For Winthrop's quotation from Shakespeare's *King John*, I am indebted to Greenberg's *Manifest Manhood*; see Robert Charles Winthrop, *A Memoir of Robert C. Winthrop* (Boston: Little, Brown, 1897), pp. 39–40. See too Greenberg, who cites this.

For the army camp in Corpus Christi in 1845–1846, see: Daniel Harvey Hill, "The Army in Texas," *Southern Quarterly Review* 9 (April 1846), pp. 434–57; Darwin Payne, "Camp Life in the Army of Occupation," *Southwestern Historical Quarterly* 73 (July 1969–April 1970), pp. 326–42. For the fighting and carousing in the camp, see Edward S. Wallace, *General William Jenkins Worth: Monterey's Forgotten Hero* (Dallas: Southern Methodist University Press, 1953), p. 66; and *Fifty Years in Camp and Field, Diary of Major-General Ethan Allen Hitchcock*, ed. W.A. Croffut (New York: G. P. Putnam's Sons, 1909), p. 203.

For the theatricals at Corpus Christi: Longstreet's unpublished interview can be found in the Hamlin Garland papers, Collection no. 0200, Special Collections, USC Libraries, University of Southern California, where he also remembered the men, including Grant, who performed in John Baldwin Buckstone's light farce, *The Irish Lion*; a contemporary acting edition calls for its female characters to appear in bonnets and white muslin dresses; James Longstreet, *From Manassas to Appomattox* (Philadelphia: J. B. Lippincott, 1896); Jeffrey D. Wert, *General James Longstreet: The Confederacy's Most Controversial Soldier—A Biography* (New York: Simon and Schuster, 1993). See too: William Seaton Henry, *Campaign Sketches of the War with Mexico* (New York: Harper, 1847); George Gordon Meade, *The Life and Letters of George Gordon Meade*, 2 vols. (New York: Charles Scribner's Sons, 1913); Thomas M. Settles, *John Bankhead Magruder: A Military Reappraisal* (Louisiana State

University Press, 2009), p. 40; *The Daily Picayune*, January 20, 1846, p. 2; and the *Corpus Christi Gazette*, January 8, 1846. For *Othello* in the antebellum South, see Charles B. Lower, "Othello as Black on Southern Stages," in Philip C. Kolin, ed., *Shakespeare in the South: Essays on Performance* (Jackson: University Press of Mississippi, 1983); and on Knowles's *The Wife*, see *The Spectator* (April 27, 1833), p. 18. On the dating of rehearsals of *Othello*: on January 2, 1846, Grant wrote to Julia that he has just returned from "a tour of one month through Texas," so he could not have rehearsed the part in December—and Mrs. Hart had arrived and was acting with the company by early January (*The Papers of Ulysses S. Grant*, vol. 1, 1837-1861). Apparently, Mr. Hart (likely married to Mrs. Hart) and his fellow professional actors who performed in the Union Theater followed the troops on the campaign, and enlisted volunteers to flesh out the performances; see: J. Jacob Oswandel in his *Notes of the Mexican War 1846–47–48* (Philadelphia: n.p., 1885).

On *Romeo and Juliet* in the nineteenth century, see James N. Loehlin, ed., *Romeo and Juliet*, Shakespeare in Production (Cambridge: Cambridge University Press, 2002); Anne Russell, "Gender, Passion, and Performance in Nineteenth-Century Women Romeos," *Essays in Theatre* 11 (1993), pp. 153–67; Jill L. Levenson, *Romeo and Juliet* (Manchester: Manchester University Press, 1987); Joseph N. Ireland, *Records of the New York Stage, from 1750 to 1860*, 2 vols. (New York: T. H., Morrell, 1867); and George C. D. Odell, *Annals of the New York Stage*, vol. 1. See too: William Winter, *Shakespeare on the Stage*, 2nd series (New York: Moffat, Yard and Co., 1915), p. 201.

On Charlotte Cushman's life and theatrical career, see Cushman Papers, in the Library of Congress, including the scrapbook she kept of reviews of her London debut as Romeo; Clara Clement, *Charlotte Cushman* (Boston: Osgood and Co., 1882); Emma Stebbins, *Charlotte Cushman: Her Letters and Memories of Her Life* (Boston: Houghton, Osgood, 1878); Lawrence Barrett, *Charlotte Cushman* (New York: The Dunlap Society, 1889), which includes an appendix on the roles she played; Joseph Leach, *Bright Particular Star: The Life & Times of Charlotte Cushman* (New Haven: Yale University Press, 1970); Lisa Merrill, *When Romeo Was a Woman: Charlotte Cushman and Her Circle of Female Spectators* (Ann Arbor: University of Michigan Press, 1999); Sharon Marcus, *Between Women: Friendship, Desire, and Marriage in Victorian England*

(Princeton: Princeton University Press, 2007); and Susan S. Cole, "Charlotte Saunders Cushman," *Notable Women in the American Theatre: A Biographical Dictionary*, ed. Alice M. Robinson, Vera Mowry Roberts, and Milly S. Barranger (New York: Greenwood Press, 1989); and for Cushman's diary, see Charlotte Cushman, "Diary" 1844–45, Dramatic Museum Collection, Rare Book and Manuscript Library, Columbia University. For her success in breeches parts, see the letter of W. E. Burton quoted in Leach, p. 130: and for her other roles, see the appendix to Barrett's *Charlotte Cushman*. For Grant going to seeing Cushman perform, see Library of Congress, Charlotte Cushman papers, 1823–1941, Bound Correspondence, 1824–1876, box 6, no. 1751.

On the reception of Cushman's Romeo, see: Elizabeth M. Puknat, "Romeo Was a Lady: Charlotte Cushman's London Triumph," *Theatre Annual* 51 (1951), pp. 59–69; George Fletcher, *Studies of Shakespeare* (London: Longman, Brown, Green, and Longmans, 1847), pp. 378–82; Yvonne Shafer, "Women in Male Roles: Charlotte Cushman and others," in *Women in American Theatre*, ed. Helen Krich Chinoy and Linda Walsh Jenkins, 3rd ed. (New York: Theatre Communications Group, 2006), pp. 65–72; Anne Russell, "Gender, Passion, and Performance in Nineteenth-Century Women Romeos," *Essays in Theatre* 11 (1993), pp. 153–67, and her "Tragedy, Gender, Performance: Women as Tragic Heroes on the Nineteenth-Century Stage," *Comparative Drama* 30 (Summer, 1996), pp. 135–157; Elizabeth Reitz Mullenix, *Wearing the Breeches: Gender on the Antebellum Stage* (New York: St. Martin's Press, 2000); and Denise A. Walen, "'Such a Romeo as We Had Never Ventured to Hope For': Charlotte Cushman," in *Passing Performances: Queer Readings of Leading Players in American Theater History*, eds. Robert A. Schanke and Kim Marra (Ann Arbor: University of Michigan Press, 1998).

For contemporary commentary on and reviews of her Romeo from which I quote, see William Winter, *Other Days: Being Chronicles and Memories of the Stage* (New York: Moffat, Yard and Co., 1908); "Theaters and Music," *John Bull*, January 3, 1846; the London *Times*, December 15, 1845; the *Athenaeum*, January 4, 1846; *Morning Chronicle*, December 30, 1845; *English Gentleman*, January 3, 1846; on her mind becoming masculine, London *Observer*, March 2, 1845; *New York Evening Post*, May 14, 1850; *Spirit of the Times*, July 4, 1846, and June 12, 1858; and "Amusements," *New York Times*, November 16, 1860.

For Queen Victoria's response, see George Rowell, *Queen Victoria Goes to the Theatre* (London: P. Elek, 1978), p. 74; on there being no trick to her Romeo, see "Sheridan Knowles' Criticism of Miss Cushman's Romeo," rpt. in the Baltimore *Sun*, June 27, 1846; John Coleman, *Fifty Years of an Actor's Life*, 2 vols. (New York: James Pott and Co., 1904); for how she prepared for the part, see especially: George Vandenhoff, *Leaves from an Actor's Note-book* (New York: D. Appleton and Co., 1860), pp. 217–18; George William Bell's essay, cited in Walen, p. 47; on her relationships with Forrest and Macready, see, in addition to the modern biographies, Karl Kippola's excellent *Acts of Manhood: The Performance of Masculinity on the American Stage, 1828–1865* (New York: Palgrave Macmillan, 2012) and Vandenhoff. I am also indebted to Richard Foulkes's fine *Dictionary of National Biography* entry on Macready. And for the poem likening Cushman to Macready, see Dutton Cook, *Hours with the Players* (London: Chatto and Windus, 1881); the poem was written for *Almanack of the Month*). On the crowds that came to see her at the end of her career, see the *New York Herald*, October 15, 1850.

On Cushman's status as an American actor, see Charles H. Shattuck, *Shakespeare on the American Stage*; see too, Lisa Merrill, *When Romeo Was a Woman*. On her Romeo as a "dangerous young man," see J. M. W. [Jessie Meriton White?], "First Impressions of Miss Cushman's Romeo," *People's Journal*, vol. 2, ed. John Saunders (London: People's Journal Office, 1847). And for Cushman's own recollections of the role, see La Salle Corbell Pickett, *Across My Path: Memories of People I Have Known* (New York: Brentano's, 1916). I am indebted to Olivia Ball's MA Columbia University essay, "'I am the man': Charlotte Cushman, America's Shakespearean Actress" (2017). See as well: Gay Smith, *Lady Macbeth in America: From the Stage to the White House* (New York: Palgrave, 2010), pp. 95–104. And on gender and cross-dressing in nineteenth-century theater more generally, see: Marjorie Garber, *Vested Interests: Cross-Dressing and Cultural Anxiety* (New York: Routledge, 1992); and Kippola, *Acts of Manhood*.

CHAPTER 3: 1849

The Astor Place riots have attracted a great deal of commentary, including a pair of fine books: Nigel Cliff, *The Shakespeare Riots: Revenge, Drama, and*

Death in Nineteenth-Century America (New York: Random House, 2007), and Richard Moody, *The Astor Place Riot* (Bloomington: Indiana University Press, 1958). For the best contemporary description of the riots, see the anonymous *Account of the Terrific and Fatal Riot at the New-York Astor Place Opera House* (New York: H. M. Ranney, 1849), rpt. in my *Shakespeare in America*, pp. 62–104, from which I quote on the laxness with which authorities treated theatrical rioting, as well as on the riots being about the rich versus the poor.

The riots (and the precipitating controversies) were extensively covered in the local, national, and international press. Many important articles have helpfully been collected in an online site: "Edwin Forrest, William Macready, and the Astor Place Riot in contemporary newspapers," http://www.merry-coz.org/voices/astor/articles.xhtml#62. For those wishing to follow up on a particular citation, use a phrase search and consult (as I have) the Library of Congress's free and invaluable website Chronicling America: Historic American Newspapers, as well as "American Historical Newspapers," part of Readex's Archive of Americana database. For the quotation about what "began in madness ended in blood," see the *New Orleans Daily Crescent*, May 21, 1849; and for the local report of how "Our city has been intensely agitated," see the *New-York Semi-Weekly Tribune*, May 16, 1849. For the events of May 7, I draw heavily on the *Weekly Herald*, May 12, 1849, and the *Boston Daily Atlas*, May 9, 1849. And for the events of May 11, including the language of the posters, I draw a great deal from the account in the *Herald* as well as (for rumors) the *Hartford Daily Courant*, May 14, 1849, and for the threatened call for police reform, the *Evening Post*, May 10, 1849. And for a pair of contemporary (if highly partisan) collections of material on the background of the theatrical controversy, see: *The Replies from England, etc., to Certain Statements Circulated in this Country Respecting Mr. Macready* (New York: Stringer and Townsend, 1849), and An American Citizen, *A Rejoinder to the Replies from England, Etc.* (New York: Stringer and Townsend, 1849), esp. pp. 110–111, from which I quote.

The Astor Place riots have also generated some first-rate historical analysis, and I have found the following especially helpful: Leo Hershkowitz, "An Anatomy of a Riot: Astor Place Opera House, 1849," *New York History* 87 (Summer 2006), pp. 277–311 (especially for suggestions about the consequences of the riots), and Peter Buckley's no less deeply researched "To the Opera

House: Culture and Society in New York City, 1820–1860" (PhD diss., State University of New York at Stony Brook, 1984), including his insights into how Astor Place was located where Broadway and the Bowery collided. Valuable chapters or articles on the riots can be found in Karl Kippola, *Acts of Manhood*; Gretchen Sween, "Rituals, Riots, Rules, and Rights: The Astor Place Theater Riot of 1849 and the Evolving Limits of Free Speech," *Texas Law Review* 81 (December 2002), pp. 679–713, including on the fallout of the riots; David Grimsted, *Melodrama Unveiled: American Theatre and Culture, 1800–1850* (Berkeley: University of California Press, 1968; rpt. 1987); Sean McEvoy, *Theatrical Unrest: Ten Riots in the History of the Stage, 1601–2004* (New York: Routledge, 2016); and Lawrence W. Levine's seminal, "William Shakespeare and the American People: A Study in Cultural Transformation," *American Historical Review*, vol. 89, (February 1984), pp. 34–66, reprinted in his *Highbrow/Lowbrow*. I have also found useful Elizabeth Williamson, "Fireboys and Burning Theatres: Performing the Astor Place Riot," *Journal of American Drama and Theatre* 25 (Winter 2013), pp. 5–26; Jerrey Ullom, "Critiquing the 'Huzza': The Historiography of the Astor Place Riot," *Journal of American Drama and Theatre* 11 (Fall 1999), pp. 16–29; and Heather Nathans, "'Blood Will Have Blood': Violence, Slavery, and *Macbeth* in the Antebellum Literary Imagination," in *Weyward Macbeth: Intersections of Race and Performance*, ed. Scott L. Newstok and Ayanna Thompson (New York: Palgrave Macmillan, 2010), pp. 35–44.

For the careers and adversarial relationship of William Macready and Edwin Forrest, see, for Macready: William Charles Macready, *The Journal of William Charles Macready, 1832–1851*, abridged and edited by J. C. Trewin (London: Longmans, 1967); *The Diaries of William Charles Macready, 1833–1851*, ed. William Toynbee (London: Chapman and Hall, 1912); Alan S. Downer, *The Eminent Tragedian: William Charles Macready* (Cambridge, MA: Harvard University Press, 1966); J. C. Trewin, *Mr Macready* (London: George G. Harrap and Co., 1955); and Richard Foulkes's entry in the *Oxford Dictionary of National Biography*. For Forrest, see: James Rees, *The Life of Edwin Forrest, with Reminiscences and Personal Recollections* (Philadelphia: T. B. Peterson and Brothers, 1874); William Rounseville Alger, *Life of Edwin Forrest, the American Tragedian* (Philadelphia: J. B. Lippincott, 1877); Lawrence Barrett, *Edwin*

Forrest (Boston: J. R. Osgood, 1881); Richard Moody, *Edwin Forrest, First Star of the American Stage* (New York: Knopf, 1960); and Montrose Moses, *The Fabulous Forrest: the Record of an American Actor* (Boston: Little, Brown, 1929). For how each performed Macbeth, I have drawn on many reviews readily available in historical newspapers, including *The Musical World*, September 4, 1845, and the *Theatrical Examiner*, October 4, 1835, from which I quote. Downer's study of Macready is also very helpful on this (esp. pp. 71–78), as are Lawrence Barrett's and Noah Ludlow's recollections. For Forrest's death, see the *Manchester Guardian*, January 14, 1873, and for Forrest's patriotic remarks in Kentucky, see the *Louisville Morning Courier*, October 13, 1846. For the recommendation to see Macready's farewell tour, see the *Albion: A Journal of News, Politics and Literature*, May 5, 1849, p. 212. For Hamlet running mad, see Anthony Scoloker, *Daiphantus* (London, 1604), sig. A2r, as well as *Eastward Ho!* (1605) where a character says, "Sfoot, Hamlet, Are you mad? Whither run you now?" (3.2.8).

For rioting in antebellum New York City, see: Joel Tyler Headley, *The Great Riots of New York, 1712–1873* (New York: E. B. Treat, 1873), esp. p. 114, from which I quote; Paul A. Gilje, *The Road to Mobocracy: Popular Disorder in New York City, 1763–1834* (Chapel Hill: University of North Carolina Press, 1987), from which I draw on the number of riots between 1816 and 1834; and David Grimsted, "Rioting in Its Jacksonian Setting," *American Historical Review* 77 (April 1972), pp. 361–397. On the Farren Riot, I have drawn on Theodore Shank, "The Bowery Theatre, 1826–1836" (PhD diss., Stanford University, 1956), pp. 378–84; Gilje, *The Road to Mobocracy;* Bruce A. McConachie, "'The Theatre of the Mob': Apocalyptic Melodrama and Preindustrial Riots in Antebellum New York," in Bruce A. McConachie and Daniel Friedman eds., *Theatre for the Working-Class Audiences in the United States, 1980–1980* (Westport, CT: Greenwood, 1985), pp. 17–46; Linda K. Kerber, "Abolitionists and Amalgamators: The New York City Race Riots of 1834," *New York History* 48 (January, 1967), pp. 28–39; Herbert Asbury, "That Was New York: The Abolition Riots of 1834," *New Yorker*, November 5, 1932; and *Evening Star*, January 18, 1834. For Rynders, see Tyler Anbinder, "Isaiah Rynders and the Ironies of Popular Democracy in Antebellum New York," in *Contested Democracy: Freedom, Race, and Power in American History*, eds. Manisha Sinha and Penny Von Eschen (New York: Columbia University Press, 2007), pp. 31–53. See too his obituary in the *New York Times*, January 14, 1885. For Ned Buntline, see Jay Monaghan, *The Great Rascal: The Life and Adventures of Ned Buntline* (Boston: Little, Brown and Co., 1952), from which I quote from *Ned Buntline's Own* (p. 172). And for nineteenth-century interpretations of *Hamlet* (and what "idle" meant, see H. H. Furness, *Hamlet*, A New Variorum edition of Shakespeare, 2 vols. (Philadelphia: J. B. Lippincott, 1877).

For the social and economic history of New York City at this time, see, for contemporary perspectives: Edmund M. Blunt, *Stranger's Guide to the City of New-York* (New York, J. Seymour, 1817); Ezekiel Porter Belden, *New-York, Past, Present, and Future: Comprising a History of the City of New-York* (New York: G. P. Putnam, 1849); and Seth Low, *New York in 1850 and 1890* (New York: New York Historical Society, 1892). See too: the *History of Wages in the United States from Colonial Times to 1928. Revision of Bulletin No. 499 with Supplement, 1929–1933* (Washington, DC: United States Government Printing Office, 1934); and Luc Sante, *Low-Life: Lures and Snares of Old New York* (New York: Farrar, Straus and Giroux, 1991). I have found Sean Wilentz's *Chants Democratic: New York City and the Rise of the American Working Class, 1788–1850* (New York: Oxford University Press, 1984) exceptionally helpful, and I quote from p. 327.

On theater culture in antebellum New York, see Thomas Allston Brown, *A History of the New York Stage from the First Performance in 1732 to 1901*, 3 vols. (New York: Dodd, Mead and Co., 1903); Don B. Wilmeth and C. W. E. Bigsby, *The Cambridge History of American Theatre: Beginnings to 1870* (New York: Cambridge University Press, 1998); Rosemary K. Bank, *Theatre Culture in America, 1825–1860* (New York: Cambridge University Press, 1997); Bruce A. McConachie, *Melodramatic Formations: American Theatre and Society, 1820–1870* (Iowa City: University of Iowa Press, 1992); Robert G. Allen, *Horrible Prettiness: Burlesque and American Culture* (Chapel Hill: University of North Carolina Press, 1991); Barry Witham, *Theatre in the United States: 1750–1915* (Cambridge: Cambridge University Press, 1996); and Eric Lott, *Love and Theft: Blackface Minstrelsy and the American Working Class* (New York: Oxford University Press, 1993). For a useful account of the various theaters, see Mary C. Henderson, *The City and the Theatre: The History of New York Playhouses: A 250 Year*

Journey from Bowling Green to Times Square, foreword by Gerald Schoenfeld, rev. and expanded ed. (New York: Back Stage Books, 2004). I have relied heavily on volume 5 of George C. D. Odell's invaluable *Annals of the New York Stage*. See too, William Winter, *Shakespeare on the Stage*, 2nd series. And for Alexis de Tocqueville, see *Democracy in America*, vol. 3, chapter 19, "Some Observations on the Drama amongst Democratic Nations," pp. 163–73.

On the Opera House and its environs, see: *Spirit of the Times*, February 6, 1847; *Home Journal*, November 13, 1847; *New York Herald*, November 23, 1847; *Squints through an Opera Glass, by a Young Gent. Who Hadn't Anything Else to Do*, 2nd ed. (New York: Merchants' Day-Book, 1850); George G. Foster, *New York Naked* (New York: De Witt and Davenport, 1851); Edmund T. Delaney, *New York's Greenwich Village: A Retrospective View of Things Past with an Appreciation of the Good and Vital in the Village Today* (Barre, MA: Barre Publishers, 1968), pp. 82–87; and Terry Miller, *Greenwich Village and How It Got that Way* (New York: Crown, 1990). And for the lyrics on the upscale Opera House, see "Pompey's Rambles," in *White's New Book of Plantation Melodies* (n.d.), pp. 15–16, quoted by Lott, *Love and Theft*, p. 65.

For the buildings in and around Astor Place, see Luther S. Harris, *Around Washington Square: An Illustrated History of Greenwich Village* (Baltimore: Johns Hopkins University Press, 2003); Edwin G. Burrow and Mike Wallace, *Gotham: A History of New York City to 1898* (New York: Oxford University Press, 1999); John R. G. Hassard, "The New York Mercantile Library," *Scribner's Monthly* (February 1871), pp. 353–67; Alex Madsen, *John Jacob Astor: America's First Multimillionaire* (New York: John Wiley and Sons, 2001); Tyler Anbinder, *Five Points: The Nineteenth Century New York City Neighborhood that Invented Tap Dance, Stole Elections, and Became the World's Most Notorious Slum* (New York: Free Press, 2001); and Eric Homberger, *Mrs. Astor's New York: Money and Social Power in a Gilded Age* (New Haven: Yale University Press, 2002). For Central Park, see Roy Rosenzweig and Elizabeth Blackmar, *The Park and the People: A History of Central Park* (Ithaca, NY: Cornell University Press, 1992), p. 18.

Thousands of New Yorkers witnessed the riots and quite a few recorded their recollections of them. Those I have found especially useful include: William Knight Northall, *Before and Behind the Curtain, or Fifteen Years'*

Observations Among the Theatres of New York (New York: W. F. Burgess, 1851), including remarks on how aristocrats tried to cover up their involvement; Noah Ludlow, *Dramatic Life as I Found It* (St. Louis: G. I. Jones and Co., 1880); George Templeton Strong, *Diary of George Templeton Strong*, eds. Allan Nevins and Milton Halsey Thomas (New York: Macmillan, 1952); George W. Walling, *Recollections of a New York Chief of Police* (New York: Caxton Book Concern, Ltd. 1887); Philip Hone, *The Diary of Philip Hone, 1828–1851*, ed. Bayard Tuckerman (New York: Dodd, Mead and Co. 1889), which I quote for details of the Farren Riot; John Coleman, *Fifty Years of an Actor's Life*; Thomas Addis Emmett, *Incidents of My Life* (New York: G. P. Putnam's Sons, 1911); and Alvin Harlow, *Old Bowery Days* (New York: D. Appleton and Co., 1931). For a contemporary sermon on the rioting, see Henry W. Bellows, *A Sermon Occasioned by the Late Riot in New York, Preached in the Church of the Divine Unity, on Sunday Morning, May 13, 1849* (New York: C. S. Francis, 1849).

For Melville and the Astor Place riots, see Dennis Berthold, "Class Acts: The Astor Place Riots and Melville's 'The Two Temples,'" *American Literature* 71 (1999), pp. 429–61 (one of a number of critics who discuss the slurs on Frederick Douglass and Pete Williams); John Evelev, *Tolerable Entertainment: Herman Melville and Professionalism in Antebellum New York* (Amherst: University of Massachusetts Press, 2006); and Harry Brinton Henderson III, "Young America and the Astor Place Riot" (MA thesis, Columbia University, 1963). On a future American Shakespeare, see too Melville's review, "Hawthorne and His Mosses," *The Literary World*, August 17 and 24, 1850.

For citations on the aftermath and afterlife of Astor Place, see Buckley; the *Alexandria Gazette*, May 15, 1849; the Philadelphia *Public Ledger*, May 16, 1849; and the *New York Courier and Enquirer*, May 15, 1849. Nathaniel Parker Willis's "After-Lesson of the Astor-Place Riot" was published in *Home Journal*, May 26, 1849, which he edited; I also quote from it earlier, regarding "the spontaneous cohesion of interest and sympathy which alone binds a republic." Henry James's reflections are quoted from a review of "Macready's Reminiscences" in the *Nation* 20 (1875), pp. 297–98. I rely on online sources for the recent history of Astor Place and rioting there: "The Ghosts of Clinton Hall: Riots, Fire, and Scandal on Astor Place," Kate Drew, http://bedfordandbowery.com/2015/12/the-ghosts-of-clinton-hall-riots-fire-and-scandal-on-astor-place, December 23, 2015; for Kushner, https://ny.curbed.com/2011/1/14/10487002/ivanka-trumps-hubby-puts-astor-place-pad-on-the-market; and for the recent riot, https://www.dnainfo.com/new-york/20120415/greenwich-village-soho/anarchists-attack-cops-starbucks-noho-police-say.

CHAPTER 4: 1865

The literature on Booth and Lincoln (and their relationship to Shakespeare) is enormous. I have relied heavily on four superb studies of Booth: Arthur F. Loux, *John Wilkes Booth: Day by Day* (Jefferson, NC: McFarland and Co., Inc., 2014); Deirdre L. Kincaid's exhaustively researched account of his theatrical career, "'Rough Magic': The Theatrical Life of John Wilkes Booth" (PhD diss., University of Hull, 2000); for Booth's own words, John Wilkes Booth, *Right or Wrong, God Judge Me: The Writings of John Wilkes Booth*, eds. John Rhodehamel and Louise Taper (Urbana: University of Illinois Press, 1997); and the recent and definitive biography: Terry Alford, *Fortune's Fool: The Life of John Wilkes Booth* (New York: Oxford University Press, 2015). BoothieBarn.com is also an invaluable resource. Alford also edited and introduced the rich mine of information about Booth's life provided by his sister, Asia Booth Clarke, *John Wilkes Booth: A Sister's Memoir* (Jackson: University Press of Mississippi, 1996). I have also consulted its posthumously published original, *The Unlocked Book: A Memoir of John Wilkes Booth by His Sister Asia Booth Clarke* (New York: G. P. Putnam's Sons, 1938). Asia had no plans to publish it in her lifetime and kept the manuscript from her husband, who would surely have destroyed it. She gave it for safekeeping to an English friend, B. L. Farjeon, whose daughter Eleanor finally published it in 1938. See too: Asia Booth, *Passages, Incidents, and Anecdotes in the Life of Junius Brutus Booth (The Elder) by His Daughter* (New York: Henry L. Hinton, 1870). Other important studies are: John F. Andrews, "Was the Bard Behind It? Old Light on the Lincoln Assassination," *Atlantic* (October 1990); John Andrews and Dwight Pitcaithley, "Cry Havoc," *New York Times*, February 19, 2011; Nora Titone, *My Thoughts Be Bloody: The Bitter Rivalry between Edwin and John Wilkes Booth that Led to an American Tragedy* (New York: Free Press, 2010); Stephen M. Archer, *Junius Brutus Booth: Theatrical Prometheus* (Carbondale:

Southern Illinois University Press, 2010); Michael W. Kauffman, *American Brutus: John Wilkes Booth and the Lincoln Conspiracies* (New York: Random House, 2004); Gene Smith, *American Gothic: The Story of America's Legendary Theatrical Family—Junius, Edwin, and John Wilkes Booth* (New York: Simon and Schuster, 1992); Stanley Kimmel, *The Mad Booths of Maryland* (Indianapolis: Bobbs-Merrill Co., 1940); Edwina Booth Grossman, *Edwin Booth: Recollections of His Daughter* (New York: Century Co., 1902); Eleanor Ruggles, *Prince of Players: Edwin Booth* (New York: W. W. Norton, 1953); and Coppélia Kahn, "Junius Brutus Booth," in *A New Literary History of America*, ed. Greil Marcus and Werner Sollors (Cambridge, MA: Harvard University Press, 2009). For the assassination, I have also relied on Frank J. Williams and Michael Burkhimer, eds., *The Lincoln Assassination Riddle: Revisiting the Crime of the Nineteenth Century* (Kent, OH: Kent State University Press, 2016); Thomas A. Bogar, *Backstage at the Lincoln Assassination: The Untold Story of the Actors and Stagehands at Ford's Theatre* (Washington, DC: Regnery History, 2013); and Edward Steers, Jr., *Lincoln's Assassination* (Carbondale: Southern Illinois University Press, 2014). For Charles Wyndham on John Wilkes's Hamlet, see Gordon Samples, *Lust for Fame: The Stage Career of John Wilkes Booth* (Jefferson, NC: McFarland and Co., 1982), p. 113.

For the "Lost Cause" of the Confederacy, see Edward Alfred Pollard, *The Lost Cause: A New Southern History of the War of the Confederates* (New York: E. B. Treat and Co., 1866), esp. pp. 744–52, as well as Pollard's *The Lost Cause Regained* (New York: G. W. Carleton and Co., 1868); Rollin G. Osterweis, *The Myth of the Lost Cause* (Hamden, CT: Archon Books, 1973); Gary W. Gallagher and Alan T. Noland, eds., *The Myth of the Lost Cause and Civil War History* (Bloomington: Indiana University Press, 2000); William C. Davis, *The Cause Lost: Myths and Realities of the Confederacy* (Lawrence: University Press of Kansas, 1996); and Gaines M. Foster, *Ghosts of the Confederacy: Defeat, the Lost Cause, and the Emergence of the New South, 1865 to 1913* (New York: Oxford University Press, 1987). For Henry Timrod, see Christina Murphy, "The Artistic Design of Societal Commitment: Shakespeare and the Poetry of Henry Timrod," *Shakespeare and Southern Writers: A Study of Influence*, ed. Philip C. Kolin (Jackson: University Press of Mississippi, 1985). Henry Timrod's poem circulated widely in the Confederacy, appearing in the *Southern*

Literary Messenger, the *Charleston Daily Courier,* the *Southern Illustrated News,* and the *Magnolia Weekly.* For Mary Preston, see her *Studies in Shakspeare: A Book of Essays* (Philadelphia: Claxton, Remsen, and Haffelfinger, 1869). For the (apparently only) review of Mary Preston's book, see the *Aegis and Intelligencer* for Friday, May 7, 1869, written by "C." from "Vineyard, Harford C., Md." I have also drawn on William R. Taylor, *Cavalier and Yankee: The Old South and American National Character* (New York: Braziller, 1961; rpt. New York: Oxford University Press, 1993).

For Booth's formative experience of Shakespeare, see especially Alford, as well as Asia's recollections in *John Wilkes Booth: A Sister's Memoir;* for Edwin's view of his brother, see his letter to Nahum Capen of July 28, 1881, quoted in that volume. And for Alfriend's recollections, see "John Wilkes Booth: The Recollections of Him by an Early Acquaintance," Baltimore *Sun,* October 13, 1901, rpt. in Edward M. Alfriend, "Recollections of John Wilkes Booth," *The Era* 8 (October 1901), pp. 603–605. For more on Booth's affinity for the role of Brutus, see: George Alfred Townsend, *The Life, Crime, and Capture of John Wilkes Booth* (New York: Pick and Fitzgerald, 1865), p. 40. And for praise of Booth as a Brutus, see as well: Portland (Maine) *Daily Eastern Argus,* April 17, 1865, and the *Evening Star,* April 20, 1865.

For the background to the benefit for Shakespeare's statue in Central Park in 1864, see Asia's and Edwin's recollections as well as the *New York Daily Tribune,* April 25, 1864; "A Notable Performance," *Castle Square Theatre Magazine,* June 2, 1913; "Memorable Night on the American Stage," *San Francisco Chronicle,* July 9, 1899; and for Chester's remark, the *New York Herald,* November 26, 1864. For John Wilkes Booth's belief that Lincoln would be king, see Asia's *Memoir.* See too: Edwina Booth Grossman, *Edwin Booth: Recollections of His Daughter* (New York: Century Co., 1902), pp. 167–72. And for the arson that night, in addition to the *New York Times,* Nov 27, 1864, see Nat Brandt, *The Man Who Tried to Burn New York* (Syracuse: Syracuse University Press, 1986). On *Sic Semper Tyrannis,* see Edward Steers, Jr., "Sic Semper Terrible!" *Surratt Courier* 24 (1999), pp. 5–6. On disagreements over what Booth actually cried out, see Timothy S. Good, *We Saw Lincoln Shot: One Hundred Eyewitness Accounts* (Jackson: University Press of Mississippi, 1995), pp. 20–22.

For Booth's earlier words and threats against Lincoln, in addition to *Right or Wrong, God Judge Me: The Writings of John Wilkes Booth*, see *Personal Memoirs of Edwin A. Ely*, ed. Ambrose E. Vanderpoel (New York: Charles Francis Press, 1926), p. 231, and https://boothiebarn.com/2012/05/31/booth-at-lincolns-second-inauguration/; and for Con Murphy, see Vincent Starrett, "Lincolnana: The Assassination Premeditated," *Reedy's Mirror* 27 (February 8, 1918), pp. 77–78. Alford quotes a friend of Booth's—the actor John M. Barron—who also blamed the assassination on the theater: "the characters he assumed, all breathing death to tyrants, impelled him to do the deed" (p. 246). For Booth's racist response to hearing that Lincoln admired his acting, see George A. Townsend's recollections in the *New York World*, April 19, 1865, cited in John Hay, *Inside Lincoln's White House*, p. 325.

For accusations that Lincoln was a tyrant, and for support for Booth after the assassination, see John McKee Barr's illuminating *Loathing Lincoln: An American Tradition from the Civil War to the Present* (Baton Rouge: Louisiana State University Press, 2014), including, from p. 2, the *Texas Republican*, May 5, 1865. And for the poetic tribute to Booth, see Alfred W. Arrington, "A Tribute to John Wilkes Booth," rpt. in Francis Wilson, *John Wilkes Booth: Fact and Fiction of Lincoln's Assassination* (Boston: Houghton Mifflin Company, 1929), p. 304. See too, Thomas Reed Turner, *Beware the People Weeping: Public Opinion and the Assassination of Abraham Lincoln* (Baton Rouge: Louisiana State University Press, 1982), p. 97, for the poem "Our Brutus." For Ford's recollections, see: "Wilkes Booth's Crime: Story of the Great Tragedy as Told by John T. Ford," *Louisville Courier Journal*, June 20, 1878. For Lincoln as Brutus, see *Southern Illustrated News* 2 (October 31, 1863), pp. 135–36; from the August 15, 1863 issue of the London *Punch*.

The best book on Lincoln's Shakespeare is Michael Anderegg's *Lincoln and Shakespeare* (Lawrence, KS: University Press of Kansas, 2015). I have also found helpful: Tim McNeese, "'I Must Have Some Relief or It Will Kill Me': Abraham Lincoln's Reliance on Shakespeare," *Journal of the Wooden O Symposium* 11 (2011), pp. 113–29; Fred Kaplan, *Lincoln: The Biography of a Writer* (New York: Harper, 2008); Robert Berkelman, "Lincoln's Interest in Shakespeare." *Shakespeare Quarterly* 2 (October 1951), pp. 303–312; Stephen Dickey's wonderful "Lincoln and Shakespeare," in *Shakespeare in Ameri-*

can Life, Folger Shakespeare Library, http://www.shakespeareinamerican-life.org; Joseph George, Jr., "The Night John Wilkes Booth Played before Abraham Lincoln," *Lincoln Herald* 59 (Summer 1957), pp. 11–15; Roy P. Basler, *A Touchstone for Greatness: Essays, Addresses, and Occasional Pieces about Abraham Lincoln* (Westport, CT: Greenwood Press, 1973); Paul F. Boller, Jr., "The American Presidents and Shakespeare," *White House History* 30 (Fall 2011); Robert N. Reeves, "Abraham Lincoln's Knowledge of Shakespeare," *Overland Monthly* 43 (1904), pp. 336–42, which must be cited with caution, as Reeves has a tendency to embellish; R. Gerald McMurtry, "Lincoln Knew Shakespeare," *Indiana Magazine of History* 31 (1935), pp. 265–77; John C. Briggs, "Steeped in Shakespeare," *Claremont Review of Books* 9 (Winter 2008/2009); and David Bromwich, "Shakespeare, Lincoln, and Ambition," *New York Review of Books*, April 11, 2014.

For general studies of Lincoln and the Civil War that have also shaped my thinking, see: Eric Foner, *The Fiery Trial: Abraham Lincoln and American Slavery* (New York: W. W. Norton, 2010); Edmund Wilson, *Patriotic Gore: Studies in the Literature of the American Civil War* (New York: Farrar, Straus and Giroux, 1962); Joshua Wolf Shenk, *Lincoln's Melancholy: How Depression Challenged a President and Fueled His Greatness* (Boston: Houghton Mifflin, 2005); Doris Kearns Goodwin, *Team of Rivals: The Political Genius of Abraham Lincoln* (New York: Simon and Schuster, 2005); Adam Gopnik, *Angels and Ages: A Short Book about Darwin, Lincoln, and Modern Life* (New York: Knopf, 2009); and Elizabeth Brown Pryor, *Six Encounters with Lincoln: A President Confronts Democracy and Its Demons* (New York: Viking, 2017).

For what Lincoln is recorded as saying, see *Recollected Words of Abraham Lincoln*, eds. Don E. Fehrenbacher and Virginia Fehrenbacher (Stanford: Stanford University Press, 1996), and for his speeches, *The Collected Works of Abraham Lincoln*, ed. Roy Prentice Basler, 11 vols. (New Brunswick: Rutgers University Press, 1953–1990). For what was reported to Herndon, see Douglas L. Wilson, Rodney O. Davis, Terry Wilson, William Henry Herndon, and Jesse W. Weik, *Herndon's Informants: Letters, Interviews, and Statements about Abraham Lincoln* (Urbana: University of Illinois Press, 1998); and *Herndon on Lincoln: Letters*, ed. Douglas L. Wilson and Rodney O. Davis (Urbana: Knox College Lincoln Studies Center and the University of Illinois Press, 2016); and

William H. Herndon and Jesse W. Weik, *Herndon's Lincoln: The True Story of a Great Life* (Chicago: Belford, Clarke, and Co., 1889). See Anderegg, *Lincoln and Shakespeare* (p. 114) for what Secretary of State Seward reported about Lincoln telling Charlotte Cushman in 1861 of his admiration for *Macbeth*.

For recollections of Lincoln's reading Shakespeare aloud, see *Lincoln and the Civil War in the Diaries and Letters of John Hay*, ed. Tyler Dennett (New York, Dodd, Mead and Co., 1939); *Inside Lincoln's White House: The Complete Civil War Diary of John Hay*, ed. Michael Burlingame and John R. Turner Ettlinger (Carbondale: Southern Illinois University Press, 1999); John Hay, "Abraham Lincoln: Life in the White House in the Time of Lincoln," *Century Magazine* (November 1890), pp. 33–37; *At Lincoln's Side: John Hay's Civil War Correspondence and Selected Writings*, ed. Michael Burlingame (Carbondale: Southern Illinois University Press, 2000); F. B. Carpenter, *Six Months at the White House with Abraham Lincoln* (1866), rpt. as *The Inner Life of Abraham Lincoln: Six Months at the White House* (New York: Hurd and Houghton, 1868); James Edward Murdoch and J. Bunting, *The Stage: Or, Recollections of Actors and Acting from an Experience of Fifty Years* (Philadelphia: J. M. Stoddart, 1880); Egbert L. Viele, "A Trip with Lincoln, Chase and Stanton," *Scribner's Monthly* (October 1878), pp. 813–823; John W. Forney, *Anecdotes of Public Men*, 2 vols. (New York: Harper and Brothers, 1881), vol. 2, pp. 180–81; Adolphe de Pineton, Marquis de Chambrun, *Impressions of Lincoln and the Civil War: A Foreigner's Account* (New York: Random House, 1952), pp. 82–86, and his "Personal Recollections of Mr. Lincoln," *Scribner's Magazine* (January 1893), pp. 26–39; David Homer Bates, *Lincoln Stories* (New York: William Edwin Rudge, 1926), pp. 44–45; Auguste Laugel, "A Portion of the Diary of August Laugel," translated in the *Nation* 75 (July 31, 1902), p. 88, as well as Laugel, *The United States During the War* (New York: Ballière Brothers, 1866), pp. 278–79; Le Grand B. Cannon to Herndon, October 7, 1889, in *Herndon's Informants*; William O. Stoddard, *Inside the White House in War Times: Memoirs and Reports of Lincoln's Secretary*, ed. Michael Burlingame (Lincoln: University of Nebraska Press, 2010), pp. 105–6; and for John McDonough's visit to the White House, see William D. Kelley, in *Reminiscences of Abraham Lincoln by Distinguished Men of His Time*, ed. Allen Thorndike Rice (New York, North American Review, 1888), pp. 262–66.

For Lincoln's early life and interest in reading Shakespeare, I draw on: "Mr. Lincoln's Early Life," *New York Times*, September 4, 1864 (for his limited schooling); David J. Harkness and R. Gerald McMurtry, *Lincoln's Favorite Poets* (Knoxville: University of Tennessee Press, 1959); Earl Schenck Miers, et. al., eds., *Lincoln Day by Day: A Chronology, 1809–1865*, 3 vols. (Dayton, OH: Morningside, 1991); for his use of Scott, see, in addition to Anderegg: Louis Austin Warren, *Lincoln's Youth: Indiana Years, Seven to Twenty-One, 1816–1830* (New York: Appleton, Century, Crofts, 1959), p. 76; Robert Bray, *Reading with Lincoln* (Carbondale: Southern Illinois University Press, 2010); and for the anecdote about Lincoln's bookseller, see the *New York Herald*, February 20, 1861. For Lincoln as theatergoer: see Leonard Grover, "Glimpses of Lincoln in War Time," *Century Magazine* (January 1895), pp. 457–467, as well as his "Lincoln's Interest in the Theater," *Century Magazine* (April 1909), pp. 943–950; Bogar, *American Presidents Attend the Theatre*; and for the story of Lincoln's reaction to Forrest's criticism in the theater, see William J. Ferguson, "I Saw Lincoln Shot! And Here is My Story—Told Now for the First Time," *American Magazine* (August 1920). On Lincoln's visit to Richmond, see: Margarita Spalding Gerry, ed., William H. Crook, *Through Five Administrations: Reminiscences of Colonel William H. Crook*, pp. 58–59; *Recollected Words of Abraham Lincoln*, pp. 256–57; Elizabeth Keckley, *Behind the Scenes: Thirty Years a Slave, and Four Years in the White House* (1868: rpt., Buffalo, NY: Stansil and Lee, 1931), p. 168; and Edward L. Pierce, *Memoir and Letters of Charles Sumner* (Boston, Roberts Brothers, 1894). And to discover what plays were staged in the nation's capital on any given night, see that day's *Washington Evening Star*.

For Lincoln's afterlife and Shakespeare's role in it, see: Merrill D. Peterson, *Lincoln in American Memory* (New York: Oxford University Press, 1994); Martha Elizabeth Hodes, *Mourning Lincoln* (New Haven: Yale University Press, 2015); Richard Wightman Fox, *Lincoln's Body: A Cultural History* (New York: W. W. Norton, 2015); and Benjamin Brown French, *Witness to the Young Republic: A Yankee's Journal, 1828–1870*, eds. Donald B. Cole and John J. McDonough (Hanover, NH: University Press of New England, 1989), p. 52. See too Rev. Pliny H. White, *A Sermon, Occasioned by the Assassination of Abraham Lincoln, President of the United States*, April 23, 1865, Coventry, Vermont (Brattleboro: Vermont Record Office, 1865); Alexander H. Stephens, *Recollections of Alexander H. Stephens: His Diary Kept When a Prisoner at Fort Warren, Boston Harbour, 1865, Giving Incidents and Reflections of His Prison Life and Some Letters and Reminiscences*, ed. Myrta Lockett Avary (New York: Doubleday, Page, 1910), p. 552; William R. Williams, et al., *Our Martyr President, Abraham Lincoln: Voices from the Pulpit of New York and Brooklyn* (New York: Tibbals and Whiting, 1865); John Carroll Power, *Abraham Lincoln: His Life, Public Services, Death and Great Funeral Cortege* (Chicago: H. W. Rokker, 1889), 145; B. F. Morris, *Memorial Record of the Nation's Tribute to Abraham Lincoln* (Washington, DC, 1865), 183; Michael Burlingame, *Abraham Lincoln: A Life*, online edition, 2 vols. (Baltimore: Johns Hopkins University Press, 2008), 2: chap. 36, p. 4055, http:// www.knox.edu/about-knox/lincoln-studies-center/burlingame-abraham-lincoln-a-life; and "Fanny Seward's Diary," transcript, p. 195, "Lincoln and His Circle," University of Rochester Rare Books and Special Collections, https://rbscp.lib.rochester.edu/lincoln/fanny-seward-diary/entry?Print=436.

For Jefferson Davis's alleged echo of *Macbeth*, see John Armor Bingham, Mary E. Surratt, David E. Herold, Lewis Payne, George A. Atzerodt, Michael O'Laughlin, Samuel Alexander Mudd, Edward Spangler, and Samuel Arnold, *Trial of the Conspirators, for the Assassination of President Lincoln* (Washington, DC: Government Printing Office, 1865). For the quotation about Duncan from Holinshed's *Chronicles*, see Raphael Holinshed, *The First and Second Volumes of Chronicles*, "The Historie of Scotland" (London, 1587), p. 168. Booth's claim that America was formed for the white man appears in an undated letter from around November, 1864, "To Whom It May Concern," that he wrote justifying the kidnapping plot, in *Right or Wrong, God Judge Me*, pp. 124–30.

CHAPTER 5: 1916

I'm indebted to the pathbreaking work of two friends on Percy MacKaye's *Caliban by the Yellow Sands* in the context of immigration: Thomas Cartelli's *Repositioning Shakespeare*, and Coppélia Kahn's "Caliban at the Stadium: Shakespeare and the Making of Americans," *Massachusetts Review* 41 (2000), pp. 256–84.

For the stage history of *The Tempest* in America and Britain, see Virginia Mason Vaughan and Alden T. Vaughan, ed. *The Tempest*, The Arden Shakespeare (London: Thomas Nelson, 1999); David Lindley, ed., *The Tempest*, The New Cambridge Shakespeare (Cambridge: Cambridge University Press, 2002); Alden T. Vaughan and Virginia Mason Vaughan, *Shakespeare's Caliban: A Cultural History* (Cambridge: Cambridge University Press, 1991); Mary M. Nilan, "*The Tempest* at the Turn of the Century: Cross Currents in Production," *Shakespeare Survey* 25 (1972), pp. 113–23; Christine Dymkowski, ed., *The Tempest*, Shakespeare in Production (Cambridge: Cambridge University Press, 2000); Charles H. Shattuck, *Shakespeare on the American Stage*, vol. 2 (Washington, DC: Folger Shakespeare Library, 1987); and Trevor R. Griffith, "'This Island's Mine': Caliban and Colonialism," *The Yearbook of English Studies* 13 (1983), pp. 159–80. And for the few productions across America, see the *Chicago Times*, June 24, 1889; the *Louisville Courier Journal*, November 11, 1902; the *Washington Post*, May 19, 1906; the *New York Times*, May 7, 1916; the *New-York Tribune*, March 27, 1916; and the Boston *Globe*, November 18, 1928. For an influential Darwinian take on Caliban, see Daniel Wilson, *Caliban: The Missing Link* (London: Macmillan and Co., 1873). Benson's trip to the zoo is recounted in Lady Benson, *Mainly Players: Bensonian Memoirs* (London: Thornton Butterworth, 1926), p. 179.

For the history of *The Tempest* in connection with the New World, see Richard Sill [Charles Dirrill], *Remarks on Shakespeare's Tempest* (Cambridge: Benjamin Flowers, 1797); Edmond Malone, *An Account of the Incidents, from Which the Title and Part of the Story of Shakespeare's Tempest Were Derived* (London: C. and R. Baldwin, 1808); Charles Frey, "*The Tempest* and the New World," *Shakespeare Quarterly* 30 (Winter, 1979), pp. 29–41; Sidney Lee, "The Call of the West: America and Elizabethan England" in *Scribner's Magazine* 42 (1907), pp. 313–30, rpt. in Sidney Lee, *Elizabethan and Other Essays*, ed. Frederick S. Boas (Oxford: Clarendon Press, 1929); and Frank M. Bristol, *Shakespeare and America*. For a groundbreaking postcolonial American reading of the play, see Leslie Fiedler, *The Stranger in Shakespeare* (New York: Stein and Day, 1972).

The literature on immigration is considerable. For primary materials, I have found the Publications of the Immigration Restriction League (including numbers 1 and 15), extremely useful (facsimiles are viewable through the

Harvard University Library Open Collections Program). For more on the League, see Lillian C. Pollan, "The Immigration Restriction League: Its Impact on National Immigration Policy" (MA thesis, Columbia University, 1964). For Fiske, see *Letters of John Fiske*, ed. Ethel F. Fisk (New York: Macmillan, 1940), pp. 666–670. The studies of immigration I have drawn on most heavily are: Royal Dixon, *Americanization* (New York: Macmillan, 1916); Prescott F. Hall, "Present-Day Immigration with Special Reference to the Japanese," *The Annals of the American Academy of Political and Social Science* 93 (January 1921), pp. 190–193; Gino Speranza, *Race or Nation: A Conflict of Divided Loyalties* (Indianapolis: Bobbs-Merrill, 1925); Madison Grant and Chas. Stewart Davison, eds., *The Alien in Our Midst, or 'Selling Our Birthright for a Mess of Pottage'* (New Haven: Galton Publishing Co., 1930); Barbara Miller Solomon, "The Intellectual Background of the Immigration Restriction Movement in New England," *New England Quarterly* 25 (March 1952), pp. 47–59, as well as her *Ancestors and Immigrants: A Changing New England Tradition* (Cambridge, MA: Harvard University Press, 1956); Samuel Lubell, *The Future of American Politics,* 2nd ed. (Garden City, NY: 1956); John Higham's seminal *Strangers in the Land: Patterns of American Nativism, 1860–1925* (New Brunswick: Rutgers University Press, 1955); Robert A. Divine, *American Immigration Policy, 1924–1952* (New York: Da Capo Press, 1972); Edward P. Hutchinson, *Legislative History of American Immigration Policy* (Philadelphia: University of Pennsylvania Press, 1981); Mae M. Ngai, "The Architecture of Race in American Immigration Law: A Reexamination of the Immigration Act of 1924," *Journal of American History* 86 (1999), pp. 67–92; Desmond King, *Making Americans: Immigration, Race, and the Origins of the Diverse Democracy* (Cambridge, MA: Harvard University Press, 2000); Cheryl Shanks, *Immigration and the Politics of American Sovereignty, 1890–1990* (Ann Arbor: University of Michigan Press, 2001); Ericka Lee, *At America's Gates: Chinese Immigration During the Exclusion Era, 1882–1943* (Chapel Hill: University of North Carolina Press, 2003); Roger Daniels, *Guarding the Golden Door: American Immigration Policy and Immigrants Since 1882* (New York: Hill and Wang, 2004); Bill Ong Hing, *Defining America Through Immigration Policy* (Philadelphia: Temple University Press, 2004); Brian Gratton, "Race or Politics?: Henry Cabot Lodge and the Origins of the Immigration Restriction Movement in the United States," *Journal of Policy History* 30 (2018), pp. 128–157; Vincent Cannato, "Comments on Brian Gratton's 'Race and Politics,'" *Journal of Policy History* 30 (2018), pp. 161–164; and Joel Perlmann's outstanding *America Classifies the Immigrants: From Ellis Island to the 2020 Census* (Harvard, 2018), which deals at length with Lodge. See too: Neil Swidey, "Trump's Anti-Immigration Playbook was Written 100 Years Ago. In Boston," *Boston Globe*, February 9, 2017. See as well, *Shakespeare and Immigration*, ed. Ruben Espinosa and David Ruiter (Burlington, VT: Ashgate, 2014). See too Daniel Okrent's excellent *The Guarded Gate: Bigotry, Eugenics, and the Law That Kept Two Generations of Jews, Italians, and Other European Immigrants Out of America* (New York: Scribner, 2019), which came out too late for me to draw on in my research.

For discussions of the literacy test in particular, see Henry Pratt Fairchild, "The Literacy Test and Its Making," *Quarterly Journal of Economics* 31 (May, 1917), pp. 447–460; and Nancy C. Carnevale, "Language, Race, and the New Immigrants: The Example of Southern Italians," in *Immigration Research for a New Century: Multidisciplinary Perspectives*, eds. Nancy Foner, Rubén G. Rumbaut, and Steven J. Gold (New York: Russell Sage Foundation, 2000). For the language of the 1917 bill, see *An Act to Regulate the Immigration of Aliens to, and the Residence of Aliens in, the United States*, H.R. 10384; Pub.L. 301; 39 Stat. 874. And for President Woodrow Wilson's veto message of January 28, 1915, see Gerhard Peters and John T. Woolley, *The American Presidency Project* (https://www.presidency.ucsb.edu/documents/veto-message-0).

For Anglo-Saxonism in the United States, see A. E. Campbell, *Great Britain and the United States: 1895–1903* (London: Longmans, 1960); Reginald Horsman, *Race and Manifest Destiny*; Stuart Anderson, *Race and Rapprochement: Anglo-Saxonism and Anglo-American Relations, 1894–1904* (Rutherford, NJ: Fairleigh Dickinson University Press, 1981); Allen J. Frantzen and John D. Niles, eds., *Anglo-Saxonism and the Construction of Social Identity* (Gainsville: University Press of Florida, 1997); and David T. Gleeson, ed., *English Ethnicity and Culture in North America* (Columbus: The University of South Carolina Press, 2017). For the roots of this theory, see Richard Verstegen, *Restitution of Decayed Intelligence* (London, 1605).

For Henry Cabot Lodge, see John A. Garraty, *Henry Cabot Lodge, a Bi-*

ography (New York: Knopf, 1953), which includes the photograph of Lodge dressed as Lady Macbeth; and Karl Schriftgiesser, *The Gentleman from Massachusetts: Henry Cabot Lodge* (Boston: Little, Brown, 1944). For Lodge's interest in Shakespeare, see as well his eulogy: "Address by William Lawrence Before the Joint Session of the General Court in Memory of Henry Cabot Lodge, April 1, 1925," The Commonwealth of Massachusetts, Senate No. 431, p. 39; as well as Lodge's own *Early Memories* (New York: C. Scribner's Sons, 1913). For Lodge's letters on Shakespeare to Matthews, see the Brander Matthews Papers, 1877–1962, Columbia University, Special Collections, box numbers 13 and 14. For Lodge's writings in 1891: Lodge, "Restriction of Immigration," *North American Review* 152 (January, 1891), pp. 27–36, which Lodge had read into the Congressional Record; Lodge, "Distribution of Ability in the United States," *Century Magazine* 20 (September 1891), pp. 687–94; and Lodge, "Lynch Law and Unrestricted Immigration," *North American Review* 152 (May 1891), pp. 602–612. See too his early and anonymous "Limited Sovereignty in the United States, *Atlantic Monthly* 53 (February 1879), pp. 185–87; Henry Cabot Lodge, *Speeches by Henry Cabot Lodge* (Boston: Houghton Mifflin and Company, 1892); and Henry Cabot Lodge, ed., *Selections from the Correspondence of Theodore Roosevelt and Henry Cabot Lodge, 1884–1918*, 2 vols. (New York: Scribner, 1924), vol. 1, pp. 216–18. For Lodge on the American setting of *The Tempest*, see his introduction to Edward Everett Hale, *Prospero's Island*, Discussions of the Drama III (New York: Dramatic Museum of Columbia University, 1919).

For Edward Alsworth Ross, see his: "Racial Consequences of Immigration," *Century Illustrated Monthly Magazine* 87 (1914), pp. 615–622, rpt. in his *The Old World in the New: The Significance of Past and Present Immigration* (New York: The Century Co., 1914). See too Ross's *Social Control: A Survey of the Foundations of Order* (New York: Macmillan, 1901), p. 356, where he writes of Caliban: "Prospero busies himself with the teaching of Caliban . . . The proselyting, missionary spirit is awakened and inspires the minority to leaven the entire lump with their new idea." And for Dr. Taylor's allusion to Caliban, see the *Los Angeles Times*, December 3, 1915.

For Charles Mills Gayley, see his *Shakespeare and the Founders of Liberty in America* (New York: Macmillan, 1917). Gayley's poem "Heart of the Race" was republished in Israel Gollancz, ed., *A Book of Homage to Shakespeare* (Oxford: Oxford University Press, 1916), pp. 34–41. For my account of Gayley, I am deeply indebted to Coppélia Kahn's "Poet of America: Charles Mills Gayley's Anglo-Saxon Shakespeare," *Power, Citizenship, and Performance*, eds. Coppélia Kahn, Heather S. Nathans, and Mimi Godfrey (Newark: University of Delaware Press, 2011), pp. 201–15. See too: Benjamin P. Kurtz, *Charles Mills Gayley: The Glory of a Lighted Mind* (1943). For a critique of Gayley's book, see Elmer Edgar Stoll, "Certain Fallacies in the Literary Scholarship of the Day," *Studies in Philology* 24 (1927), pp. 485–508. For more on Shakespeare and America, see Joseph Watson, "Shakespeare in America," *New York Herald*, February 26, 1877, p. 6; Kim Sturgess, *Shakespeare and the American Nation*; and Andrew Carlson and Charlotte M. Canning, "Shakespeare, Once and Future American," *American Theatre*, August 3, 2016, https://www.americantheatre.org/2016/08/03/shakespeare-once-and-future -american/.

For the text of *Caliban*, see Percy MacKaye, *Caliban by the Yellow Sands* (Garden City, New York: Doubleday, Page and Co., 1916). For the New York program, see *The New York City Shakespeare Tercentenary Committee Presents the Community Masque of the Art of the Theatre: Caliban by the Yellow Sands, by Percy MacKaye, Produced at the Stadium of the College of the City of New York on the Evenings of May 23, 24, 25, 26, and 27, 1916*. And for responses to it, in addition to Cartelli and Kahn, see Michael Peter Mehler's outstanding dissertation, *Percy MacKaye: Spatial Formations of a National Character* (University of Pittsburgh, 2010). Monika Smialkowska has written extensively and illuminatingly on MacKaye's masque in the context of 1916. See her: "'A democratic art at a democratic price': American Celebrations of the Shakespeare Tercentenary, 1916," *Transatlantica* (2010); "Shakespeare and 'Native Americans': Forging Identities through the 1916 Shakespeare Tercentenary," *Critical Survey* 22 (2010), pp. 76–90; "Conscripting Caliban: Shakespeare, America, and the Great War," *Shakespeare* 7 (2011), pp. 192–207; "An Englishman in New York?: Celebrating Shakespeare in America, 1916," in *Locating the English Diaspora, 1500–2010*, eds. Tanja Bueltmann, David T. Gleeson, and Donald M. MacRaild (Liverpool University Press, 2012), pp. 205–21; and "Patchwork Shakespeare: Community Events at the American Shakespeare Tercentenary

(1916)," in *OuterSpeares: Shakespeare, Intermedia, and the Limits of Adaptation*, ed. Daniel Fischlin (Toronto: University of Toronto Press, 2014), pp. 321–46. See too: John Collier, "*Caliban of the Yellow Sands*: The Shakespeare Pageant and Masque Reviewed Against a Background of American Pageantry," *Survey* 36 (July 1, 1916), pp. 343–350; David Glassberg, "Restoring a 'Forgotten Childhood': American Play and the Progressive Era's Elizabethan Past," *American Quarterly* 32 (1980), pp. 351–368; Vilma Raskin Potter, "Percy MacKaye's *Caliban* for a Democracy," *Journal of American Culture* 19 (Winter 1996), pp. 71–79; and Mel Gordon, "Percy MacKaye's Masque of *Caliban*," *Tulane Drama Review* 20 (1976), pp. 93–107. For biographical background, see: Arvia MacKaye Ege, *The Power of the Impossible*: *The Life Story of Percy and Marion MacKaye* (Falmouth, ME: Kennebec River Press, 1992), and *Percy MacKaye*: *A Sketch of His Life with Bibliography of His Works*, rpt. from the *Twenty-fifth Anniversary Report of the Class of 1897* (Cambridge, MA: Harvard University Press, 1922). For MacKaye's related writings, see his *A Substitute for War* (New York: Macmillan, 1915); *The Immigrants: A Lyric Drama* (New York: Huebsch, 1915); *Saint Louis: A Civic Masque* (New York: Doubleday, Page, 1914) and *The New Citizenship* (New York: Macmillan, 1915); and "How I Came to Write Caliban," *Caliban News*, July 12, 1917. His interview with Joyce Kilmer ran in the *New York Times* on May 14, 1916. For Otto H. Kahn's remarks, see "Art and the People," *Art World* 1 (March 1917), pp. 404–407. And for Cecil Sharp's observation, see Maud Karpeles, *Cecil Sharp: His Life and Work* (London: Routledge and Kegan Paul, 1967), p. 133. For responses to *Caliban*, see: John Collier, "*Caliban of the Yellow Sands*: The Shakespeare Pageant and Masque Reviewed Against a Background of American Pageantry," *Survey* 36 (July 1, 1916), pp. 343–350; and Jane P. Franck, "*Caliban* at Lewisohn Stadium, 1916," *Shakespeare Encomium*, ed. Anne Paolucci, The City College Papers I (New York: The City College, 1964), pp. 154–68. Florence Ripley Mastin's poem "Caliban at the Stadium" first appeared in the *New York Times* on May 31, 1916, and was reprinted in her collection, *Green Leaves* (New York: James T. White and Co., 1918). For the controversy surrounding the playing of the national anthem in 1916, see the *New York Times*, July 25, 2016, and September 3, 1916. For the African American production of *Othello* in 1916, see "Negroes Give *Othello*," *New York Times*, April 25, 1916, as well as "Theatrical Jottings,"

New York Age, April 27, 1916. And for Shakespeare in Yiddish in America, see Joel Berkowitz, *Shakespeare on the American Yiddish Stage* (Iowa City: University of Iowa Press, 2002).

For the life of Joseph Quincy Adams, see the tributes to him by Stanley King and Lane Cooper in *Joseph Quincy Adams: Memorial Studies*, ed. James G. McManaway, Giles E. Dawson, and Edwin E. Willoughby (Washington, DC: Folger Shakespeare Library, 1948), as well as George L. Sioussat, *Joseph Quincy Adams (1881–1946)*, pp. 233–37, rpt. from the *Year Book of the American Philosophy Society* (1947), pp. 233–237. For his writings, see *Bibliography of Joseph Quincy Adams, 1904–1943* (Washington, DC, Privately Printed, 1943); Joseph Quincy Adams, "A Shakespeare Memorial for America," *Shakespeare Association Bulletin* 5 (1930), pp. 169–73; Joseph Q. Adams, "A Norman Origin for Shakespeare," *Sewanee Review* 29 (October 1921), pp. 386–391; and for Adams's unpublished talk on "Shakespeare and Virginia," see the bound typescript dated April 12, 1943, in the Folger Shakespeare Library, Washington, DC, MS.Add.37. Adams's inaugural talk was published in the *Spinning Wheel*, 12:9–10 (June-July 1932), pp. 229–232, and is reprinted in my anthology, *Shakespeare in America*. For a contemporary report of his talk, see James Waldo Fawcett, "Folger Library, Memorial to Shakespeare, Dedicated," *Washington Post*, April 24, 1932.

CHAPTER 6: 1948

I'm indebted to Anne Melissa Potter, a doctoral student at Columbia University, whose Master's Essay on *Kiss Me, Kate*—part of which appeared as "The Taming of 'Kiss Me, Kate,'" *American Theatre* (January 2019)—galvanized my interest in this story, and whose archival discovery of an early draft in which Katherine cross-dresses is a major contribution to our understanding of the making of the musical.

For information about early drafts of *Kiss Me, Kate* as well as the correspondence of those who created it, I have relied heavily on the Samuel and Bella Spewack Papers in the Rare Book and Manuscript Library of Columbia University Libraries. For biographical and autobiographical information that I cite, see box 100, and box 37; for letters that I quote from, see box E, box 1, and box 21; for early drafts, see the successive and mostly undated versions in box 26 and box 27. For an audio version of the 1970 BBC television program *The Making of Kiss Me, Kate*, in which Bella Spewack and Arnold Saint Subber appear, see box 136. I have also made use of "Patricia Morison, The Original Kate, Recalls the Broadway Production," an interview with Miles Kreuger, as well as Kreuger's liner notes for a CD of *Kiss Me, Kate* (London Sinfonietta and Ambrosian Chorus, EMI, 1990). Unfortunately, the Spewack archive is incomplete, for Kreuger took vital materials from Bella Spewack, which were never returned and are presumably lost; see Jess Bravin, "Musical Archivist Hits Sour Note as Lawsuit Claims He Stole Papers," *Wall Street Journal*, June 3, 1998. I have also made use of a video recording of the raw footage of Michael Kantor's 2002 interview with Patricia Morison, in the New York Public Library for the Performing Arts Research Collection, where I also consulted the annotated Lunt and Fontanne promptbook of their 1935 production of *The Taming of the Shrew*.

For the published text of *Kiss Me, Kate*, see *Kiss Me, Kate: A Musical Play*, book by Samuel and Bella Spewack, lyrics by Cole Porter (New York: Knopf, 1953); for a vocal score, see *Kiss Me, Kate*, music and lyrics by Cole Porter, book by Samuel and Bella Spewack, eds. David Charles Abell and Seann Alderking, Critical Edition (The Cole Porter Musical and Literary Property Trusts, Chappell and Co., and Artlomin, Ltd., 2014).

For a performance history of *The Taming of the Shrew*, see: *The Taming of the Shrew*, ed. Elizabeth Schafer, Shakespeare in Production (Cambridge: Cambridge University Press, 2002); *The Taming of the Shrew*, ed. Barbara Hodgdon, The Arden Shakespeare (London: Methuen Drama, 2010); and William Winter, *Shakespeare on the Stage*, 2nd series, pp. 524–38. For how unruly Elizabethan women were punished, see Linda Boose, "Scolding Brides and Bridling Scolds: Taming the Woman's Unruly Member," *Shakespeare Quarterly* 42 (Summer 1991), pp. 179–213.

For Lunt and Fontanne's production of *The Taming of the Shrew*, see George Freedley, *The Lunts* (New York: Macmillan Co., 1958); Maurice Zolotow, *Stagestruck: The Romance of Alfred Lunt and Lynn Fontanne* (New York: Harcourt, Brace and World, 1964); Jared Brown, *The Fabulous Lunts: A Biography of Alfred Lunt and Lynn Fontanne* (New York: Athenaeum, 1986); Margot Peters, *Design for Living: Alfred Lunt and Lynn Fontanne* (New York:

Knopf, 2003); Helen Ormabee, *New York Herald Tribune*, September 29, 1935; *Boston Globe*, January 22, 1936; Richard Watts, Jr., *New York Herald Tribune*, February 6, 1940; John D. Beaufort, *Christian Science Monitor*, February 6, 1940; and Burns Mantle, *New York Daily News*, February 6, 1940. See too: Sam Abel, "Staging Heterosexuality: Alfred Lunt and Lynn Fontanne's Design for Living," Robert A. Schanke and Kim Marra, eds., *Passing Performances: Queer Readings of Leading Players in American Theater History* (Ann Arbor: University of Michigan Press, 1998), pp. 175–96.

For scholarship on women, work, and domestic violence in 1940s America, I have drawn on: Maureen Honey, *Creating Rosie the Riveter: Class, Gender and Propaganda During World War II* (Amherst: University of Massachusetts Press, 1984); Kristin Celello, *Making Marriage Work: A History of Marriage and Divorce in the Twentieth-Century United States* (Chapel Hill: University of North Carolina Press, 2009); Susan M. Hartmann, *The Home Front and Beyond: American Women in the 1940s* (Boston: Twayne, 1982); Susan M. Hartmann, "Prescriptions for Penelope: Literature on Women's Obligations to Returning World War II Veterans," *Women's Studies* 5 (1978), pp. 223–39; Elaine Tyler May, *Great Expectations: Marriage and Divorce in Post-Victorian America* (Chicago: University of Chicago Press, 1980); Elaine Tyler May, *Homeward Bound: American Families in the Cold War Era* (New York: Basic Books, 1988); William Chafe, *The American Woman: Her Changing Social, Economic, and Political Roles, 1920–1970* (New York: Oxford University Press, 1972), revised as *The Paradox of Change: American Women in the 20th Century* (New York: Oxford University Press, 1991); D'Ann Campbell, *Women at War with America: Private Lives in a Patriotic Era* (Cambridge, MA: Harvard University Press, 1984); Steven Mintz and Susan Kellogg, *Domestic Revolutions: A Social History of American Family Life* (New York: Free Press, 1988); Geoffrey Perrett, *A Dream of Greatness: The American People, 1945–1963* (New York: Coward, McCann and Geoghegan, 1979); Lori Rotskoff, *Love on the Rocks: Men, Women, and Alcohol in Post-World War II America* (Chapel Hill: University of North Carolina Press, 2002); Sheryl J. Grana, *Women and (In)justice: The Criminal and Civil Effects of the Common Law on Women's Lives* (Boston: Allyn and Bacon, 2002); *America's Working Women*, ed. Rosalyn Baxandall, Linda Gordon, and Susan Reverby (New York: Vintage Books, 1976); Nancy Lemon, *Domes-*

tic Violence Law: A Comprehensive Overview of Cases and Sources (San Francisco: Austin and Winfield, 1996); David Peterson del Mar, *What Trouble I Have Seen: A History of Violence Against Wives* (Cambridge, MA: Harvard University Press, 1996); R. Emerson Dobash and Russell P. Dobash, *Women, Violence, and Social Change* (New York: Routledge, 1992); Karen Anderson, *Wartime Women: Sex Roles, Family Relations, and the Status of Women during World War II* (Westport, CT, Greenwood Press, 1981); and George Hutchinson, *Facing the Abyss: American Literature and Culture in the 1940s* (New York: Columbia University Press, 2018). For statistics on women workers, see Women's Bureau, *Women as Workers, A Statistical Guide* (Washington, DC, 1953), pp. 15–17, cited in Campbell, *Women at War*.

For contemporary discussions of these issues, I have consulted: Ferdinand Lundberg and Marynia Farnham, *Modern Woman: The Lost Sex* (New York: Harper and Brothers, 1947), and their earlier article: "Men Have Lost Their Women," *Ladies' Home Journal* 61 (November 1944), pp. 23, 132–136, 139; their influence was pervasive and provocative enough to generate an angry refutation, nearly two decades later, in Betty Friedan's *The Feminine Mystique* (New York: W. W. Norton, 1963). See as well, Joanne Meyerowitz, "Beyond the Feminine Mystique: A Reassessment of Postwar Mass Culture, 1946–1958," *Journal of American History* 79 (March 1993), pp. 1455–1482. See too: Leslie B. Hohman, "Married Strangers," *Ladies' Home Journal* (October 1944), pp. 156–57; Rudolf Dreikurs, "Getting Along in Marriage," *Ladies' Home Journal* (November 1946), p. 260; William K. Reed, Jr., "One Out of Three Breaks Up," *New Republic* (March 24, 1947), pp. 17–20; Samuel G. Kling, "Why Marriages Fail," *Better Homes and Gardens* (December 1947), pp. 46, 144–46; "Divorces: A New High for U.S.," *U.S. News & World Report* (October 4, 1946), pp. 30–31; and "Divorce: The Postwar Wave," *Newsweek* (October 7, 1946), p. 33; Douglas Larsen, "Wear and Tear on Wives Is Terrific As Men in Service Come Home and Spank Their Cares Away," *Austin Statesman* (January 26, 1946); and Alanson H. Edgerton, *Readjustment or Revolution: A Guide to Economic, Educational, and Social Readjustment of War Veterans, Ex-War Workers, and Oncoming Youth* (New York: Whittlesey House, McGraw-Hill, 1946). For Willard Waller, see his *The Veteran Comes Back* (New York: Dryden Press, 1944), *War and the Family* (New York: Dryden Press, 1940), as well as his op-ed that ran in the *New York Herald Tribune* (February 18, 1945), and also appeared in the Baltimore *Sun*, the *Los Angeles Times*, the Atlanta *Constitution*, and other national newspapers. For Eleanor Roosevelt's response, see *New York Times*, February 20, 1945, and Hartford *Courant*, February 26, 1945. See too, on male sexuality: Alfred C. Kinsey, *Sexual Behavior in the Human Male* (Philadelphia: W. B. Saunders Co., 1948).

On spanking in the play, the musical, and in midcentury American culture, see Andrew Heisel, "'I Don't Know Whether to Kiss You or Spank You': A Half Century of Fear of an Unspanked Woman," https://pictorial.jezebel. com/i-dont-know-whether-to-kiss-you-or-spank-you-a-half-ce-1769140132; Larsen, "Wear and Tear on Wives," *Austin Statesman*, January 26, 1946; and for evidence of a 1922 German production of *The Taming of the Shrew*, directed by Max Reinhardt, in which Katherine is spanked—the first recorded instance of this in a staging of the play—see https://mainstreamspanking.wordpress.com/2017/04/04/the-value-and-risks-of-wearing-a-practical-skirt/. See too: https://flashbak.com/women-being-spanked-in-vintage-comic-books-62908/ and https://mainstreamspanking.word press.com/2015/05/04/there-isnt-a-spanking-scene-in-the-taming-of-the-shrew/. See too Steven Pinker, *The Better Angels of Our Nature: Why Violence Has Declined* (New York: Viking, 2011). For the photograph accompanying Brooks Atkinson's review of the production, see the *New York Times*, December 31, 1948.

For additional biographical information on Bella Spewack, see Elizabeth Drorbaugh, "Bella Spewack," in *Jewish American Women Writers*, ed. Ann R. Shapiro (Westport, CT: Greenwood Press, 1994); and her memoir: Bella Cohen Spewack, *Streets: A Memoir of the Lower East Side*, introduction by Ruth Limmer, afterword by Lois Raeder Elias (New York: Feminist Press, 1995). And for Cole Porter, see: George Eells, *The Life that Late He Led: A Biography of Cole Porter* (London: W. H. Allen, 1967), as well as the invaluable William McBrien, *Cole Porter: A Biography* (New York: Knopf, 1998); Don M. Randel, Matthew Shaftel, and Susan Forscher Weiss, eds., *A Cole Porter Companion* (Urbana: University of Illinois Press, 2016), especially Lynn Laitman Siebert's essay on *Kiss Me, Kate*. There is no biography of Saint Subber. I am also indebted to Forrest A. Newlin, "The New York Stage Designs of Lemuel Ayers" (PhD diss., University of Nebraska, 1978).

For scholarship on *Kiss Me, Kate* and the Shakespeare Broadway musical in general, I am indebted to the brilliant essay by John R. Severn, which has shaped my thinking about the social contexts of the musical, "A (White) Woman's (Ironic) Place in *Kiss Me, Kate* and Post-war America," *Studies in Musical Theatre* 6 (2012), pp. 173–86. I have also found especially helpful: Dan Rebellato, "'No Theatre Guild Attraction Are We': *Kiss Me, Kate* and the Politics of the Integrated Musical," *Contemporary Theatre Review* 19 (2009), pp. 61–73; Geoffrey Block, *Enchanted Evenings: The Broadway Musical from 'Show Boat' to Sondheim and Lloyd Webber* (New York: Oxford University Press, 2009); Irene G. Dash, *Shakespeare and the American Musical* (Bloomington: Indiana University Press, 2010); Joseph P. Swain, *The Broadway Musical: A Critical and Musical Survey* (New York: Oxford University Press, 1990); Larry Stempel, *Showtime: A History of the Broadway Musical Theater* (New York: W. W. Norton, 2010); Carol E. Silverberg's excellent PhD dissertation, "If It's Good Enough for Shakespeare: The Bard and the American Musical" (State University of New York at Binghamton, 2009); Jennifer S. Horn's valuable PhD dissertation, "The Rehabilitation of *The Shrew*: Romance, Spankings, Feminism, and the Search for a Happy Ending in Stage and Film Adaptations of Shakespeare's Play" (University of London, 2006); Fran Teague, "Shakespeare, Beard of Avon," in Richard Burt, ed., *Shakespeare After Mass Media* (New York: Palgrave, 2002), pp. 221–42; Robert Lawson-Peebles, "Brush Up Your Shakespeare: The Case of *Kiss Me, Kate*," in *Approaches to the American Musical*, ed. Robert Lawson-Peebles (Exeter: University of Exeter Press, 1996); Andrea Most, *Making Americans: Jews and the Broadway Musical* (Cambridge, MA: Harvard University Press, 2004); Raymond Knapp, *The American Musical and the Performance of Personal Identity* (Princeton: Princeton University Press, 2006); Ethan Mordden, *Beautiful Mornin': The Broadway Musical in the 1940s* (New York: Oxford University Press, 1999); Raymond Knapp, *The American Musical and the Formation of National Identity* (Princeton: Princeton University Press, 2004); and Scott McMillan, *The Musical as Drama* (Princeton: Princeton University Press, 2006). Also useful for the comedy of remarriage: Stanley Cavell, *Pursuits of Happiness: The Hollywood Comedy of Remarriage* (Cambridge, MA: Harvard University Press, 1981).

For *Swingin' the Dream*, see: Frances Teague, *Shakespeare and the American Popular Stage*; Alan Corrigan, "Jazz, Shakespeare, and Hybridity: A Script from *Swingin' the Dream*," *Borrowers and Lenders: The Journal of Shakespeare and Appropriation* 1 (March 2005); Errol Hill, *Shakespeare in Sable: A History of Black Shakespearean Actors* (Amherst: The University of Massachusetts Press, 1984); Lewis A. Erenberg, *Swingin' the Dream: Big Band Jazz and the Rebirth of American Culture* (Chicago: University of Chicago Press, 1998); and the review in *Theatre Arts Monthly* (February 1940), p. 93.

For the announcement in early 1949 of the future musical *West Side Story*, see Louis Calta, "'Romeo' to Receive Musical Styling: Bard's Play to Undergo Local Renovation by Bernstein, Robbins and Laurents," *New York Times*, January 27, 1949. And for reviews of the 1953 film that I quote from, see John Beaufort, *Christian Science Monitor*, November 27, 1953, and Otis L. Guernsey, Jr., *New York Herald Tribune*, November 6, 1953. The 1953 film earned $2 million in North American movie houses; at an average price at the time of fifty cents a ticket, that meant that roughly four million North American moviegoers saw the film.

CHAPTER 7: 1998

This chapter relies heavily on a major archive as well as a few key sources. Tom Stoppard's archive is in the Harry Ransom Center at the University of Texas at Austin. I am especially grateful to Stephen Ennis, director of the Ransom Center, as well as his colleagues Aaron Pratt and Eric Colleary. I have drawn on interviews found on the Collector's DVD of *Shakespeare in Love*, which also provided outtakes cut from the film. I have also drawn on interviews included in Linda Seger's *And the Best Screenplay Award Goes to . . . : Learning from the Winners: Sideways, Shakespeare in Love, Crash* (Studio City: Michael Wiese; Enfield: Publishers Group, 2008). For information about Harvey Weinstein's involvement in the film I have depended heavily on Peter Biskind's outstanding *Down and Dirty Pictures: Miramax, Sundance and the Rise of Independent Film* (New York: Simon and Schuster, 2004), which offers an incisive account, based on extensive interviews, of the film's making. Alisa Perren's *Indie, Inc.: Miramax and the Transformation of Hollywood in the 1990s* (Austin: University of Texas Press, 2012) has also been useful. For other quotations from the principal figures and for accounts of the making of the film, see Susan Bullington Katz, "Rhyme and Reason: A Conversation with *Shakespeare in Love*'s Marc Norman and Tom Stoppard," in *Written By* (March 1999), pp. 19–27; Ira Nadel's richly detailed *Double Act: The Life of Tom Stoppard* (London: Methuen, 2004); Karen Hollinger, "The First Lady of Miramax: Gwyneth Paltrow," in *The Actress: Hollywood Acting and the Female Star* (New York: Routledge, 2006); James Spada, *Julia: Her Life* (New York: St. Martin's, 2004); and Valerie Marino, *Gwyneth* (Toronto: ECW Press, 2000).

For the drafts on which I offer my extended account of early versions of the play (including Marc Norman's, which I accessed through Stoppard's copy of Norman's script), consult the Finding Aid for Tom Stoppard's holdings at the Ransom Center related to *Shakespeare in Love*, especially: containers 50–51, container 117, as well as his correspondence for these years, both catalogued and uncatalogued, including G12345 (both 4, which contains his outlines, and 5) and G12573. Stoppard didn't put all of his drafts in chronological order and only a few are dated. Stoppard's letter to Barry Isaacson about overhauling Norman's draft is dated June 20, 1992; his letter to Edward Zwick about "Susan's" studio rewrite is dated June 10, 1997. For quotations from the published version of the screenplay, see Marc Norman and Tom Stoppard, *Shakespeare in Love: A Screenplay* (New York: Miramax Film Corp and Universal Studios, 1998).

The film has generated a good deal of critical commentary. I have drawn on: Michael Anderegg, "James Dean Meets the Pirate's Daughter: Passion and Parody in *William Shakespeare's Romeo + Juliet* and *Shakespeare in Love*," in Richard Burt and Lynda Boose, eds., *Shakespeare the Movie, II: Popularizing the Plays on Film, TV, Video, and DVD* (New York: Routledge, 2003), pp. 56–71; Elizabeth Klett, "Shakespeare in Love and the End(s) of History," *Retrovisions: Reinventing the Past in Film and Fiction*, eds. Deborah Cartmell, I. Q. Hunter, and Imelda Whelehan (London: Pluto Press, 2001), pp. 25–40; Courtney Lehmann, "*Shakespeare in Love*: Romancing the Author, Mastering the Body," in *Spectacular Shakespeare: Critical Theory and Popular Cinema*, eds. Courtney Lehmann and Lisa J. Starks (Madison: Fairleigh Dickinson University Press, 2002), pp. 125–45; Paul J. C. M. Franssen, "Shakespeare's

Life on Film and Television: *Shakespeare in Love* and *A Waste of Shame*," in *Adaptation, Intermediality and the British Celebrity Biopic* (Farnham, Surrey: Ashgate, 2014), pp. 101–13; Emma French, *Selling Shakespeare to Hollywood: The Marketing of Filmed Shakespeare Adaptations from 1989 into the New Millennium* (Hatfield: University of Hertfordshire Press, 2006), pp. 133–68; Deborah Cartmell, "Marketing Shakespeare Films: From Tragedy to Biopic," in *Shakespeare's Cultural Capital: His Economic Impact from the Sixteenth to the Twenty-First Century* (London: Palgrave Macmillan, 2016), pp. 57–76; Russell Jackson, "Working with Shakespeare: Confessions of an Advisor," *Cineaste* 24 (1999), pp. 42–44; Kenneth Rothwell, "*Elizabeth* and *Shakespeare in Love*," *Cineaste* 24 (1999), pp. 78–80; Sujata Iyengar, "Shakespeare in Love," *Literature/Film Quarterly* 29 (2001), pp. 122–27; Richard Burt, "Shakespeare in Love and the End of Shakespeare," *Shakespeare, Film, Fin-de-siècle*, eds. Mark T. Burnett and Ramona Wray (Basingstoke: Macmillan, 2000); Todd F. Davis and Kenneth Womack, "Reading (and Writing) the Ethics of Authorship: *Shakespeare in Love* as Postmodern Metanarrative," in *"The Real Thing": Essays on Tom Stoppard in Celebration of His 75th Birthday*, ed. William Baker and Amanda Smothers (Newcastle upon Tyne: Cambridge Scholars Publishing, 2013), pp. 136–49; Sarah Mayo, "'A Shakespeare for the people'? Negotiating the Popular in *Shakespeare in Love* and Michael Hoffman's *A Midsummer Night's Dream*," *Textual Practice* 17 (2003), pp. 295–315; Sarah Werner, *Shakespeare and Feminist Performance: Ideology on Stage* (London: Routledge, 2001); Stephen Greenblatt, "About that Romantic Sonnet," *New York Times*, February 6, 1999; and for an excellent account of the ending of the film, including what was cut, see John Blakely, "Shakespearean Relocations: The Final Scene of John Madden's *Shakespeare in Love*," *Shakespeare Bulletin* 27 (2009), pp. 249–59.

For Harvey Weinstein's campaign to win Academy Awards, see Nikki Finke's important "Much Ado about Oscar," *New York Magazine*, March 15, 1999, as well as Sarah Martindale, "The Golden [Statuette] Age: How Miramax Sold Shakespeare to the Academy," *Networking Knowledge* 7(4) (2014); and Rebecca Keegan and Nicole Sperling, "*Shakespeare in Love* and Harvey Weinstein's Dark Oscar Victory," *Vanity Fair*, December 8, 2017. For contemporary reviews of the film, see especially: Janet Maslin, "Shakespeare Saw a Therapist?" *New York Times*, December 11, 1998; Grace Bradbury, "Love Turns

Bard," *London Times*, February 5, 1999; Peter Clark, "The Divine Gwyneth and Shakespeare in Love," *Evening Standard*, January 20, 1999; Martin Harries, "Hollywood in Love," *Chronicle of Higher Education* 45, April 16, 1999; and A. O. Scott, "Stoppard in Love: The Playwright's Infatuation with Smart Fun . . . and with Himself," *Slate*, March 20, 1999.

For *Romeo and Juliet* and the Monica Lewinsky scandal, see: Nigel Cawthorne, *The Mammoth Book of Sex Scandals* (London: Constable and Robinson, Ltd., 2012); "Valentine Ad in Paper Thrilled Bill, Tape Says," *New York Daily News*, January 27, 1998; https://www.washingtonpost.com/wp-srv/politics/special/clin ton/icreport/6narritvi.htm; and Susan Schmidt and Peter Baker, "Lewinsky Gives Starr Detailed Testimony Offer," *Washington Post*, January 27, 1998. I'm grateful to Richard McCoy for telling me about Lewinsky's ad. My account of *Two Gentlemen of Queens* is based on the account provided in Nadel as well as the quoted passage from George Rush, Joanna Molloy, and Marcus Baram, "Spielberg, Benigni: A 'Beautiful' Friendship," *New York Daily News*, March 22, 1999, and Frank DiGiacomo, "A Tense Best-Picture Victory for the Miramax Mogul Who Stormed Oscar Beach," *The Observer*, March 29, 1999. For Stuart Klawans, see his "Oscar Who?," the *Nation*, February 25, 1999. And for Willa Cather, Frederick Wadsworth Loring, and Moncure Conway, see my anthology, *Shakespeare in America*.

I include a number of statistics in this chapter. My source for how much Shakespeare films have earned is the invaluable online site *Box Office Mojo*. For figures on *Shakespeare in Love*'s test audiences, and for the pressure from Weinstein and the other producers, see Biskind, pp. 330–31. For the average ticket price in 1999—$5.08—see https://www.the-numbers.com/market/. The adult population (18 or over) of the US in 1999 was 207,094,130 (http://datacenter.kidscount.org/data/tables/99-total-population-by-child-and-adult#detailed/1/any/false/870,573,10/39,40,41/416,417); for polling on divorce and other moral issues, see http://news.gallup.com/poll/183413/americans-continue-shift-left-key-moral-issues.aspx and https://www.usnews.com/news/national/articles/2008/03/27/how-common-are-cheating-spouses.

For a list of the more than eighty women who have accused Weinstein of sexual misconduct, see: https://www.usatoday.com/story/life/people/2017/10/27/wein stein-scandal-complete-list-accusers/804663001/.

And for Brad Pitt and Robert Lindsay's confrontations with Harvey Weinstein, see http://www.kansascity.com/entertainment/article178239306. html and http://www.nydailynews.com/entertainment/movies/robert-lindsay-weinstein-fired-movie-article-1.3575014, as well as "Gwyneth Paltrow: Brad Pitt Threatened to Kill Weinstein over Alleged Assault," *Guardian*, May 24, 2018.

For information about American attitudes toward gays and lesbians in the 1990s, see especially "LGBT Rights Timeline," http://breakingprejudice.org/assets/AHAA/Activities/Gay%20Rights%20Movement%20Timeline%20Activity/LGBT%20Rights%20Timeline.pdf; https://www.theatlantic.com/politics/archive/2013/04/how-america-got-past-the-anti-gay-politics-of-the-90s/266976/; and https://www.vanityfair.com/news/1999/13/matthew-shepard-199903. And for 9/11 and the warnings leading up to it, see the official report: "9/11 and Terrorist Travel: Staff Report of the National Commission on Terrorist Attacks Upon the United States" (https://govinfo.library.unt.edu/911/staff_state ments/911_TerrTrav_Monograph.pdf).

CONCLUSION: 2017

On the Culture Wars, see, for example: James Davison Hunter, *Culture Wars: The Struggle to Define America* (New York: Basic Books, 1991); Roger Kimball, *Tenured Radicals* (New York: Harper & Row, 1990); Ivo Kamps, *Shakespeare Left and Right* (New York: Routledge, 1991); and Allan Bloom, *The Closing of the American Mind* (New York: Simon and Schuster, 1987). On colorblind casting, see Ayanna Thompson, ed., *Colorblind Shakespeare: New Perspectives on Race and Performance* (New York: Routledge, 2006), and Charlene Widener, "The Changing Face of American Theatre: Colorblind and Uni-Racial Casting at the New York Shakespeare Festival under the Direction of Joseph Papp" (PhD diss., University of Missouri-Columbia, 2006). On American presidents and Shakespeare, see Bogar, *American Presidents Attend the Theatre*. For statistics on the decline of English majors, see, for example, Colleen Flaherty, "The Evolving English Major," *Inside Higher Ed* (July 18, 2018).

As noted previously, much of my information in this chapter is based on what I saw, on data shared with me by the Public Theater, and on extended interviews I conducted with Oskar Eustis, Patrick Willingham, Rosalind

Barbour, Ruth E. Sternberg, Jeremy Adams, and Tom McCann at the Public Theater.

On Steve Bannon, Shakespeare, *Julius Caesar*, and *Coriolanus*, see Lauren Gambino, "Steve Bannon Renews Call for War on Republican Establishment," *Guardian*, October 14, 2017; Connie Bruck, "How Hollywood Remembers Steve Bannon," *New Yorker*, May 1, 2017; Todd Van Luling, "Steve Bannon's Failed 'Star Wars'-Meets-Shakespeare Movie Script," *Huffington Post*, May 10, 2017; Daniel Pollack-Pelzner, "Behold, Steve Bannon's Hip-Hop Shakespeare Rewrite: *Coriolanus*," *New York Times*, December 17, 2016; Rex Weiner, "Titus in Space: Steve Bannon's Obsession with Shakespeare's Goriest Play," *Paris Review*, November 29, 2016; and Asawin Suebsaeng, "*The Thing I Am*: Steve Bannon, Donald Trump's Campaign CEO, Once Wrote a Rap Musical," *Daily Beast*, August 23, 2016. On Bannon's desire for the destruction of institutions ("I want to bring everything crashing down and destroy all of today's establishment") see *Guardian*, February 6, 2017. To see and hear a staged table reading of Bannon's adaptation of *Coriolanus*, through which his script can be accessed, see the link to https://nowthisnews.com /steve-bannon-hip-hop-rap-musical provided by Jon Blistein, "'He Approaches the Baby Gangsta': Watch Steve Bannon's Rap Musical," *Rolling Stone*, May 3, 2017. The script, in addition to being recited, is reproduced on the bottom of the screen. See too: Joshua Green, *Devil's Bargain: Steve Bannon, Donald Trump, and the Storming of the Presidency* (New York: Penguin Press, 2017). And for background on the Rodney King riots in LA, see Mark Baldassare, ed., *The Los Angeles Riots: Lessons for the Urban Future* (Boulder, CO: Westview Press, 1994), and Nathan Cohen, ed., *The Los Angeles Riots: A Socio-Psychological Study*, published in cooperation with the Institute of Government and Public Affairs, University of California, Los Angeles (New York: Praeger, 1970).

For Mike Cernovich and Pizzagate, see https://www.sfgate.com/entertainment/the-wrap/article/Mike-Cernovich-a-Timeline-From-Choking-Advice-13102048.php. For his offer of payment to disrupt the show, see Elliot Hannon, "Right-Wing Protesters Rush Stage, Disrupt Trump-Themed *Julius Caesar* Production," *Slate*, June 17, 2017, which names the pair who interrupted the show: Laura Loomer and Jack Posobiec. For the threats to other theaters across America, see Jeremy Gerard, "Free Theaters Threatened in

Fallout From *Julius Caesar* as Supporters Plan Rally," *Deadline Hollywood*, June 14, 2017, and Malcolm Gay, "Knives Are Out for Theaters that Bear the Name 'Shakespeare,'" *Boston Globe*, June 16, 2017. Tom Finkelpearl's support for the production is quoted from Michael Paulson and Sopan Deb, "How Outrage Built Over a Shakespearean Depiction of Trump," *New York Times*, June 12, 2017. And for threats to the Eustis family, see Tina Moore and Max Jaeger, *"Julius Caesar*'s Director Gets Death Threats at Home," *New York Post*, June 21, 2017. Clips of the disruption of the Delacorte production, a tape of Joe Piscopo's show, the *Fox & Friends* show, Ben Shapiro's critique, and the *Inside Edition* clip can all be accessed on YouTube.

For Summer Shakespeare Festivals in America, see https://www.sta-home.org. For the percentage of American secondary schools that taught Shakespeare in the 1980s, see Valerie Strauss, "A Shakespeare for All Ages," *Washington Post*, March 7, 1999. For Shakespeare in the Common Core standards, see http://www.cores tandards.org/ELA-Literacy/RL/11-12/. And for the National Endowment for the Arts program Shakespeare in American Communities, see Amanda Giguere, *Shakespeare in American Communities*: *Conservative Politics, Appropriation, and the NEA* (Saarbrücken, Germany: VDM Verlag, 2010) and the US government website https://www.arts.gov/partnership/shakespeare-american-communities.

And for the pulling down of London's theaters in 1642, see N. W. Bawcutt, "Puritanism and the Closing of the Theaters in 1642," *Medieval & Renaissance Drama in England* 22 (2009), pp. 179–200.

Credits

IMAGE 12: David Parfitt, Donna Gigliotti, Harvey Weinstein, Gwyneth Paltrow, Edward Zwick, and Marc Norman at the 71st Academy Awards, March 21, 1999. Courtesy of ImageCollect.

IMAGE 13: Cropped screen grab of the assassination scene in *Julius Caesar* at the Delacorte Theater in Central Park, June 2017, *Inside Edition*, YouTube.

TEXT CREDITS

BRUSH UP YOUR SHAKESPEARE (from "Kiss Me, Kate"). Words and Music by COLE PORTER © 1949 by COLE PORTER. © Renewed and Assigned to John F. Wharton. Trustee of the COLE PORTER MUSICAL AND LITERARY PROPERTY TRUSTS. CHAPPELL & CO. Owner of Publication and Allied Rights Throughout the World. All Rights Reserved. Used By Permission of ALFRED PUBLISHING, LLC.

Index

Figures in *italics* refer to pages with illustrations.